WI]

MW01532240

LOGIC

INDUCTIVE AND DEDUCTIVE

Elibron Classics
www.elibron.com

Logic

Inductive and Deductive

By WILLIAM MINTO, M.A.

HON. LL.D., ST. ANDREWS

LATE PROFESSOR OF LOGIC IN THE UNIVERSITY OF ABERDEEN

WITH A FEW DIAGRAMS

LONDON

JOHN MURRAY, ALBEMARLE STREET

1893

ABERDEEN UNIVERSITY PRESS.

PREFACE.

In this little treatise two things are attempted that at first might appear incompatible. One of them is to put the study of logical formulæ on a historical basis. Strangely enough, the scientific evolution of logical forms, is a bit of history that still awaits the zeal and genius of some great scholar. I have neither ambition nor qualification for such a *magnum opus*, and my life is already more than half spent; but the gap in evolutionary research is so obvious that doubtless some younger man is now at work in the field unknown to me. All that I can hope to do is to act as a humble pioneer according to my imperfect lights. Even the little I have done represents work begun more than twenty years ago, and continuously pursued for the last twelve years during a considerable portion of my time.

The other aim, which might at first appear inconsistent with this, is to increase the power of Logic as a practical discipline. The main purpose of this practical science, or scientific art, is conceived to be the organisation of reason against error, and error in its various kinds is made the basis of the division of the subject. To carry out this practical aim along with the historical one is not hopeless, because throughout its long history Logic has been a practical science; and, as I have tried to show at some length in introductory chapters, has concerned itself at different periods with the risks of error peculiar to each.

To enumerate the various books, ancient and modern, to which I have been indebted, would be a vain parade. Where I have consciously adopted any distinctive recent contribution to the long line of tradition, I have made particular acknowledgment. My greatest obligation is to my old professor, Alexander Bain, to whom I owe my first interest in the subject, and more details than I can possibly separate from the general body of my knowledge.

W. M.

ABERDEEN, *January*, 1893.

SINCE these sentences were written, the author of this book has died; and Professor Minto's *Logic* is his last contribution to the literature of his country. It embodies a large part of his teaching in the philosophical class-room of his University, and doubtless reflects the spirit of the whole of it.

Scottish Philosophy has lost in him one of its typical representatives, and the University of the North one of its most stimulating teachers. There have been few more distinguished men than William Minto in the professoriate of Aberdeen; and the memory of what he was, of his wide and varied learning, his brilliant conversation, his urbanity, and his rare power of sympathy with men with whose opinions he did not agree, will remain a possession to many who mourn his loss.

It will be something if this little book keeps his memory alive, both amongst the students who owed so much to him, and in the large circle of friends who used to feel the charm of his personality.

WILLIAM KNIGHT.

CONTENTS.

INTRODUCTION.

I.

BOOK I.

THE LOGIC OF CONSISTENCY—SYLLOGISM AND DEFINITION.

PART I.

THE ELEMENTS OF PROPOSITIONS.

CHAPTER I.

CHAPTER II.

(ix)

PART II.

DEFINITION.

CHAPTER I.

PART III.

THE INTERPRETATION OF PROPOSITIONS.

CHAPTER I.

PART IV.

THE INTERDEPENDENCE OF PROPOSITIONS.

CHAPTER I.

BOOK II.

INDUCTIVE LOGIC, OR THE LOGIC OF SCIENCE.

Contents.

INTRODUCTION.

I.—THE ORIGIN AND SCOPE OF LOGIC.

THE question has sometimes been asked, Where should we begin in Logic? Particularly within the present century has this difficulty been felt, when the study of Logic has been revived and made intricate by the different purposes of its cultivators.

Where did the founder of Logic begin? Where did Aristotle begin? This seems to be the simplest way of settling where we should begin, for the system shaped by Aristotle is still the trunk of the tree, though there have been so many offshoots from the old stump and so many parasitic plants have wound themselves round it that Logic is now almost as tangled a growth as the Yews of Borrowdale—

> An intertwisted mass of fibres serpentine
> Upcoiling and inveterately convolved.

It used to be said that Logic had remained for two thousand years precisely as Aristotle left it. It was an example of a science or art perfected at one stroke by the genius of its first inventor. The bewildered student must often wish that this were so : it is only superficially true. Much of Aristotle's nomenclature and his central formulæ have been retained, but they have been very variously supplemented and interpreted to very different purposes—often to no purpose at all.

The Cambridge mathematician's boast about his new theorem—"The best of it all is that it can never by any possibility be made of the slightest use to anybody for anything"—might be made with truth about many of the later developments of Logic. We may say the same, indeed, about the later developments of any subject that has been a playground for generation after generation of acute intellects, happy in their own disinterested exercise. Educational subjects —subjects appropriated for the general schooling of young minds—are particularly apt to be developed out of the lines of their original intention. So many influences conspire to pervert the original aim. The convenience of the teacher, the convenience of the learner, the love of novelty, the love of symmetry, the love of subtlety ; easy-going indolence on the one hand and intellectual restlessness on the other—all these motives act from within on traditional matter without regard to any external purpose whatever. Thus in Logic difficulties have been glossed over and simplified for the dull understanding, while acute minds have revelled in variations and new and ingenious manipulations of the old formulæ, and in multiplication and more exact and symmetrical definition of the old distinctions.

To trace the evolution of the forms and theories of Logic under these various influences during its periods of active development is a task more easily conceived than executed, and one far above the ambition of an introductory treatise. But it is well that even he who writes for beginners should recognise that the forms now commonly used have been evolved out of a simpler tradition.   Without entering into the details of the process, it is possible to indicate its main stages, and thus furnish a clue out of the modern labyrinthine confusion of purposes.

How did the Aristotelian Logic originate ?   Its central feature is the syllogistic forms.   In what circumstances did Aristotle invent these ?   For what purpose ?   What use did he contemplate for them ? In rightly understanding this, we shall understand the original scope or province of Logic, and thus be in a position to understand more clearly how it has been modified, contracted, expanded, and supplemented.

Logic has always made high claims as the *scientia scientiarum*, the science of sciences.   The builders of this Tower of Babel are threatened in these latter days with confusion of tongues.   We may escape this danger if we can recover the designs of the founder, and of the master-builders who succeeded him.

Aristotle's Logic has been so long before the world in abstract isolation that we can hardly believe that its form was in any way determined by local accident.   A horror as of sacrilege is excited by the bare suggestion that the author of this grand and venerable work, one of the most august monuments of transcendent intellect, was in his day and generation only a pre-eminent tutor or schoolmaster, and that his logical writings were designed for the accomplishment of his pupils in a special art in which every intellectually ambitious young Athenian of the period aspired to excel.   Yet such is the plain fact, baldly stated. Aristotle's Logic in its primary aim was as practical as a treatise on Navigation, or " Cavendish on Whist ".   The latter is the more exact of the two comparisons. It was in effect in its various parts a series of handbooks for a temporarily fashionable intellectual game, a peculiar mode of disputation or dialectic,[1] the game of Question and Answer, the game so fully illustrated in the Dialogues of Plato, the game identified with the name of Socrates.

We may lay stress, if we like, on the intellectuality of the game, and the high topics on which it was exercised. It was a game that could flourish only among a peculiarly intellectual people; a people less acute would find little sport in it. The Athenians still take a singular delight in disputation. You

---

[1] We know for certain—and it is one of the evidences of the importance attached to this trivial-looking pastime—that two of the great teacher's logical treatises, the Topics and the Sophistical Refutations, were written especially for the guidance of Questioners and Respondents. The one instructs the disputant how to qualify himself methodically for discussion before an ordinary audience, when the admissions extracted from the respondent are matters of common belief, the questioner's skill being directed to make it appear that the respondent's position is inconsistent with these. The other is a systematic exposure of sophistical tricks, mostly verbal quibbles, whereby a delusive appearance of victory in debate may be obtained. But in the concluding chapter of the *Elenchi*, where Aristotle claims not only that his method is superior to the empirical methods of rival teachers, but that it is entirely original, it is the Syllogism upon which he lays stress as his peculiar and chief invention. The Syllogism, the pure forms of which are expounded in his Prior Analytics, is really the centre of Aristotle's logical system, whether the propositions to which it is applied are matters of scientific truth as in the Posterior Analytics, or matters of common opinion as in the Topics. The treatise on Interpretation, *i.e.*, the interpretation of the Respondent's "Yes" and "No," is preliminary to the Syllogism, the reasoning of the admissions together. Even in the half-grammatical half-logical treatise on the Categories, the author always keeps an eye on the Syllogistic analysis.

cannot visit Athens without being struck by it. You may still see groups formed round two protagonists in the cafés or the squares, or among the ruins of the Acropolis, in a way to remind you of Socrates and his friends. They do not argue as Gil Blas and his Hibernians did with heat and temper, ending in blows. They argue for the pure love of arguing, the audience sitting or standing by to see fair play with the keenest enjoyment of intellectual thrust and parry. No other people could argue like the Greeks without coming to blows. It is one of their characteristics now, and so it was in old times two thousand years ago. And about a century before Aristotle reached manhood, they had invented this peculiarly difficult and trying species of disputative pastime, in which we find the genesis of Aristotle's logical treatises.

To get a proper idea of this debate by Question and Answer, which we may call Socratic disputation after its most renowned master, one must read some of the dialogues of Plato. I will indicate merely the skeleton of the game, to show how happily it lent itself to Aristotle's analysis of arguments and propositions.

A thesis or proposition is put up for debate, *e.g.*, that knowledge is nothing else than sensible perception,[1] that it is a greater evil to do wrong than to suffer wrong,[2] that the love of gain is not reprehensible.[3] There are two disputants, but they do not speak on the question by turns, so many minutes being allowed to each as in a modern encounter of wits. One of the two, who may be called the Questioner, is limited to asking

---

[1] Theætetus, 151 E.   [2] Gorgias, 473 D.
[3] Hipparchus, 225 A.

questions, the other, the Respondent, is limited to answering. Further, the Respondent can answer only " Yes " or " No," with perhaps a little explanation : on his side the Questioner must ask only questions that admit of the simple answer " Yes " or " No ". The Questioner's business is to extract from the Respondent admissions involving the opposite of what he has undertaken to maintain. The Questioner tries in short to make him contradict himself. Only a very stupid Respondent would do this at once : the Questioner plies him with general principles, analogies, plain cases; leads him on from admission to admission, and then putting the admissions together convicts him out of his own mouth of inconsistency.[1]

Now mark precisely where Aristotle struck in with his invention of the Syllogism, the invention on which he prided himself as specially his own, and the forms of which have clung to Logic ever since, even in the usage of those who deride Aristotle's Moods and Figures as antiquated superstitions. Suppose yourself the Questioner, where did he profess to help you with his mechanism ? In effect, as the word Syllogism indicates, it was when you had obtained a number of admissions,

---

[1] In its leading and primary use, this was a mode of debate, a duel of wits, in which two men engaged before an audience. But the same form could be used, and was used, notably by Socrates, not in an eristic spirit but as a means of awakening people to the consequences of certain admissions or first principles, and thus making vague knowledge explicit and clear. The mind being detained on proposition after proposition as assent was given to it, dialectic was a valuable instrument of instruction and exposition. But whatever the purpose of the exercise, controversial triumph, or solid grounding in first principles—"the evolution of in-dwelling conceptions "—the central interest lay in the syllogising or reasoning together of the separately assumed or admitted propositions.

and wished to reason them together, to demonstrate how they bore upon the thesis in dispute, how they hung together, how they necessarily involved what you were contending for. And the essence of his mechanism was the reduction of the admitted propositions to common terms, and to certain types or forms which are manifestly equivalent or inter-dependent. Aristotle advised his pupils also in the tactics of the game, but his grand invention was the form or type of admissions that you should strive to obtain, and the effective manipulation of them when you had got them.

An example will show the nature of this help, and what it was worth. To bring the thing nearer home, let us, instead of an example from Plato, whose topics often seem artificial to us now, take a thesis from last century, a paradox still arguable, Mandeville's famous —some would say infamous—paradox that Private Vices are Public Benefits. Undertake to maintain this, and you will have no difficulty in getting a respondent prepared to maintain the negative. The plain men, such as Socrates cross-questioned, would have declared at once that a vice is a vice, and can never do any good to anybody. Your Respondent denies your proposition simply : he upholds that private vices never are public benefits, and defies you to extract from him any admission inconsistent with this. Your task then is to lure him somehow into admitting that in some cases what is vicious in the individual may be of service to the State. This is enough : you are not concerned to establish that this holds of all private vices. A single instance to the contrary is enough to break down his universal negative. You cannot, of course, expect him to make the necessary admission in direct terms :

you must go round about. You know, perhaps, that he has confidence in Bishop Butler as a moralist. You try him with the saying: " To aim at public and private good are so far from being inconsistent that they mutually promote each other ". Does he admit this ?

Perhaps he wants some little explanation or exemplification to enable him to grasp your meaning. This was within the rules of the game. You put cases to him, asking for his " Yes " or " No " to each. Suppose a man goes into Parliament, not out of any zeal for the public good, but in pure vainglory, or to serve his private ends, is it possible for him to render the State good service ? Or suppose a milk-seller takes great pains to keep his milk pure, not because he cares for the public health, but because it pays, is this a benefit to the public ?

Let these questions be answered in the affirmative, putting you in possession of the admission that some actions undertaken for private ends are of public advantage, what must you extract besides to make good your position as against the Respondent ? To see clearly at this stage what now is required, though you have to reach it circuitously, masking your approach under difference of language, would clearly be an advantage. This was the advantage that Aristotle's method offered to supply. A disputant familiar with his analysis would foresee at once that if he could get the Respondent to admit that all actions undertaken for private ends are vicious, the victory was his, while nothing short of this would serve.

Here my reader may interject that he could have seen this without any help from Aristotle, and that anybody may see it without knowing that what he has to do is, in Aristotelian language, to construct a syllogism in Bokardo. I pass this over. I am not concerned at this point to defend the utility of Aristotle's method. All that I want is to illustrate the kind of use that it was intended for. Perhaps if Aristotle had not habituated men's minds to his analysis, we should none of us have been able to discern coherence and detect incoherence as quickly and clearly as we do now.

But to return to our example. As Aristotle's pupil, you would have seen at the stage we are speaking of that the establishment of your thesis must turn upon the definition of virtue and vice. You must proceed, therefore, to cross-examine your Respondent about this. You are not allowed to ask him what he means by virtue, or what he means by vice. In accordance with the rules of the dialectic, it is your business to propound definitions, and demand his Yes or No to them. You ask him, say, whether he agrees with Shaftesbury's definition of a virtuous action as an action undertaken purely for the good of others. If he assents, it follows that an action undertaken with any suspicion of a self-interested motive cannot be numbered among the virtues. If he agrees, further, that every action must be either vicious or virtuous, you have admissions sufficient to prove your original thesis. All that you have now to do to make your triumph manifest, is to display the admissions you have obtained in common terms.

> Some actions done with a self-interested motive are public benefits.
> All actions done with a self-interested motive are private vices.

From these premisses it follows irresistibly that

> Some private vices are public benefits.

This illustration may serve to show the kind of disputation for which Aristotle's logic was designed, and thus to make clear its primary uses and its limitations.

To realise its uses, and judge whether there is anything analogous to them in modern needs, conceive the chief things that it behoved Questioner and Respondent in this game to know. All that a proposition necessarily implies; all that two propositions put together imply; on what conditions and to what extent one admission is inconsistent with another; when one admission necessarily involves another; when two necessarily involve a third. And to these ends it was obviously necessary to have an exact understanding of the terms used, so as to avoid the snares of ambiguous language.

That a Syllogistic or Logic of Consistency should emerge out of Yes-and-No Dialectic was natural. Things in this world come when they are wanted: inventions are made on the spur of necessity. It was above all necessary in this kind of debate to avoid contradicting yourself: to maintain your consistency. A clever interrogator spread out proposition after proposition before you and invited your assent, choosing forms of words likely to catch your prejudices and lure you into self-contradiction. An organon, instrument, or discipline calculated to protect you as Respondent and guide you as Questioner by making clear what an admission led to, was urgently called for, and when the game had been in high fashion for more than a century Aristotle's genius devised what was wanted, meeting at the same time, no doubt, collateral needs that had arisen from the application of Dialectic to various kinds of subject-matter.

The thoroughness of Aristotle's system was doubtless due partly to the searching character of the dialectic in which it had its birth. No other mode of disputation makes such demands upon the disputant's intellectual agility and precision, or is so well adapted to lay bare the skeleton of an argument.

The uses of Aristotle's logical treatises remained when the fashion that had called them forth had passed.[1] Clear and consistent thinking, a mastery of the perplexities and ambiguities of language, power to detect identity of meaning under difference of expression, a ready apprehension of all that a proposition implies, all that may be educed or deduced from it— whatever helps to these ends must be of perpetual use. " To purge the understanding of those errors which lie in the confusion and perplexities of an inconsequent thinking," is a modern description of the main scope of Logic.[2] It is a good description of the branch of Logic that keeps closest to the Aristotelian tradition.

---

[1] Like every other fashion, Yes-and-No Dialectic had its period, its rise and fall. The invention of it is ascribed to Zeno the Eleatic, the answering and questioning Zeno, who flourished about the middle of the fifth century B.C. Socrates (469-399) was in his prime at the beginning of the great Peloponnesian War when Pericles died in 429. In that year Plato was born, and lived to 347, "the olive groves of Academe" being the established centre of his teaching from about 386 onwards. Aristotle (384-322), who was the tutor of Alexander the Great, established his school at the Lyceum when Alexander became king in 336 and set out on his career of conquest. That Yes-and-No Dialectic was then a prominent exercise, his logical treatises everywhere bear witness. The subsequent history of the game is obscure. It is probable that Aristotle's thorough exposition of its legitimate arts and illegitimate tricks helped to destroy its interest as an amusement.

[2] Hamilton's *Lectures*, iii. p. 37.

The limitations as well as the uses of Aristotle's logic
may be traced to the circumstances of its origin.   Both
parties to the disputation, Questioner and Respondent
alike, were mainly concerned with the inter-dependence
of the propositions put forward.   Once the Respondent
had given his assent to a question, he was bound in
consistency to all that it implied.   He must take all
the consequences of his admission.   It might be true
or it might be false as a matter of fact : all the same
he was bound by it : its truth or falsehood was
immaterial to his position as a disputant.   On the
other hand, the Questioner could not go beyond the
admissions of the Respondent.   It has often been
alleged as a defect in the Syllogism that the conclusion
does not go beyond the premisses, and ingenious
attempts have been made to show that it is really an
advance upon the premisses.   But having regard to the
primary use of the syllogism, this was no defect, but a
necessary character of the relation.   The Questioner
could not in fairness assume more than had been
granted by implication.   His advance could only be an
argumentative advance : if his conclusion contained a
grain more than was contained in the premisses, it was
a sophistical trick, and the Respondent could draw
back and withhold his assent.   He was bound in consistency to stand by his admissions ; he was not
bound to go a fraction of an inch beyond them.

We thus see how vain it is to look to the Aristotelian
tradition for an organon of truth or a criterion of
falsehood.   Directly and primarily, at least, it was not
so ; the circumstances of its origin gave it a different
bent.   Indirectly and secondarily, no doubt, it served
this purpose, inasmuch as truth was the aim of all
serious thinkers who sought to clear their minds and

the minds of others by Dialectic. But in actual debate truth was represented merely by the common-sense of the audience. A dialectician who gained a triumph by outraging this, however cleverly he might outwit his antagonist, succeeded only in amusing his audience, and dialecticians of the graver sort aimed at more serious uses and a more respectful homage, and did their best to discountenance merely eristic disputation. Further, it would be a mistake to conclude because Aristotle's Logic, as an instrument of Dialectic, concerned itself with the syllogism of propositions rather than their truth, that it was merely an art of quibbling. On the contrary, it was essentially the art of preventing and exposing quibbling. It had its origin in quibbling, no doubt, inasmuch as what we should call verbal quibbling was of the essence of Yes-and-No Dialectic, and the main secret of its charm for an intellectual and disputatious people; but it came into being as a safeguard against quibbling, not a serviceable adjunct.

The mediæval developments of Logic retained and even exaggerated the syllogistic character of the original treatises. Interrogative dialectic had disappeared in the Middle Ages whether as a diversion or as a discipline : but errors of inconsistency still remained the errors against which principally educated men needed a safeguard. Men had to keep their utterances in harmony with the dogmas of the Church. A clear hold of the exact implications of a proposition, whether singly or in combination with other propositions, was still an important practical need. The Inductive Syllogism was not required, and its treatment dwindled to insignificance in mediæval text-books, but the Deductive Syllogism and the formal apparatus for the definition of terms held the field.

It was when observation of Nature and its laws became a paramount pursuit that the defects of Syllogistic Logic began to be felt. Errors against which this Logic offered no protection then called for a safeguard—especially the errors to which men are liable in the investigation of cause and effect. "Bring your thoughts into harmony one with another," was the demand of Aristotle's age. "Bring your thoughts into harmony with authority," was the demand of the Middle Ages. "Bring them into harmony with fact," was the requirement most keenly felt in more recent times. It is in response to this demand that what is commonly but not very happily known as Inductive Logic has been formulated.

In obedience to custom, I shall follow the now ordinary division of Logic into Deductive and Inductive. The titles are misleading in many ways, but they are fixed by a weight of usage which it would be vain to try to unsettle. Both come charging down the stream of time each with its cohort of doctrines behind it, borne forward with irresistible momentum.

The best way of preventing confusion now is to retain the established titles, recognise that the doctrines behind each have a radically different aim or end, and supply the interpretation of this end from history. What they have in common may be described as the prevention of error, the organisation of reason against error. I have shown that owing to the bent impressed upon it by the circumstances of its origin, the errors chiefly safeguarded by the Aristotelian logic were the errors of inconsistency. The other branch of Logic, commonly called Induction, was really a separate evolution, having its origin in a different practical need. The history of this I will trace separately after we have seen our way through the Aristotelian tradition and its accretions. The Experimental Methods are no less manifestly the germ, the evolutionary centre or starting-point, of the new Logic than the Syllogism is of the old, and the main errors safeguarded are errors of fact and inference from fact.

At this stage it will be enough to indicate briefly the broad relations between Deductive Logic and Inductive Logic.

Inductive Logic, as we now understand it—the Logic of Observation and Explanation—was first formulated and articulated to a System of Logic by J. S. Mill. It was he that added this wing to the old building. But the need of it was clearly expressed as early as the thirteenth century. Roger Bacon, the Franciscan friar (1214-1292), and not his more illustrious namesake Francis, Lord Verulam, was the real founder of Inductive Logic. It is remarkable that the same century saw Syllogistic Logic advanced to its most complete development in the system of Petrus Hispanus, a Portuguese scholar who under the title of John XXI. filled the Papal Chair for eight months in 1276-7.

A casual remark of Roger Bacon's in the course of his advocacy of Experimental Science in the *Opus Majus* draws a clear line between the two branches of Logic. " There are," he says, "two ways of knowing, by Argument and by Experience. Argument concludes a question, but it does not make us feel certain, unless the truth be also found in experience."

On this basis the old Logic may be clearly distinguished from the new, taking as the general aim of Logic the protection of the mind against the errors to which it is liable in the acquisition of knowledge.

All knowledge, broadly speaking, comes either from Authority, *i.e.*, by argument from accepted premisses, or from Experience. If it comes from Authority it comes through the medium of words : if it comes from Experience it comes through the senses. In taking in knowledge through words we are liable to certain errors ; and in taking in knowledge through the senses we are liable to certain errors. To protect against the one is the main end of " Deductive " Logic : to protect against the other is the main end of " Inductive " Logic. As a matter of fact the pith of treatises on Deduction and Induction is directed to those ends respectively, the old meanings of Deduction and Induction as formal processes (to be explained afterwards) being virtually ignored.

There is thus no antagonism whatever between the two branches of Logic. They are directed to different ends. The one is supplementary to the other. The one cannot supersede the other.

Aristotelian Logic can never become superfluous as long as men are apt to be led astray by words. Its ultimate business is to safeguard in the interpretation of the tradition of language. The mere syllogistic, the bare forms of equivalent or consistent expression, have a very limited utility, as we shall see. But by cogent sequence syllogism leads to proposition, and proposition to term, and term to a close study of the relations between words and thoughts and things.

II.—LOGIC AS A PREVENTIVE OF ERROR OR FALLACY.—THE INNER SOPHIST.

Why describe Logic as a system of defence against error? Why say that its main end and aim is the organisation of reason against confusion and falsehood? Why not rather say, as is now usual, that its end is the attainment of truth? Does this not come to the same thing?

Substantially, the meaning is the same, but the latter expression is more misleading. To speak of Logic as a body of rules for the investigation of truth has misled people into supposing that Logic claims to be an art of Discovery, that it claims to lay down rules by simply observing which investigators may infallibly arrive at new truths. Now, this does not hold even of the Logic of Induction, still less of the older Logic, the precise relation of which to truth will become apparent as we proceed. It is only by keeping men from going astray and by disabusing them when they think they have reached their destination that Logic helps men on the road to truth. Truth often lies hid in the centre of a maze, and logical rules only help the searcher onwards by giving him warning when he is on the wrong track and must try another. It is the searcher's own impulse that carries him forward : Logic does not so much beckon him on to the right path as beckon him back from the wrong. In laying down the conditions of correct interpretation, of valid argument, of trustworthy evidence, of satisfactory explanation, Logic shows the inquirer how to test and purge his conclusions, not how to reach them.

To discuss, as is sometimes done, whether Fallacies lie within the proper sphere of Logic, is to obscure the real connexion between Fallacies and Logic. It is the existence of Fallacies that calls Logic into existence; as a practical science Logic is needed as a protection against Fallacies. Such historically is its origin. We may, if we like, lay down an arbitrary rule that a treatise on Logic should be content to expound the correct forms of interpretation and reasoning and should not concern itself with the wrong. If we take this view we are bound to pronounce Fallacies extra-logical. But to do so is simply to cripple the usefulness of Logic as a practical science. The manipulation of the bare logical forms, without reference to fallacious departures from them, is no better than a nursery exercise. Every correct form in Logic is laid down as a safeguard against some erroneous form to which men are prone, whether in the interpretation of argument or the interpretation of experience, and the statement and illustration of the typical forms of wrong procedure should accompany *pari passu* the exposition of the right procedure.

In accordance with this principle, I shall deal with special fallacies, special snares or pitfalls—misapprehension of words, misinterpretation of propositions, misunderstanding of arguments, misconstruction of facts, evidences, or signs—each in connexion with its appropriate safeguard. This seems to me the most profitable method. But at this stage, it may be worth while, by way of emphasising the need for Logic as a science of rational belief, to take a survey of the most general tendencies to irrational belief, the chief kinds of illusion or bias that are rooted in the human constitution. We shall then better appreciate the magnitude of the task that Logic attempts in seeking to protect reason against its own fallibility and the pressure of the various forces that would usurp its place.

It is a common notion that we need Logic to protect us against the arts of the Sophist, the dishonest juggler with words and specious facts. But in truth the Inner Sophist, whose instruments are our own inborn propensities to error, is a much more dangerous enemy. For once that we are the victims of designing Sophists, we are nine times the victims of our own irrational impulses and prejudices. Men generally deceive themselves before they deceive others.

Francis Bacon drew attention to these inner perverting influences, these universal sources of erroneous belief, in his *De Augmentis* and again in his *Novum Organum,* under the designation of *Idola* (εἴδωλα), deceptive appearances of truth, illusions. His classification of *Idola*—*Idola Tribus,* illusions common to all men, illusions of the race ; *Idola Specus,* personal illusions, illusions peculiar to the " den " in which each man lives ; *Idola Fori,* illusions of conversation, vulgar prejudices embodied in words ; *Idola Theatri,* illusions of illustrious doctrine, illusions imposed by the dazzling authority of great names—is defective as a classification inasmuch as the first class includes all the others, but like all his writings it is full of sagacious remarks and happy examples. Not for the sake of novelty, but because it is well that matters so important should be presented from more than one point of view, I shall follow a division adapted from the more scientific, if less picturesque, arrangement of Professor Bain, in his chapter on the Fallacious Tendencies of the Human Mind.[1]

[1] Bain's *Logic,* bk. vi. chap. iii. Bacon intended his *Idola* to bear the same relation to his *Novum Organum* that Aristotle's

The illusions to which we are all subject may best be classified according to their origin in the depths of our nature. Let us try to realise how illusory beliefs arise.

What is a belief? One of the uses of Logic is to set us thinking about such simple terms. An exhaustive analysis and definition of belief is one of the most difficult of psychological problems. We cannot enter upon that : let us be content with a few simple characters of belief.

First, then, belief is a state of mind. Second, this state of mind is outward-pointing : it has a reference beyond itself, a reference to the order of things outside us. In believing, we hold that the world as it is, has been, or will be, corresponds to our conceptions of it. Third, belief is the guide of action : it is in accordance with what we believe that we direct our activities. If we want to know what a man really believes, we look at his action. This at least is the clue to what he believes at the moment. " I cannot," a great orator once said, " read the minds of men." This was received with ironical cheers. " No," he retorted, " but I can construe their acts." Promoters of companies are expected to invest their own money as a guarantee of good faith. If a man says he believes the world is coming to an end in a year, and takes a lease of a house for fifteen years, we conclude that his belief is not of the highest degree of strength.

Fallacies or Sophistical Tricks bore to the old Organum. But in truth, as I have already indicated, what Bacon classifies is our inbred tendencies to form *idola* or false images, and it is these same tendencies that make us liable to the fallacies named by Aristotle. Some of Aristotle's, as we shall see, are fallacies of Induction.

The close connexion of belief with our activities, enables us to understand how illusions, false conceptions of reality,.arise. The illusions of Feeling and the illusions of Custom are well understood, but other sources of illusion, which may be designated Impatient Impulse and Happy Exercise, are less generally recognised. An example or two will show what is meant. We cannot understand the strength of these perverting influences till we realise them in our own case. We detect them quickly enough in others. Seeing that in common speech the word illusion implies a degree of error amounting almost to insanity, and the illusions we speak of are such as no man is ever quite free from, it is perhaps less startling to use the word *bias*.

The Bias of Impatient Impulse.

As a being formed for action, not only does healthy man take a pleasure in action, physical and mental, for its own sake, irrespective of consequences, but he is so charged with energy that he cannot be comfortable unless it finds a free vent. In proportion to the amount and excitability of his energy, restraint, obstruction, delay is irksome, and soon becomes a positive and intolerable pain. Any bar or impediment that gives us pause is hateful even to think of: the mere prospect annoys and worries.

Hence it arises that belief, a feeling of being prepared for action, a conviction that the way is clear before us for the free exercise of our activities, is a very powerful and exhilarating feeling, as much a necessity of happy existence as action itself. We see this when we consider how depressing and uncomfortable a condition is the opposite state to belief, namely, doubt, perplexity, hesitation, uncertainty as to our course. And realising this, we see how strong a bias we have in this fact of our nature, this imperious inward necessity for action ; how it urges us to act without regard to consequences, and to jump at beliefs without inquiry. For, unless inquiry itself is our business, a self-sufficient occupation, it means delay and obstruction.

This ultimate fact of our nature, this natural inbred constitutional impatience, explains more than half of the wrong beliefs that we form and persist in. We must have a belief of some kind : we cannot be happy till we get it, and we take up with the first that seems to show the way clear. It may be right or it may be wrong : it is not, of course, necessarily always wrong : but that, so far as we are concerned, is a matter of accident. The pressing need for a belief of some sort, upon which our energies may proceed in anticipation at least, will not allow us to stop and inquire. Any course that offers a relief from doubt and hesitation, any conviction that lets the will go free, is eagerly embraced.

It may be thought that this can apply only to beliefs concerning the consequences of our own personal actions, affairs in which we individually play a part. It is from them, no doubt, that our nature takes this set : but the habit once formed is extended to all sorts of matters in which we have no personal interest. Tell an ordinary Englishman, it has been wittily said, that it is a question whether the planets are inhabited, and he feels bound at once to have a confident opinion on the point. The strength of the conviction bears no proportion to the amount of reason spent in reaching it, unless it may be said that as a general rule the less a belief is reasoned the more confidently it is held.

"A grocer," writes Mr. Bagehot in an acute essay on "The Emotion of Conviction," [1] "has a full creed as to foreign policy, a young lady a complete theory of the Sacraments, as to which neither has any doubt. A girl in a country parsonage will be sure that Paris never can be taken, or that Bismarck is a wretch." An attitude of philosophic doubt, of suspended judgment, is repugnant to the natural man. Belief is an independent joy to him.

This bias works in all men. While there is life, there is pressure from within on belief, tending to push reason aside. The force of the pressure, of course, varies with individual temperament, age, and other circumstances. The young are more credulous than the old, as having greater energy: they are apt, as Bacon puts it, to be " carried away by the sanguine element in their temperament". Shakespeare's Laertes is a study of the impulsive temperament, boldly contrasted with Hamlet, who has more discourse of reason. When Laertes hears that his father has been killed, he hurries home, collects a body of armed sympathisers, bursts into the presence of the king, and threatens with his vengeance—the wrong man. He never pauses to make inquiry: like Hotspur he is "a wasp-stung and impatient fool"; he must wreak his revenge on somebody, and at once. Hamlet's father also has been murdered, but his reason must be satisfied before he proceeds to his revenge, and when doubtful proof is offered, he waits for proof more relative.

Bacon's *Idola Tribus* and Dr. Bain's illustrations of

---

[1] Bagehot's *Literary Studies*, ii. 427.

incontinent energy, are mostly examples of unreasoning intellectual activity, hurried generalisations, unsound and superficial analogies, rash hypotheses. Bacon quotes the case of the sceptic in the temple of Poseidon, who, when shown the offerings of those who had made vows in danger and been delivered, and asked whether he did not now acknowledge the power of the god, replied : " But where are they who made vows and yet perished ? " This man answered rightly, says Bacon. In dreams, omens, retributions, and such like, we are apt to remember when they come true and to forget the cases when they fail. If we have seen but one man of a nation, we are apt to conclude that all his countrymen are like him ; we cannot suspend our judgment till we have seen more. Confident belief, as Dr. Bain remarks, is the primitive attitude of the human mind : it is only by slow degrees that this is corrected by experience. The old adage, " Experience teaches fools," has a meaning of its own, but in one sense it is the reverse of the truth. The mark of a fool is that he is not taught by experience, and we are all more or less intractable pupils, till our energies begin to fail.

The Bias of Happy Exercise.

If an occupation is pleasant in itself, if it fully satisfies our inner craving for action, we are liable to be blinded thereby to its consequences. Happy exercise is the fool's Paradise. The fallacy lies not in being content with what provides a field for the full activity of our powers : to be content in such a case may be the height of wisdom : but the fallacy lies in claiming for our occupation results, benefits, utilities that do not really attend upon it. Thus we see subjects of study, originally taken up for some purpose, practical, artistic, or religious, pursued into elaborate detail far beyond their original purpose, and the highest value, intellectual, spiritual, moral, claimed for them by their votaries, when in truth they merely serve to consume so much vacant energy, and may be a sheer waste of time that ought to be otherwise employed.

But as I am in danger of myself furnishing an illustration of this bias—it is nowhere more prevalent than in philosophy—I will pass to our next head.

The Bias of the Feelings.

This source of illusion is much more generally understood. The blinding and perverting influence of passion on reason has been a favourite theme with moralists ever since man began to moralise, and is acknowledged in many a popular proverb. " Love is blind ; " " The wish is father to the thought ; " " Some people's geese are all swans ; " and so forth.

We need not dwell upon the illustration of it. Fear and Sloth magnify dangers and difficulties ; Affection can see no imperfection in its object : in the eyes of Jealousy a rival is a wretch. From the nature of the case we are much more apt to see examples in others than in ourselves. If the strength of this bias were properly understood by everybody, the mistake would not so often be committed of suspecting bad faith, conscious hypocrisy, when people are found practising the grossest inconsistencies, and shutting their eyes apparently in deliberate wilfulness to facts held under their very noses. Men are inclined to ascribe this

human weakness to women.   Reasoning from feeling
is said to be feminine logic.   But it is a human
weakness.

To take one very powerful feeling, the feeling of
self-love or self-interest—this operates in much more
subtle ways than most people imagine, in ways so
subtle that the self-deceiver, however honest, would
fail to be conscious of the influence if it were pointed
out to him.   When the slothful man saith, There is a
lion in the path, we can all detect the bias to his
belief, and so we can when the slothful student says
that he will work hard to-morrow, or next week, or
next month ; or when the disappointed man shows an
exaggerated sense of the advantages of a successful
rival or of his own disadvantages.   But self-interest
works to bias belief in much less palpable ways than
those.   It is this bias that accounts for the difficulty
that men of antagonistic interests have in seeing the
arguments or believing in the honesty of their
opponents.   You shall find conferences held between
capitalists and workmen in which the two sides, both
represented by men incapable of consciously dishonest
action, fail altogether to see the force of each other's
arguments, and are mutually astonished each at the
other's blindness.

The Bias of Custom.

That custom, habits of thought and practice, affect
belief, is also generally acknowledged, though the
strength and wide reach of the bias is seldom realised.
Very simple cases of unreasoning prejudice were
adduced by Locke, who was the first to suggest a
general explanation of them in the " Association of

Ideas" (*Human Understanding*, bk. ii. ch. xxxiii.). There is, for instance, the fear that overcomes many people when alone in the dark. In vain reason tells them that there is no real danger; they have a certain tremor of apprehension that they cannot get rid of, because darkness is inseparably connected in their minds with images of horror. Similarly we contract unreasonable dislikes to places where painful things have happened to us. Equally unreasoning, if not unreasonable, is our attachment to customary doctrines or practices, and our invincible antipathy to those who do not observe them.

Words are very common vehicles for the currency of this kind of prejudice, good or bad meanings being attached to them by custom. The power of words in this way is recognised in the proverb: " Give a dog a bad name, and then hang him ". These verbal prejudices are Bacon's *Idola Fori*, illusions of conversation. Each of us is brought up in a certain sect or party, and accustomed to respect or dishonour certain sectarian or party names, Whig, Tory, Radical, Socialist, Evolutionist, Broad, Low, or High Church. We may meet a man without knowing under what label he walks and be charmed with his company: meet him again when his name is known, and all is changed.

Such errors are called Fallacies of Association to point to the psychological explanation. This is that by force of association certain ideas are brought into the mind, and that once they are there, we cannot help giving them objective reality. For example, a doctor comes to examine a patient, and finds certain symptoms. He has lately seen or heard of many cases of influenza, we shall say; influenza is running in his

head.   The idea once suggested has all the advantage
of possession.

But why is it that a man cannot get rid of an idea ?
Why does it force itself upon him as a belief ?   Association, custom, explains how it got there, but not why it
persists in staying.

To explain this we must call in our first fallacious
principle, the Impatience of Doubt or Delay, the
imperative inward need for a belief of some sort.

And this leads to another remark, that though for
convenience of exposition, we separate these various
influences, they are not separated in practice.   They
may and often do act all together, the Inner Sophist
concentrating his forces.

Finally, it may be asked whether, seeing that
illusions are the offspring of such highly respectable
qualities as excess of energy, excess of feeling, excess
of docility, it is a good thing for man to be disillusioned.   The rose-colour that lies over the world for
youth is projected from the abundant energy and
feeling within : disillusion comes with failing energies,
when hope is " unwilling to be fed ".   Is it good then
to be disillusioned ?   The foregoing exposition would
be egregiously wrong if the majority of mankind did
not resent the intrusion of Reason and its organising
lieutenant Logic.   But really there is no danger that
this intrusion succeeds to the extent of paralysing
action and destroying feeling, and uprooting custom.
The utmost that Logic can do is to modify the excess
of these good qualities by setting forth the conditions
of rational belief.   The student who masters those
conditions will soon see the practical wisdom of
applying his knowledge only in cases where the
grounds of rational belief are within his reach.   To

apply it to the consequences of every action would be to yield to that bias of incontinent activity which is, perhaps, our most fruitful source of error.

III.—THE AXIOMS OF DIALECTIC AND OF SYLLOGISM.

There are certain principles known as the Laws of Thought or the Maxims of Consistency. They are variously expressed, variously demonstrated, and variously interpreted, but in one form or another they are often said to be the foundation of all Logic. It is even said that all the doctrines of Deductive or Syllogistic Logic may be educed from them. Let us take the most abstract expression of them, and see how they originated. Three laws are commonly given, named respectively the Law of Identity, the Law of Contradiction and the Law of Excluded Middle.

1. *The Law of Identity.* A is A. Socrates is Socrates. Guilt is guilt.

2. *The Law of Contradiction.* A is not not-A. Socrates is not other than Socrates. Guilt is not other than guilt. Or A is not at once *b* and not-*b*. Socrates is not at once good and not-good. Guilt is not at once punishable and not-punishable.

3. *The Law of Excluded Middle.* Everything is either A or not-A ; or, A is either *b* or not-*b*. A given thing is either Socrates or not-Socrates, either guilty or not-guilty. It must be one or the other: no middle is possible.

Why lay down principles so obvious, in some interpretations, and so manifestly sophistical in others ? The bare forms of modern Logic have been reached by a process of attenuation from a passage in Aristotle's *Metaphysics*[1] (iii. 3, 4, 1005*b* – 1008). He is there laying down the first principle of demonstration, which he takes to be that " it is impossible that the same predicate can both belong, and not belong, to the same subject, at the same time, and in the same sense ".[2] That Socrates knows grammar, and does not know grammar—these two propositions cannot both be true at the same time, and in the same sense. Two contraries cannot exist together in the same subject. The double answer Yes and No cannot be given to one and the same question understood in the same sense.

But why did Aristotle consider it necessary to lay down a principle so obvious ? Simply because among the subtle dialecticians who preceded him the principle had been challenged. The Platonic dialogue Euthydemus shows the farcical lengths to which such quibbling was carried. The two brothers vanquish all opponents, but it is by claiming that the answer No does not preclude the answer Yes. " Is not the honourable honourable, and the base base ? " asks Socrates. " That is as I please," replies Dionysodorus. Socrates concludes that there is no arguing with such men : they repudiate the first principles of dialectic.

There were, however, more respectable practitioners

---

[1] The first statement of the Law of Identity in the form *Ens est ens* is ascribed by Hamilton (*Lectures*, iii. 91) to Antonius Andreas, a fourteenth century commentator on the *Metaphysics*. But Andreas is merely expounding what Aristotle sets forth in iii. 4, 1006 *a*, *b*. *Ens est ens* does not mean in Andreas what A is A means in Hamilton.

[2] τὸ γὰρ αὐτὸ ἅμα ὑπάρχειν τε καὶ μὴ ὑπάρχειν ἀδύνατον τῷ αὐτῷ καὶ κατὰ τὸ αὐτὸ, . . . αὕτη δὴ πασῶν ἐστὶ βεβαιοτάτη τῶν ἀρχῶν. iii. 3, 1005*b*, 19-23.

who canvassed on more plausible grounds any form into which ultimate doctrines about contraries and contradictions, truth and falsehood, could be put, and therefore Aristotle considered it necessary to put forth and defend at elaborate length a statement of a first principle of demonstration. "Contradictions cannot both be true of the same subject at the same time and in the same sense." This is the original form of the Law of Contradiction.

The words " of the same subject," " at the same time," and " in the same sense," are carefully chosen to guard against possible quibbles. "*Socrates knows grammar.*" By Socrates we must mean the same individual man. And even of the same man the assertion may be true at one time and not at another. There was a time when Socrates did not know grammar, though he knows it now. And the assertion may be true in one sense and not in another. It may be true that Socrates knows grammar, yet not that he knows everything that is to be known about grammar, or that he knows as much as Aristarchus.

Aristotle acknowledges that this first principle cannot itself be demonstrated, that is, deduced from any other. If it is denied, you can only reduce the denier to an absurdity. And in showing how to proceed in so doing, he says you must begin by coming to an agreement about the words used, that they signify the same for one and the other disputant.[1]

---

[1] Hamilton credits Andreas with maintaining, "against Aristotle," that "the principle of Identity, and not the principle of Contradiction, is the one absolutely first". Which comes first, is a scholastic question on which ingenuity may be exercised. But in fact Aristotle put the principle of Identity first in the above plain sense, and Andreas only expounded more formally what Aristotle had said.

No dialectic is possible without this understanding. This first principle of Dialectic is the original of the Law of Identity. While any question as to the truth or falsehood of a question is pending, from the beginning to the end of any logical process, the words must continue to be accepted in the same sense. Words must have an identical reference to things.

Incidentally in discussing the Axiom of Contradiction (ἀξίωμα τῆς ἀντιφάσεως),[1] Aristotle lays down what is now known as the Law of Excluded Middle. Of two contradictories one or other must be true : we must either affirm or deny any one thing of any other : no mean or middle is possible.

In their origin, then, these so-called Laws of Thought were simply the first principles of Dialectic and Demonstration. Consecutive argument, coherent ratiocination, is impossible unless they are taken for granted.

If we divorce or abstract them from their original application, and consider them merely as laws of thinking or of being, any abstract expression, or illustration, or designation of them may easily be pushed into antagonism with other plain truths or first principles equally rudimentary. Without entering into the perplexing and voluminous discussion to which these laws have been subjected by logicians within the last hundred years, a little casuistry is necessary to enable the student to understand within what limits they hold good.

Socrates is Socrates. The name Socrates is a name

---

[1] Μεταξὺ ἀντιφάσεως ἐνδέχεται εἶναι οὐθέν, ἀλλ' ἀνάγκη ἢ φάναι ἢ ἀποφάναι ἓν καθ' ἑνὸς ὁτιοῦν. *Metaph.* iii. 7, 1011b, 23-4.

for something to which you and I refer when we use the name. Unless we have the same reference, we cannot hold any argument about the thing, or make any communication one to another about it.

But if we take *Socrates is Socrates* to mean that, "An object of thought or thing is identical with itself," "An object of thought or thing cannot be other than itself," and call this a law of thought, we are met at once by a difficulty. Thought, properly speaking, does not begin till we pass beyond the identity of an object with itself. Thought begins only when we recognise the likeness between one object and others. To keep within the self-identity of the object is to suspend thought. " Socrates was a native of Attica," " Socrates was a wise man," " Socrates was put to death as a troubler of the commonweal "—whenever we begin to think or say anything about Socrates, to ascribe any attributes to him, we pass out of his self-identity into his relations of likeness with other men, into what he has in common with other men.

Hegelians express this plain truth with paradoxical point when they say : " Of any definite existence or thought, therefore, it may be said with quite as much truth that it *is not*, as that it *is*, its own bare self".[1] Or, " A thing must other itself in order to be itself". Controversialists treat this as a subversion of the laws of Identity and Contradiction. But it is only Hegel's fun—his paradoxical way of putting the plain truth that any object has more in common with other objects than it has peculiar to itself. Till we enter into those aspects of agreement with other objects, we cannot truly be said to think at

[1] Prof. Caird's *Hegel*, p. 138.

all. If we say merely that a thing is itself, we may as well say nothing about it. To lay down this is not to subvert the Law of Identity, but to keep it from being pushed to the extreme of appearing to deny the Law of Likeness, which is the foundation of all the characters, attributes, or qualities of things in our thoughts.

That self-same objects are like other self-same objects, is an assumption distinct from the Law of Identity, and any interpretation of it that excludes this assumption is to be repudiated. But does not the law of Identity as well as the law of the likeness of mutually exclusive identities presuppose that there are objects self-same, like others, and different from others? Certainly: this is one of the presuppositions of Logic.[1] We assume that the world of which we talk and reason is separated into such objects in our thoughts. We assume that such words as *Socrates* represent individual objects with a self-same being or substance; that such words as *wisdom, humour, ugliness, running, sitting, here, there,* represent attributes, qualities, characters or predicates of individuals; that such words as *man* represent groups or classes of individuals.

Some logicians in expressing the Law of Identity have their eye specially upon the objects signified by general names or abstract names, *man, education.*[2] "A concept is identical with the sum of its characters," or, "Classes are identical with the sum of the individuals composing them". The assumptions thus expressed in technical language which will hereafter

[1] See Venn, *Empirical Logic*, 1-8.
[2] *E.g.,* Hamilton, lect. v.; Veitch's *Institutes of Logic*, chaps. xii., xiii.

be explained are undoubtedly assumptions that Logic makes : but since they are statements of the internal constitution of some of the identities that words represent, to call them the Law of Identity is to depart confusingly from traditional usage.[1]

That throughout any logical process a word must signify the same object, is one proposition : that the object signified by a general name is identical with the sum of the individuals to each of whom it is applicable, or with the sum of the characters that they bear in common, is another proposition. Logic assumes both : Aristotle assumed both : but it is the first that is historically the original of all expressions of the Law of Identity in modern text-books.

Yet another expression of a Law of Identity which is really distinct from and an addition to Aristotle's original. *Socrates was an Athenian, a philosopher, an ugly man, an acute dialectician, etc.* Let it be granted that the word Socrates bears the same signification throughout all these and any number more of predicates, we may still ask : " But what is it that Socrates signifies ? " The title Law of Identity is sometimes given[2] to a theory on this point. *Socrates is Socrates.* " An individual is the identity running through the totality of its attributes." Is this not, it may be

---

[1] The confusion probably arises in this way. First, these " laws " are formulated as laws of thought that Logic assumes. Second, a notion arises that these laws are the only postulates of Logic : that all logical doctrines can be " evolved " from them. Third, when it is felt that more than the identical reference of words or the identity of a thing with itself must be assumed in Logic, the Law of Identity is extended to cover this further assumption.

[2] *E.g.,* Bosanquet's *Logic,* ii. 207.

asked, to confuse thought and being, to resolve
Socrates into a string of words? No: real existence
is one of the admissible predicates of Socrates: one
of the attributes under which we conceive him. But
whether we accept or reject this " Law of Identity,"
it is an addition to Aristotle's dialectical " law of
identity"; it is a theory of the metaphysical nature
of the identity signified by a Singular name. And
the same may be said of yet another theory of Identity,
that, " An individual is identical with the totality of its
predicates," or (another way of putting the same theory),
" An individual is a conflux of generalities ".

To turn next to the Laws of Contradiction and
Excluded Middle. These also may be subjected to
Casuistry, making clearer what they assert by showing
what they do not deny.

They do not deny that things change, and that successive states of the same thing may pass into one
another by imperceptible degrees. A thing may be
neither here nor there : it may be on the passage
from here to there : and, while it is in motion, we
may say, with equal truth, that it is neither here nor
there, or that it is both here and there. Youth passes
gradually into age, day into night : a given man or a
given moment may be on the borderland between the
two.

Logic does not deny the existence of indeterminate
margins: it merely lays down that for purposes of
clear communication and coherent reasoning the line
must be drawn somewhere between b, and not-b.

A difference, however, must be recognised between
logical negation and the negations of common thought
and common speech. The latter are definite to a

degree with which the mere Logic of Consistency does not concern itself. To realise this is to understand more clearly the limitations of Formal Logic.

In common speech, to deny a quality of anything is by implication to attribute to it some other quality of the same kind. Let any man tell me that " the streets of such and such a town are not paved with wood," I at once conclude that they are paved with some other material. It is the legitimate effect of his negative proposition to convey this impression to my mind. If, proceeding on this, I go on to ask: " Then they are paved with granite or asphalt, or this or that ? " and he turns round and says : " I did not say they were paved at all," I should be justified in accusing him of a quibble. In ordinary speech, to deny one kind of pavement is to assert pavement of some kind. Similarly, to deny that So-and-so is not in the Twenty-first Regiment, is to imply that he is in another regiment, that he is in the army in some regiment. To retort upon this inference: " He is not in the army at all," is a quibble : as much so as it would be to retort : " There is no such person in existence ".

Now Logic does not take account of this implication, and nothing has contributed more to bring upon it the reproach of quibbling. In Logic, to deny a quality is simply to declare a repugnance between it and the subject ; negation is mere sublation, taking away, and implies nothing more. Not-*b* is entirely indefinite : it may cover anything except *b*.

Is Logic then really useless, or even misleading, inasmuch as it ignores the definite implication of negatives in ordinary thought and speech ? In ignoring this implication, does Logic oppose this implication as erroneous ? Does Logic shelter the quibbler who trades upon it? By no means : to jump to this conclusion were a misunderstanding. The fact only is that nothing beyond the logical Law of Contradiction needs to be assumed for any of the processes of Formal Logic. Aristotle required to assume nothing more for his syllogistic formulæ, and Logic has not yet included in its scope any process that requires any further assumption. " If not-b represent everything except b, everything outside b, then that A is b, and that A is not-b, cannot both be true, and one or other of them must be true."

Whether the scope of Logic ought to be extended is another question. It seems to me that the scope of Logic may legitimately be extended so as to take account both of the positive implication of negatives and the negative implication of positives. I therefore deal with this subject in a separate chapter following on the ordinary doctrines of Immediate Inference, where I try to explain the simple Law of Thought involved. When I say that the extension is legitimate, I mean that it may be made without departing from the traditional view of Logic as a practical science, conversant with the nature of thought and its expression only in so far as it can provide practical guidance against erroneous interpretations and inferences. The extension that I propose is in effect an attempt to bring within the fold of Practical Logic some of the results of the dialectic of Hegel and his followers, such as Mr. Bradley and Mr. Bosanquet, Professor Caird and Professor Wallace.[1]

The logical processes formulated by Aristotle are

[1] Bradley, *Principles of Logic ;* Bosanquet, *Logic or The Morphology of Knowledge ;* Caird, *Hegel* (in Blackwood's Philosophical Classics) ; Wallace, *The Logic of Hegel.*

merely stages in the movement of thought towards attaining definite conceptions of reality. To treat their conclusions as positions in which thought may dwell and rest, is an error, against which Logic itself as a practical science may fairly be called upon to guard. It may even be conceded that the Aristotelian processes are artificial stages, courses that thought does not take naturally, but into which it has to be forced for a purpose. To concede this is not to concede that the Aristotelian logic is useless, as long as we have reason on our side in holding that thought is benefited and strengthened against certain errors by passing through those artificial stages.

BOOK I.

THE LOGIC OF CONSISTENCY. SYLLOGISM AND
DEFINITION.

PART I.

THE ELEMENTS OF PROPOSITIONS.

CHAPTER I.

GENERAL NAMES AND ALLIED DISTINCTIONS.

To discipline us against the errors we are liable to in receiving knowledge through the medium of words—such is one of the objects of Logic, the main object of what may be called the Logic of Consistency.

Strictly speaking, we may receive knowledge about things through signs or single words, as a nod, a wink, a cry, a call, a command. But an assertory sentence, proposition, or predication, is the unit with which Logic concerns itself—a sentence in which a subject is named and something is said or predicated about it. Let a man once understand the errors incident to this regular mode of communication, and he may safely be left to protect himself against the errors incident to more rudimentary modes.

A proposition, whether long or short, is a unit, but it is an analysable unit. And the key to syllogistic analysis is the General Name. Every proposition, every sentence in which we convey knowledge to another, contains a general name or its equivalent. That is to say, every proposition may be resolved into a form in which the predicate is a general name. A knowledge of the function of this element of speech is the basis of all logical discipline. Therefore, though we must always remember that the proposition is the real unit of speech, and the general name only an analytic element, we take the general name and its allied distinctions in thought and reality first.

How propositions are analysed for syllogistic purposes will be shown by-and-by, but we must first explain various technical terms that logicians have devised to define the features of this cardinal element. The technical terms CLASS, CONCEPT, NOTION, ATTRIBUTE, EXTENSION or DENOTATION, INTENSION or CONNOTATION, GENUS, SPECIES, DIFFERENTIA, SINGULAR NAME, COLLECTIVE NAME, ABSTRACT NAME, all centre round it.

A **general name** is a name applicable to a number of different things on the ground of some likeness among them, as *man*, *ratepayer*, *man of courage*, *man who fought at Waterloo*.

From the examples it will be seen that a general name logically is not necessarily a single word. Any word or combination of words that serves a certain function is technically a general name. The different ways of making in common speech the equivalent of a general name logically are for the grammarian to consider.

In the definition of a general name attention is called to two distinct considerations, the individual objects to each of which the name is applicable, and the points of‹ resemblance among them, in virtue of which they have a common name. For those distinctions there are technical terms.

Class is the technical term for the objects, different yet agreeing, to each of which a general name may be applied.

The points of resemblance are called the common **attributes** of the class.

A class may be constituted on one attribute or on several. *Ratepayer, woman ratepayer, unmarried woman ratepayer: soldier, British soldier, British soldier on foreign service.* But every individual to which the general name can be applied must possess the common attribute or attributes.

These common attributes are also called the **Notion** of the class, inasmuch as it is them that the mind notes or should note when the general name is applied. **Concept** is a synonym perhaps in more common use than notion; the rationale of this term (derived from *con* and *capere*, to take or grasp together) being that it is by means of the points of resemblance that the individuals are grasped or held together by the mind. These common points are the one in the many, the same amidst the different, the identity signified by the common name. The name of an attribute as thought of by itself without reference to any individual or class possessing it, is called an **Abstract** name. By contradistinction, the name of an individual or a class is **Concrete.**

Technical terms are wanted also to express the relation of the individuals and the attributes to the general name. The individuals jointly are spoken of as the **Denotation,** or **Extension** or **Scope** of the

name ; the common attributes as its **Connotation,
Intension, Comprehension,** or **Ground.** The whole
denotation, etc., is the class ; the whole connotation,
etc., is the concept.[1]

---

[1] It has been somewhat too hastily assumed on the authority
of Mansel (Note to Aldrich, pp. 16, 17) that Mill inverted the
scholastic tradition in his use of the word *Connotative.* Mansel
puts his statement doubtfully, and admits that there was some
licence in the use of the word Connotative, but holds that in
Scholastic Logic an adjective was said to " signify *primarily* the
attribute, and to *connote* or *signify secondarily* (προσσημαίνειν) the
subject of inhesion ". The truth is that Mansel's view was a
theory of usage not a statement of actual usage, and he had good
reason for putting it doubtfully.

As a matter of fact, the history of the distinction follows the
simple type of increasing precision and complexity, and Mill was
in strict accord with standard tradition. By the Nominalist
commentators on the *Summulæ* of Petrus Hispanus certain names,
adjectives grammatically, are called *Connotativa* as opposed to
Absoluta, simply because they have a double function. White is
connotative as signifying both a subject, such as Socrates, of
whom "whiteness" is an attribute, and an attribute "whiteness":
the names " Socrates " and "whiteness " are Absolute, as having
but a single signification. Occam himself speaks of the subject
as the primary signification, and the attribute as the secondary,
because the answer to "What is white?" is "Something informed
with whiteness," and the subject is in the nominative case while
the attribute is in an oblique case (*Logic*, part i. chap. x.). Later
on we find that Tataretus (*Expositio in Summulas*, A.D. 1501),
while mentioning (Tract. Sept. *De Appellationibus*) that it is a
matter of **dispute** among Doctores whether a connotative name
connotat the subject or the attribute, is perfectly explicit in his
own definition, " Terminus connotativus est qui præter illud pro
quo supponit connotat aliquid adjacere vel non adjacere rei pro
qua supponit " (Tract. Sept. *De Suppositionibus*). And this
remained the standard usage as long as the distinction remained
in logical text-books. We find it very clearly expressed by
Clichtoveus, a Nominalist, quoted as an authority by Guthutius

The limits of a "class" in Logic are fixed by the common attributes. Any individual object that

in his *Gymnasium Speculativum*, Paris, 1607 (*De Terminorum Cognitione*, pp. 78-9). "Terminus absolutus est, qui solum illud pro quo in propositione supponit, significat. Connotativus autem, qui ultra idipsum, aliud importat." Thus *man* and *animal* are absolute terms, which simply stand for (supponunt pro) the things they signify. *White* is a connotative name, because "it stands for (supponit pro) a subject in which it is an accident: and beyond this, still signifies an accident, which is in that subject, and is expressed by an abstract name". Only Clichtoveus drops the verb *connotat*, perhaps as a disputable term, and says simply *ultra importat.*

So in the Port Royal Logic (1662), from which possibly Mill took the distinction: "Les noms qui signifient les choses comme modifiées, marquant premièrement et directement la chose, quoique plus confusément, et indirectement le mode, quoique plus distinctement, sont appelés *adjectifs* ou *connotatifs;* comme rond, dur, juste, prudent" (part i. chap. ii.).

What Mill did was not to invert Scholastic usage but to revive the distinction, and extend the word connotative to general names on the ground that they also imported the possession of attributes. The word has been as fruitful of meticulous discussion as it was in the Renaissance of Logic, though the ground has changed. The point of Mill's innovation was, premising that general names are not absolute but are applied in virtue of a meaning, to put emphasis on this meaning as the cardinal consideration. What he called the connotation had dropped out of sight as not being required in the Syllogistic Forms. This was as it were the point at which he put in his horn to toss the prevalent conception of Logic as Syllogistic.

The real drift of Mill's innovation has been obscured by the fact that it was introduced among the preliminaries of Syllogism, whereas its real usefulness and significance belongs not to Syllogism in the strict sense but to Definition. He added to the confusion by trying to devise forms of Syllogism based on connotation, and by discussing the Axiom of the Syllogism from this point of view. For syllogistic purposes, as we shall see, Aristotle's forms are perfect, and his conception of the proposition

possesses these is a member.   The statement of them
is the **Definition.**

To predicate a general name of any object, as,
" This is a cat," " This is a very sad affair," is to
refer that object to a class, which is equivalent to
saying that it has certain features of resemblance with
other objects, that it reminds us of them by its likeness
to them.   Thus to say that the predicate of every
proposition is a general name, expressed or implied, is
the same as to say that every predication may be
taken as a reference to a class.

Ordinarily our notion or concept of the common
features signified by general names is vague and hazy.
The business of Logic is to make them clear.   It is to
this end that the individual objects of the class are

in extension the only correct conception.   Whether the centre
of gravity in Consistency Logic should not be shifted back
from Syllogism to Definition, the latter being the true centre
of consistency, is another question.   The tendency of Mill's
polemic was to make this change.   And possibly the secret of
the support it has recently received from Mr. Bradley and Mr.
Bosanquet is that they, following Hegel, are moving in the
same direction.

In effect, Mill's doctrine of Connotation helped to fix a conception of the general name first dimly suggested by Aristotle
when he recognised that names of genera and species signify
Quality, in showing what sort a thing is.   Occam carried this a
step farther towards clear light by including among Connotative
Terms such general names as " monk," names of classes that at
once suggest a definite attribute.   The third step was made by
Mill in extending the term Connotation to such words as " man,"
" horse," the *Infimæ Species* of the Schoolmen, the Species of
modern science.

Whether connotation was the best term to use for this purpose,
rather than extension, may be questioned : but at least it was in
the line of tradition through Occam.

summoned before the mind. In ordinary thinking there is no definite array or muster of objects: when we think of "dog" or "cat," "accident," "book," "beggar," "ratepayer," we do not stop to call before the mind a host of representatives of the class, nor do we take precise account of their common attributes. The concept of "house" is what all houses have in common. To make this explicit would be no easy matter, and yet we are constantly referring objects to the class "house". We shall see presently that if we wish to make the connotation or concept clear we must run over the denotation or class, that is to say, the objects to which the general name is applied in common usage. Try, for example, to conceive clearly what is meant by house, tree, dog, walking-stick. You think of individual objects, so-called, and of what they have in common.

A class may be constituted on one property or on many. There are several points common to all houses, enclosing walls, a roof, a means of exit and entrance. For the full concept of the natural kinds, *men*, *dogs*, *mice*, etc., we should have to go to the natural historian.

Degrees of generality. One class is said to be of higher generality than another when it includes that other and more. Thus animal includes man, dog, horse, etc.; man includes Aryan, Semite, etc.; Aryan includes Hindoo, Teuton, Celt, etc.

The technical names for higher and lower classes are **Genus** and **Species.** These terms are not fixed as in Natural History to certain grades, but are purely relative one to another, and movable up and down a scale of generality. A class may be a species relatively to one class, which is above it, and a genus

relatively to one below it.   Thus Aryan is a species
of the genus man, Teuton a species of the genus
Aryan.

In the graded divisions of Natural History genus
and species are fixed names for certain grades.   Thus:
Vertebrates form a " division " ; the next subdivision,
e.g., Mammals, Birds, Reptiles, etc., is called a " class ";
the next, *e.g.*, Rodents, Carnivora, Ruminants, an
" order " ; the next, *e.g.*, Rats, Squirrels, Beavers, a
" genus " ;   the next, *e.g.*, Brown rats, Mice, a
" species ".

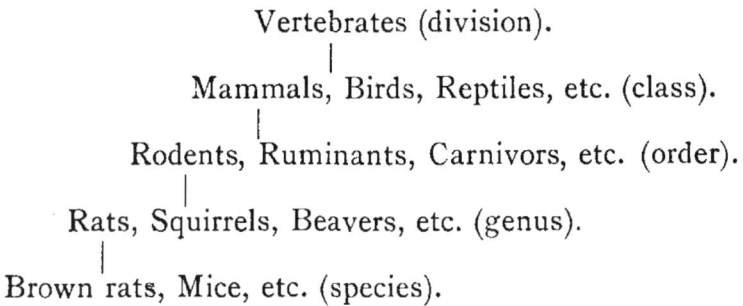

Vertebrates (division).

Mammals, Birds, Reptiles, etc. (class).

Rodents, Ruminants, Carnivors, etc. (order).

Rats, Squirrels, Beavers, etc. (genus).

Brown rats, Mice, etc. (species).

If we subdivide a large class into smaller classes,
and, again, subdivide these subdivisions, we come at
last to single objects.

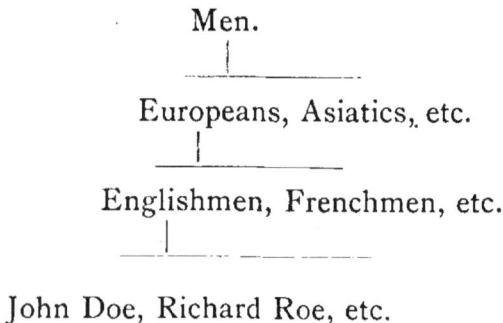

Men.

Europeans, Asiatics, etc.

Englishmen, Frenchmen, etc.

John Doe, Richard Roe, etc.

A table of higher and lower classes arranged in order has been known from of old as a *tree* of division or classification.   The following is Porphyry's " tree ":—

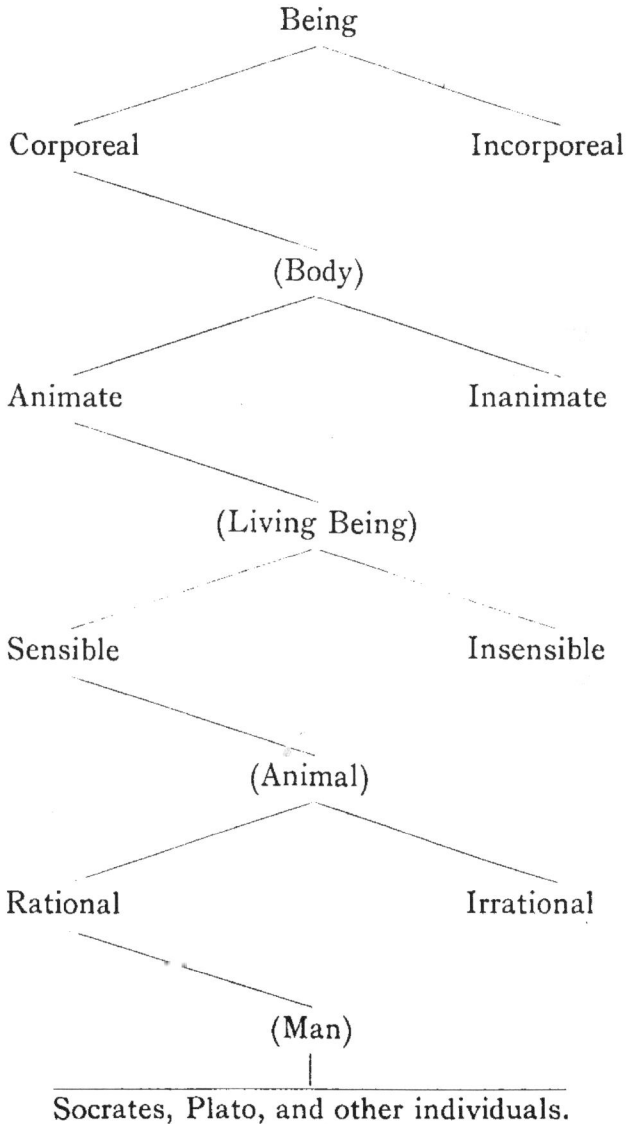

```
                    Being
          /                      \
   Corporeal                   Incorporeal
          \
           (Body)
          /      \
   Animate        Inanimate
          \
           (Living Being)
          /          \
   Sensible           Insensible
          \
           (Animal)
          /      \
   Rational        Irrational
          \
           (Man)
             |
```
Socrates, Plato, and other individuals.

The single objects are called **Individuals,** because the division cannot be carried farther. The highest. class is technically the **Summum Genus,** or *Genus generalissimum ;* the next highest class to any species is the **Proximum Genus ;** the lowest group before you descend to individuals is the **Infima Species,** or *Species specialissima.*

The attribute or attributes whereby a species is distinguished from other species of the same genus, is called its **differentia** or **differentiæ.** The various species of houses are differentiated by their several uses, dwelling-house, town-house, ware-house, public-house. ´ Poetry is a species of Fine Art, its differentia being the use of metrical language as its instrument.

A lower class, indicated by the name of its higher class qualified by´ adjectives or adjective phrases expressing its differential property or properties, is said to be described **per genus et differentiam.** Examples : " Black-bird," " note-book," " clever man," " man of Kent," " eminent British painter of marine subjects ". By giving a combination of attributes common to him with nobody else, we may narrow down the application of a name to an individual : " The Commander-in-Chief of the British forces at the battle of Waterloo ".

Other attributes of classes as divided and defined, have received technical names.

An attribute common to all the individuals of a class, found in that class only, and following from the essential or defining attributes, though not included among them, is called a **Proprium.**

An attribute that belongs to some, but not to all, or that belongs to all, but is not a necessary consequence of the essential attributes, is called an **Accident.**

The clearest examples of Propria are found in

mathematical figures. Thus, the defining property of an equilateral triangle is the equality of the sides : the equality of the angles is a proprium. That the three angles of a triangle are together equal to two right angles is a proprium, true of all triangles, and deducible from the essential properties of a triangle.

Outside Mathematics, it is not easy to find *propria* that satisfy the three conditions of the definition. It is a useful exercise of the wits to try for such. Educability—an example of the proprium in mediæval text-books—is common to men, and results from man's essential constitution ; but it is not peculiar ; other animals are educable. That man cooks his food is probably a genuine proprium.

That horses run wild in Thibet : that gold is found in California : that clergymen wear white ties, are examples of Accidents. Learning is an accident in man, though educability is a proprium.

What is known technically as an **Inseparable Accident,** such as the black colour of the crow or the Ethiopian, is not easy to distinguish from the Proprium. It is distinguished only by the third character, deducibility from the essence.[1]

---

[1] The history of the definition of the *Proprium* is an example of the tendency of distinctions to become more minute and at the same time more purposeless. Aristotle's ἴδιον was an attribute, such as the laugh of the man or the bark of the dog, common to all of a class and peculiar to the class (*quod convenit omni soli et semper*) yet not comprised in the definition of the class. Porphyry recognised three varieties of ἴδια besides this, four in all, as follows :—(1) an attribute peculiar to a species but not possessed by all, as knowledge of medicine or geometry ; (2) possessed by a whole species but not peculiar to it, as being a biped in man ; (3) peculiar to a species, and possessed by all at a certain time, as turning grey in old age ; (4) Aristotle's "proprium," peculiar and

Accidents that are both common and peculiar are often useful for distinguishing members of a class. Distinctive dresses or badges, such as the gown of a student, the hood of a D.D., are accidents, but mark the class of the individual wearer. So with the colours of flowers.

Genus, *Species*, *Differentia*, *Proprium*, and *Accidens* have been known since the time of Porphyry as the FIVE PREDICABLES. They are really only terms used in dividing and defining. We shall return to them and endeavour to show that they have no significance except with reference to fixed schemes, scientific or popular, of Division or Classification.

Given such a fixed scheme, very nice questions may be raised as to whether a particular attribute is a defining attribute, or a proprium, or an accident, or an inseparable accident. Such questions afford great scope for the exercise of the analytic intellect.

We shall deal more particularly with degrees of generality when we come to Definition. This much has been necessary to explain an unimportant but much discussed point in Logic, what is known as the inverse variation of Connotation and Denotation.

Connotation and Denotation are often said to vary inversely in quantity. The larger the connotation the smaller the denotation, and *vice versâ*. With certain qualifications the statement is correct enough, but it is a rough compendious way of expressing the facts and it needs qualification.

The main fact to be expressed is that the more

possessed by all, as risibility. The idea of the Proprium as deducible from or consequent on the essence would seem to have originated in the desire to find something common to all Porphyry's four varieties.

general a name is, the thinner is its meaning. The wider the scope, the shallower the ground. As you rise in the scale of generality, your classes are wider but the number of common attributes is less. Inversely, the name of a species has a smaller denotation than the name of its genus, but a richer connotation. *Fruit-tree* applies to fewer objects than *tree*, but the objects denoted have more in common : so with *apple* and *fruit-tree*, *Ribston Pippin* and *apple*.

Again, as a rule, if you increase the connotation you contract the area within which the name is applicable. Take any group of things having certain attributes in common, say, *men of ability :* add *courage, beauty, height of six feet, chest measurement of 40 inches*, and with each addition fewer individuals are to be found possessing all the common attributes.

This is obvious enough, and yet the expression inverse variation is open to objection. For the denotation may be increased in a sense without affecting the connotation. The birth of an animal may be said to increase the denotation : every year thousands of new houses are built : there are swarms of flies in a hot summer and few in a cold. But all the time the connotation of *animal, house*, or *fly* remains the same : the word does not change its meaning.

It is obviously wrong to say that they vary in inverse proportion. Double or treble the number of attributes, and you do not necessarily reduce the denotation by one-half or one-third.

It is, in short, the meaning or connotation that is the main thing. This determines the application of a word. As a rule if you increase meaning, you restrict scope. Let your idea, notion, or concept of *culture* be a knowledge of Mathematics, Latin and Greek :

your *men of culture* will be more numerous than if you require from each of them these qualifications *plus* a modern language, an acquaintance with the Fine Arts, urbanity of manners, etc.

It is just possible to increase the connotation without decreasing the denotation, to thicken or deepen the concept without diminishing the class. This is possible only when two properties are exactly co-extensive, as equilaterality and equiangularity in triangles.

Singular and **Proper** Names. A Proper or Singular name is a name used to designate an individual. Its function, as distinguished from that of the general name, is to be used purely for the purpose of distinctive reference.

A man is not called Tom or Dick because he is like in certain respects to other Toms or other Dicks. The Toms or the Dicks do not form a logical class. The names are given purely for purposes of distinction, to single out an individual subject. The Arabic equivalent for a Proper name, *alam,* " a mark," " a sign-post," is a recognition of this.

In the expressions " a Napoleon," " a Hotspur," " a Harry," the names are not singular names logically, but general names logically, used to signify the possession of certain attributes.

A man may be nicknamed on a ground, but if the name sticks and is often used, the original meaning is forgotten. If it suggests the individual in any one of his qualities, any point in which he resembles other individuals, it is no longer a Proper or Singular name logically, that is, in logical function. That function is fulfilled when it has called to mind the individual intended.

To ask, as is sometimes done, whether Proper names

are connotative or denotative, is merely a confusion of language. The distinction between connotation and denotation, extension and intension, applies only to general names. Unless a name is general, it has neither extension nor intension :[1] a Proper or Singular name is essentially the opposite of a general name and has neither the one nor the other.

A nice distinction may be drawn between Proper and Singular names, though they are strict synonyms for the same logical function. It is not essential to the discharge of that function that the name should be strictly appropriated to one object. There are many Toms and many Dicks. It is enough that the word indicates the individual without confusion in the particular circumstances.

This function may be discharged by words and combinations of words that are not Proper in the grammatical sense. " This man," " the cover of this book," " the Prime Minister of England," " the seer of

---

[1] It is a plausible contention that in the case of the Singular name the extension is at a minimum and the intension at a maximum, the extension being one individual, and the intension the totality of his attributes. But this is an inexact and confused use of words. A name does not *extend* beyond the individual except when it is used to signify one, or more of his prominent qualities, that is, is used with the function of a general name. The *extension* of a Singular name is zero : it has no extension. On the other hand, it suggests, in its function as a Singular name, no properties or qualities ; it suggests only a subject ; *i.e.*, it has no intension. The ambiguity of the term Denotation helps the confusion in the case of Singular names. " Denote " in common speech means to indicate, to distinguish. But when in Logic we say that a general name denotes individuals, we have no thought of indicating or distinguishing : we mean only that it is applicable to any one, without respect of individuals, either in predication or epithetic description.

Chelsea," may be Singular names as much as Honolulu or Lord Tennyson.

In common speech Singular names are often manufactured *ad hoc* by taking a general name and narrowing it down by successive qualifications till it applies only to one individual, as "The leading subject of the Sovereign of England at the present time". If it so happens that an individual has some attribute or combination peculiar to himself, he may be suggested by the mention of that attribute or combination :— "the inventor of the steam-engine," "the author of Hudibras ".

Have such names a connotation ? The student may exercise his wits on the question. It is a nice one, an excellent subject of debate. Briefly, if we keep rigid hold of the meaning of connotation, this Singular name has none. The combination is a singular name only when it is the subject of a predication or an attribution, as in the sentences, " The position of the leading subject of etc., is a difficult one," or " The leading subject of etc., wears an eyeglass". In such a sentence as " So-and-so is the leading subject of etc.," the combined name has a connotation, but then it is a general and not a singular name.

Collective Names, as distinguished from General Names. A collective name is a name for a number of similar units taken as a whole—a name for a totality of similar units, as army, regiment, mob, mankind, patrimony, personal estate.

A group or collection designated by a collective name is so far like a class that the individual objects have something in common : they are not heterogeneous but homogeneous. A mob is a collection of human beings : a regiment of soldiers ; a library of books.

The distinction lies in. this, that whatever is said of a collective name is said about the collection as a whole, and does not apply to each individual; whatever is said of a general name applies to each individual. Further, the collective name can be predicated only of the whole group, as a whole; the general name is predicable of each, distributively. " Mankind has been in existence for thousands of years;" " The mob passed through the streets." In such expressions as " An honest man's the noblest work of God," the subject is functionally a collective name.

A collective name may be used as a general name when it is extended on the ground of what is common to all such totalities as it designates. " An excited mob is dangerous;" " An army without discipline is useless." The collective name is then " connotative " of the common characters of the collection.

Material or Substantial Names. The question has been raised whether names of material, gold, water, snow, coal, are general or collective singular. In the case of pieces or bits of a material, it is true that any predicate made concerning the material, such as " Sugar is sweet," or " Water quenches thirst," applies to any and every portion. But the separate portions are not individuals in the whole signified by a material name as individuals are in a class. Further, the name of material cannot be predicated of a portion as a class name can be of an individual. We cannot say, " This is a sugar ". When we say, " This is a piece of sugar," sugar is a collective name for the whole material. There are probably words on the borderland between general names and collective names. In such expressions as " This is a *coal*," " The bonnie *water* o' Urie,"

the material name is used as a general name.   The
real distinction is between the distributive use and the
collective use of a name ; as a matter of grammatical
usage, the same word may be used either way, but
logically in any actual proposition it must be either
one or the other.

Abstract Names are names for the common attributes or concepts on which classes are constituted.   A
concrete name is a name directly applicable to an
individual in all his attributes, that is, as he exists in
the concrete.   It may be written on a ticket and pinned
to him.   When we have occasion to speak of the point
or points in which a number of individuals resemble
one another, we use what is called an abstract name.
" Generous man," " clever man," " timid man," are
concrete names; "generosity," "cleverness," "timidity,"
are abstract names.

It is disputed whether abstract names are connotative.
The question is a confused one : it is like asking
whether the name of a town is municipal.   An abstract
name is the name of a connotation as a separate
object of thought or reference, conceived or spoken of
in abstraction from individual accidents.   Strictly
speaking it is notative rather than *con*notative : it cannot be said to have a connotation because it is itself
the symbol of what is called the connotation of a
general name.[1]

---

[1] Strictly speaking, as I have tried to indicate all along, the
words Connotation and Denotation, or Extension and Intension,
apply only to general names.   Outside general names, they have
no significance.   An adjective with its noun is a general name, of
which the adjective gives part of the Connotation.   If we apply
the word connotation to signify merely the suggestion of an
attribute in whatever grammatical connexion, then an abstract

The distinction between abstract names and concrete names is virtually a grammatical distinction, that is, a distinction in mode of predication. We may use concrete names or abstract names at our pleasure to express the same meaning. To say that "John is a timid man" is the same thing as saying that "Timidity is one of the properties or characteristics or attributes of John". "Pride and cruelty generally go together;" "Proud men are generally cruel men."

General names are predicable of individuals because they possess certain attributes: to predicate the possession of those attributes is the same thing as to predicate the general name.

Abstract forms of predication are employed in common speech quite as frequently as concrete, and are, as we shall see, a great source of ambiguity and confusion.

name is undoubtedly as much connotative as an adjective. The word *Sweetness* has the same meaning as *Sweet:* it indicates or signifies, conveys to the mind of the reader the same attribute: the only difference is that it does not at the same time indicate a subject in which the attribute is found, as *sweet apple.* The meaning is not *con*noted.

Chapter II.

THE SYLLOGISTIC ANALYSIS OF PROPOSITIONS INTO TERMS.

I.—The Bare Analytic Forms.

The word " term " is loosely used as a mere synonym for a name : strictly speaking, a term (ὅρος, a boundary) is one of the parts of a proposition as analysed into Subject and Predicate. In Logic, a term is a technical word in an analysis made for a special purpose, that purpose being to test the mutual consistency of propositions.

For this purpose, the propositions of common speech may be viewed as consisting of two **Terms,** a linkword called the copula (positive or negative) expressing a relation between them, and certain symbols of quantity used to express that relation more precisely.

Let us indicate the Subject term by S, and the Predicate term by P.

All propositions may be analysed into one or other of four forms :—

All S is P,
No S is P,
Some S is P,
Some S is not P.

(62)

All S is P is called the **Universal Affirmative,** and is indicated by the symbol A (the first vowel of Affirmo).

No S is P is called the **Universal Negative,** symbol E (the first vowel of Nego).

Some S is P is called the **Particular Affirmative,** symbol I (the second vowel of *aff*Irmo).

Some S is not P is called the **Particular Negative,** symbol O (the second vowel of *neg*O).

The distinction between Universal and Particular is called a distinction in **Quantity;** between Affirmative and Negative, a distinction in **Quality.** A and E, I and O, are of the same quantity, but of different quality : A and I, E and O, same in quality, different in quantity.

In this symbolism, no provision is made for expressing degrees of particular quantity. *Some* stands for any number short of all : it may be one, few, most, or all but one. The debates in which Aristotle's pupils were interested turned mainly on the proof or disproof of general propositions ; if only a proposition could be shown to be not universal, it did not matter how far or how little short it came. In the Logic of Probability, the degree becomes of importance.

Distinguish, in this Analysis, to avoid subsequent confusion, between the Subject and the Subject Term, the Predicate and the Predicate Term. The Subject is the Subject Term quantified : in A and E,[1] "All S";

---

[1] For perfect symmetry, the form of E should be All S is not P. "No S is P" is adopted for E to avoid conflict with a form of common speech, in which All S is not P conveys the meaning of the Particular Negative. "All advices are not safe" does not mean that safeness is denied of all advices, but that safeness cannot be affirmed of all, *i.e.*, Not all advices are safe, *i.e.*, some are not.

in I and O, " Some S ".   The Predicate is the Predicate Term with the Copula, positive or negative: in
A and I, " is P "; in E and O, " is not P".

It is important also, in the interest of exactness, to
note that S and P, with one exception, represent
general names.   They are symbols for classes.   P is
so always: S also except when the Subject is an
individual object.   In the machinery of the Syllogism,
predications about a Singular term are treated as
Universal Affirmatives.   " Socrates is a wise man "
is of the form All S is P.

S and P being general names, the signification of
the symbol " is " is not the same as the " is " of
common speech, whether the substantive verb or the
verb of incomplete predication.   In the syllogistic
form, " is " means *is contained in*, " is not," *is not
contained in.*

The relations between the terms in the four forms
are represented by simple diagrams known as Euler's
circles.

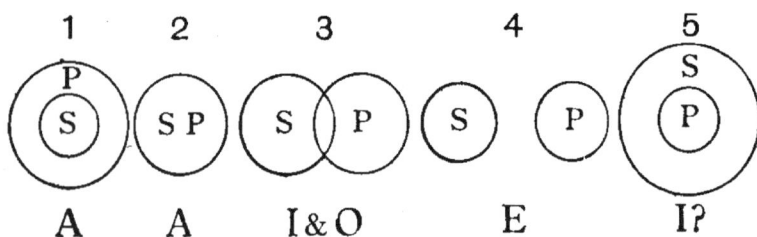

Diagram 5 is a purely artificial form, having no
representative in common speech.   In the affirmations
of common speech, P is always a term of greater
extent than S.

No. 2 represents the special case where S and P

are coextensive, as in All equiangular triangles are equilateral.

S and P being general names, they are said to be **distributed** when the proposition applies to them in their whole extent, that is, when the assertion covers every individual in the class.

In E, the Universal Negative, both terms are distributed : " No S is P " wholly excludes the two classes one from the other, imports that not one individual of either is in the other.

In A, S is distributed, but not P. S is wholly in P, but nothing is said about the extent of P beyond S.

In O, S is undistributed, P is distributed. A part of S is declared to be wholly excluded from P.

In I, neither S nor P is distributed.

It will be seen that the Predicate term of a Negative proposition is always distributed, of an Affirmative, always undistributed.

A little indistinctness in the signification of P crept into mediæval text-books, and has tended to confuse modern disputation about the import of Predication. Unless P is a class name, the ordinary doctrine of distribution is nonsense ; and Euler's diagrams are meaningless. Yet many writers who adopt both follow mediæval usage in treating P as the equivalent of an adjective, and consequently " is " as identical with the verb of incomplete predication in common speech.

It should be recognised that these syllogistic forms are purely artificial, invented for a purpose, namely, the simplification of syllogising. Aristotle indicated the precise usage on which his syllogism is based

(*Prior Analytics*, i. 1 and 4).   His form [1] for All S is P, is S is wholly in P ; for No S is P, S is wholly not in P.   His copula is not " is," but " is in," and it is a pity that this usage was not kept.   " All S is in P " would have saved much confusion.   But, doubtless for the sake of simplicity, the besetting sin of tutorial handbooks, All S is P crept in instead, illustrated by such examples as " All men are mortal ".

Thus the " is " of the syllogistic form became confused with the " is " of common speech, and the syllogistic view of predication as being equivalent to inclusion in, or exclusion from a class, was misunderstood.   The true Aristotelian doctrine is not that predication consists in referring subjects to classes, but only that for certain logical purposes it may be so regarded. The syllogistic forms are artificial forms.   They were not originally intended to represent the actual processes of thought expressed in common speech. To argue that when I say " All crows are black," I do not form a class of black things, and contemplate crows within it as one circle is within another, is to contradict no intelligent logical doctrine.

The root of the confusion lies in quoting sentences from common speech as examples of the logical forms, forgetting that those forms are purely artificial. " Omnis homo est mortalis," " All men are mortal," is not an example formally of All S is P.   P is a symbol for a substantive word or combination of words, and mortal is an adjective.   Strictly speaking, there is no formal equivalent in common speech, that is, in the forms of ordinary use—no strict grammatical

---

[1] His most precise form, I should say, for in " P is predicated of every S " he virtually follows common speech.

formal equivalent—for the syllogistic propositional symbols. We can make an equivalent, but it is not a form that men would use in ordinary intercourse. " All man is in mortal being " would be a strict equivalent, but it is not English grammar.

Instead of disputing confusedly whether All S is P should be interpreted in extension or in comprehension, it would be better to recognise the original and traditional use of the symbols S and P as class names, and employ other symbols for the expression in comprehension or connotation. Thus, let *s* and *p* stand for the connotation. Then the equivalent for All S is P would be All S has *p*, or *p* always accompanies *s*, or *p* belongs to all S.

It may be said that if predication is treated in this way, Logic is simplified to the extent of childishness. And indeed, the manipulation of the bare forms with the help of diagrams and mnemonics is a very humble exercise. The real discipline of Syllogistic Logic lies in the reduction of common speech to these forms.

This exercise is valuable because it promotes clear ideas about the use of general names in predication, their ground in thought and reality, and the liabilities to error that lurk in this fundamental instrument of speech.

II.—The Practice of Syllogistic Analysis.

The basis of the analysis is the use of general names in predication. To say that in predication a subject is referred to a class, is only another way of saying that in every categorical sentence the predicate is a general name express or implied : that it is by means of general names that we convey our thoughts about things to others.

" Milton is a great poet." " Quoth Hudibras,
I smell a rat." *Great poet* is a general name : it means
certain qualities, and applies to anybody possessing
them. *Quoth* implies a general name, a name for
persons *speaking*, connoting or meaning a certain act
and applicable to anybody in the performance of it.
Quoth expresses also past time : thus it implies another
general name, a name for persons *in past time*, connoting a quality which differentiates a species in the genus
persons speaking, and making the predicate term
" persons speaking in past time ". Thus the proposition *Quoth Hudibras*, analysed into the syllogistic
form S is in P, becomes S (Hudibras) is in P (persons
speaking in past time). The Predicate term P is a
class constituted on those properties. *Smell a rat* also
implies a general name, meaning an act or state
predicable of many individuals.

Even if we add the grammatical object of *Quoth* to
the analysis, the Predicate term is still a general name.
Hudibras is only one of the persons speaking in past
time who have spoken of themselves as being in a
certain mood of suspicion.[1]

The learner may well ask what is the use of twisting

---

[1] Remember that when we speak of a general name, we do not
necessarily mean a single word. A general name, logically
viewed, is simply the name of a *genus*, kind, or class : and
whether this is single-worded or many-worded is, strictly
speaking, a grammatical question. " Man," " man-of-ability,"
"man-of-ability-and-courage," " man-of-ability-and-courage-and-
gigantic-stature," " man-who-fought-at-Marathon "—these are
all general names in their logical function. No matter how the
constitutive properties of the class are indicated, by one word or
by a combination, that word or combination is a general name.
In actual speech we can seldom indicate by a single word the
meaning predicated.

plain speech into these uncouth forms. The use is certainly not obvious. The analysis may be directly useful, as Aristotle claimed for it, when we wish to ascertain exactly whether one proposition contradicts another, or forms with another or others a valid link in an argument. This is to admit that it is only in perplexing cases that the analysis is of direct use. The indirect use is to familiarise us with what the forms of common speech imply, and thus strengthen the intellect for interpreting the condensed and elliptical expression in which common speech abounds.

There are certain technical names applied to the components of many-worded general names, **Categorematic** and **Syncategorematic, Subject** and **Attributive.** The distinctions are really grammatical rather than logical, and of little practical value.

A word that can stand by itself as a term is said to be Categorematic. *Man, poet,* or any other common noun.

A word that can only form part of a term is Syncategorematic. Under this definition come all adjectives and adverbs.

The student's ingenuity may be exercised in applying the distinction to the various parts of speech. A verb may be said to be *Hypercategorematic,* implying, as it does, not only a term, but also a copula.

A nice point is whether the Adjective is categorematic or syncategorematic. The question depends on the definition of " term " in Logic. In common speech an adjective may stand by itself as a predicate, and so might be said to be Categorematic. " This heart is merry." But if a term is a class, or the name of a class, it is not Categorematic in the above definition.   It can only help to specify a class when attached to the name of a higher genus.

Mr. Fowler's words **Subject** and **Attributive** express practically the same distinction, except that Attributive is of narrower extent than syncategorematic. An Attributive is a word that connotes an attribute or property, as *hot, valorous*, and is always grammatically an adjective.

The **expression of Quantity,** that is, of Universality or non-universality, is all-important in syllogistic formulæ.   In them universality is expressed by *All* or *None*.   In ordinary speech universality is expressed in various forms, concrete and abstract, plain and figurative, without the use of " all " or " none ".

> Uneasy lies the head that wears a crown.
> He can't be wrong whose life is in the right.
> What cat's averse to fish ?
> Can the leopard change his spots ?
> The longest road has an end.
> Suspicion ever haunts the guilty mind.
> Irresolution is always a sign of weakness.
> Treason never prospers.

A proposition in which the quantity is not expressed is called by Aristotle **Indefinite** (ἀδιόριστος).   For " indefinite "[1] Hamilton suggests **Preindesignate,**

---

[1] The **objection** taken to the word " indefinite," that the quantity of particular propositions is indefinite, *some* meaning any quantity less than all, is an example of the misplaced and frivolous subtlety that has done so much to disorder the tradition of Logic.   By " indefinite " is simply meant not definitely expressed as either Universal or Particular, Total or Partial. The same objection might be taken to any word used to express the distinction : the degree of quantity in Some S is not " designate " any more than it is " definite " or " dioristic ".

undesignated, that is, before being received from common speech for the syllogistic mill. A proposition is **Predesignate** when the quantity is definitely indicated. All the above propositions are " Predesignate " universals, and reducible to the form All S is P, or No S is P.

The following propositions are no less definitely particular, reducible to the form I or O. In them as in the preceding quantity is formally expressed, though the forms used are not the artificial syllogistic forms :—

> Afflictions are often salutary.
> Not every advice is a safe one.
> All that glitters is not gold.
> Rivers generally[1] run into the sea.

Often, however, it is really uncertain from the form of common speech whether it is intended to express a universal or a particular. The quantity is not formally expressed. This is especially the case with proverbs and loose floating sayings of a general tendency. For example :—

> Haste makes waste.
> Knowledge is power.
> Light come, light go.
> Left-handed men are awkward antagonists.
> Veteran soldiers are the steadiest in fight.

---

[1] *Generally*. In this word we have an instance of the frequent conflict between the words of common speech and logical terminology. How it arises shall be explained in next chapter. A General proposition is a synonym for a Universal proposition (if the forms A and E are so termed) : but " generally " in common speech means "for the most part," and is represented by the symbol of particular quantity, *Some*.

Such sayings are in actual speech for the most part delivered as universals.[1]   It is a useful exercise of the Socratic kind to decide whether they are really so. This can only be determined by a survey of facts.   The best method of conducting such a survey is probably (1) to pick out the concrete subject, " hasty actions," " men possessed of knowledge," " things lightly acquired "; (2) to fix the attribute or attributes predicated; (3) to run over the individuals of the subject class and settle whether the attribute is as a matter of fact meant to be predicated of each and every one.

This is the operation of **Induction.**   If one individual can be found of whom the attribute is not meant to be predicated, the proposition is not intended as Universal.

Mark the difference between settling what is intended and settling what is true.   The conditions of truth and the errors incident to the attempt to determine it, are the business of the Logic of Rational Belief, commonly entitled Inductive Logic.   The kind of " induction" here contemplated has for its aim merely to determine the quantity of a proposition in common acceptation, which can be done by considering in what cases the proposition would generally be alleged.   This corresponds nearly as we shall see to Aristotelian Induction, the acceptance of a universal statement when no instance to the contrary is alleged.

It is to be observed that for this operation we do not

---

[1] With some logicians it is a mechanical rule in reducing to syllogistic form to treat as I or O all sentences in which there is no formal expression of quantity.   This is to err on the safe side, but common speakers are not so guarded, and it is to be presumed rather that they have a universal application in their minds when they do not expressly qualify.

practically use the syllogistic form All S is P. We do
not raise the question Is All S, P? That is, we do not
constitute in thought a class P: the class in our minds
is S, and what we ask is whether an attribute predicated
of this class is truly predicated of every individual
of it.

Suppose we indicate by p the attribute, knot of
attributes, or concept on which the class P is constituted, then All S is P is equivalent to " All S has p " :
and Has All S p? is the form of a question that we
have in our minds when we make an inductive survey
on the above method. I point this out to emphasise
the fact that there is no prerogative in the form All S
is P except for syllogistic purposes.

This inductive survey may be made a useful
Collateral Discipline. The bare forms of Syllogistic
are a useless item of knowledge unless they are
applied to concrete thought. And determining the
quantity of a common aphorism or saw, the limits
within which it is meant to hold good, is a valuable
discipline in exactness of understanding. In trying
to penetrate to the inner intention of a loose general
maxim, we discover that what it is really intended
to assert is a general connexion of attributes, and a
survey of concrete cases leads to a more exact apprehension of those attributes. Thus in considering
whether *Knowledge is power* is meant to be asserted
of all knowledge, we encounter along with such
examples as the sailor's knowledge that wetting a
rope shortens it, which enabled some masons to raise
a stone to its desired position, or the knowledge of
French roads possessed by the German invaders,—
along with such examples as these we encounter cases
where a knowledge of difficulties without a knowledge

of the means of overcoming them is paralysing to
action.   Samuel Daniel says :—

> Where timid knowledge stands considering
> Audacious ignorance has done the deed.

Studying numerous cases where " Knowledge is
power " is alleged or denied, we find that what is
meant is that a knowledge of the right means of
doing anything is power—in short, that the predicate
is not made of all knowledge, but only of a species
of knowledge.

Take, again, *Custom blunts sensibility.*   Putting this
in the concrete, and inquiring what predicate is made
about " men accustomed to anything " (S), we have
no difficulty in finding examples where such men are
said to become indifferent to it.   We find such illustrations as Lovelace's famous " Paradox " :—

> Through foul we follow fair
>   For had the world one face
> And earth been bright as air
>   We had known neither place.
> Indians smell not their nest
> The Swiss and Finn taste best
>   The spices of the East.

So men accustomed to riches are not acutely sensible
of their advantages : dwellers in noisy streets cease to
be distracted by the din : the watchmaker ceases to
hear the multitudinous ticking in his shop : the
neighbours of chemical works are not annoyed by the
smells like the casual passenger.   But we find also
that wine-tasters acquire by practice an unusual
delicacy of sense ; that the eyes once accustomed to
a dim light begin to distinguish objects that were at

first indistinguishable; and so on. What meanings of " custom " and of " sensibility " will reconcile these apparently conflicting examples? What are the exact attributes signified by the names? We should probably find that by sensibility is meant emotional sensibility as distinguished from intellectual discrimination, and that by custom is meant familiarity with impressions whose variations are not attended to, or subjection to one unvarying impression.

To verify the meaning of abstract proverbs in this way is to travel over the road by which the Greek dialecticians were led to feel the importance of definition. Of this more will be said presently. If it is contended that such excursions are beyond the bounds of Formal Logic, the answer is that the exercise is a useful one and that it starts naturally and conveniently from the formulæ of Logic. It is the practice and discipline that historically preceded the Aristotelian Logic, and in the absence of which the Aristotelian formulæ would have a narrowing and cramping effect.

Can all propositions be reduced to the syllogistic form? Probably: but this is a purely scientific inquiry, collateral to Practical Logic. The concern of Practical Logic is chiefly with forms of proposition that favour inaccuracy or inexactness of thought. When there is no room for ambiguity or other error, there is no virtue in artificial syllogistic form. The attempt so to reduce any and every proposition may lead, however, to the study of what Mr. Bosanquet happily calls the " Morphology " of Judgment, Judgment being the technical name for the mental act that accompanies the utterance of a proposition. Even in such sentences as " How hot it is ! " or " It rains," the rudiment of subject and predicate may be detected.   When a man says "How hot it is," he conveys the meaning, though there is no definitely formed subject in his mind, that the outer world at the moment of his speaking has a certain quality or attribute.   So with "It rains".   The study of such examples in their context, however, reveals the fact that the same form of Common speech may cover different subjects and predicates in different connexions.   Thus in the argument :—

> "Whatever is, is best.
> It rains : "—

the Subject is *Rain* and the Predicate *is now*, "is at the present time," "is in the class of present events".

III.—Some Technical Difficulties.

The formula for **Exclusive Propositions.**   "None but the brave deserve the fair" : "No admittance except on business" : "Only Protestants can sit on the throne of England".

These propositions exemplify different ways in common speech of naming a subject *exclusively*, the predication being made of all outside a certain term. "None that are not brave, etc. ; " "none that are not on business, etc. ; " "none that are not Protestants, etc.".   No not-S is P.   It is only about all outside the given term that the universal assertion is made : we say nothing universally about the individuals within the term : we do not say that all Protestants are eligible, nor that all persons on business are admitted, nor that every one of the brave deserves the fair.   All that we say is that the possession of the attribute named is an indispensable condition: a person may possess the attribute, and yet on other grounds may not be entitled to the predicate.

The justification for taking special note of this form in Logic is that we are apt by inadvertence to make an inclusive inference from it. Let it be said that None but those who work hard can reasonably expect to pass, and we are apt to take this as meaning that all who work hard may reasonably expect to pass. But what is denied of every Not-S is not necessarily affirmed of every S.

The expression of **Tense** or **Time** *in the Syllogistic Forms.* Seeing that the Copula in S is P or S is in P does not express time, but only a certain relation between S and P, the question arises Where are we to put time in the analytic formula ? " Wheat is dear ; " " All had fled ;" time is expressed in these propositions, and our formula should render the whole content of what is given. Are we to include it in the Predicate term or in the Subject term ? If it must not be left out altogether, and we cannot put it with the copula, we have a choice between the two terms.

It is a purely scholastic question. The common technical treatment is to view the tense as part of the predicate. " All had fled," All S is P, *i.e.*, the whole subject is included in a class constituted on the attributes of flight at a given time. It may be that the Predicate is solely a predicate of time. " The Board met yesterday at noon." S is P, *i.e.*, the meeting of the Board is one of the events characterised by having happened at a certain time, agreeing with other events in that respect.

But in some cases the time is more properly regarded as part of the subject. *E.g.*, "Wheat is dear". S does not here stand for wheat collectively, but for the wheat now in the market, the wheat of the present time : it is concerning this that the attribute of dearness is predicated ; it is this that is in the class of dear things.

The expression of **Modality** *in the Syllogistic Forms.* Propositions in which the predicate is qualified by an expression of necessity, contingency, possibility or impossibility [*i.e.*, in English by *must*, *may*, *can*, or *cannot*], were called in Mediæval Logic *Modal* Propositions. " Two and two *must* make four." " Grubs *may* become butterflies." " *Z can* paint." " Y *cannot* fly."

There are two recognised ways of reducing such propositions to the form S is P. One is to distinguish between the *Dictum* and the *Mode*, the proposition and the qualification of its certainty, and to treat the *Dictum* as the Subject and the *Mode* as the Predicate. Thus : " That two and two make four is necessary "; " That Y can fly is impossible ".

The other way is to treat the Mode as part of the predicate. The propriety of this is not obvious in the case of Necessary propositions, but it is unobjectionable in the case of the other three modes. Thus : " Grubs are things that have the potentiality of becoming butterflies "; " Z has the faculty of painting "; " Y has not the faculty of flying ".

The chief risk of error is in determining the quantity of the subject about which the Contingent or Possible predicate is made. When it is said that " Victories may be gained by accident," is the predicate made concerning All victories or Some only ? Here we are apt to confuse the meaning of the contingent assertion with the matter of fact on which in common belief it rests. It is true only that some victories have been gained by accident, and it is on this ground that we assert in the absence of certain knowledge concerning any victory that it may have been so gained. The latter is the effect of the contingent assertion : it is made about any victory in the absence of certain knowledge, that is to say, formally about all.

The history of Modals in Logic is a good illustration of intricate confusion arising from disregard of a clear traditional definition. The treatment of them by Aristotle was simple, and had direct reference to tricks of disputation practised in his time. He specified four "modes," the four that descended to mediæval logic, · and he concerned himself chiefly with the import of contradicting these modals. What is the true contradictory of such propositions as, " It is possible to be " (δυνατὸν εἶναι), " It admits of being " (ἐνδέχεται εἶναι), " It must be " (ἀναγκαῖον εἶναι), " It is impossible to be " (ἀδύνατον εἶναι) ? What is implied in saying " No " to such propositions put interrogatively ? " Is it possible for Socrates to fly ? " " No." Does this mean that it is not possible for Socrates to fly, or that it is possible for Socrates not to fly ?

A disputant who had trapped a respondent into admitting that it is possible for Socrates not to fly, might have pushed the concession farther in some such way as this : " Is it possible for Socrates not to walk ? " " Certainly." " Is it possible for him to walk ? " " Yes." " When you say that it is possible for a man to do anything do you not believe that it is possible for him to do it ? " " Yes." " But you have admitted that it is possible for Socrates not to fly ? "

It was in view of such perplexities as these that Aristotle set forth the true contradictories of his four Modals. We may laugh at such quibbles now and wonder that a grave logician should have thought them worth guarding against. But historically this is the origin of the Modals of Formal Logic, and to divert the names of them to signify other distinctions than those between modes of qualifying the certainty of a statement is to introduce confusion.

Thus we find "Alexander was a great general," given as an example of a Contingent Modal, on the ground that though as a matter of fact Alexander was so he might have been otherwise. It was not *necessary* that Alexander should be a great general : therefore the proposition is *contingent.* Now the distinction between Necessary truth and Contingent truth may be important philosophically : but it is merely confusing to call the character of propositions as one or the other by the name of Modality. The original Modality is a mode of expression : to apply the name to this character is to shift its meaning.

A more simple and obviously unwarrantable departure from tradition is to extend the name Modality to any grammatical qualification of a single verb in common speech. On this understanding "Alexander conquered Darius" is given by Hamilton as a *Pure* proposition, and "Alexander conquered Darius honourably" as a *Modal.* This is a merely grammatical distinction, a distinction in the mode of composing the predicate term in common speech. In logical tradition Modality is a mode of qualifying the certainty of an affirmation. " The conquest of Darius by Alexander was honourable," or " Alexander in conquering Darius was an honourable conqueror," is the syllogistic form of the proposition : it is simply assertory, not qualified in any " mode ".

There is a similar misunderstanding in Mr. Shedden's

treatment of " generally " as constituting a Modal in such sentences, as " Rivers *generally* flow into the sea ". He argues that as *generally* is not part either of the Subject term or of the Predicate term, it must belong to the Copula, and is therefore a *modal* qualification of the whole assertion. He overlooked the fact that the word " generally " is an expression of Quantity : it determines the quantity of the Subject term.

Finally it is sometimes held (*e.g.*, by Mr. Venn) that the question of Modality belongs properly to Scientific or Inductive Logic, and is out of place in Formal Logic. This is so far accurate that it is for Inductive Logic to expound the conditions of various degrees of certainty. The consideration of Modality is pertinent to Formal Logic only in so far as concerns special perplexities in the expression of it. The treatment of it by Logicians has been rendered intricate by torturing the old tradition to suit different conceptions of the end and aim of Logic.

PART II.

DEFINITION.

CHAPTER I.

IMPERFECT UNDERSTANDING OF WORDS AND THE REMEDIES THEREFOR. — DIALECTIC. — DEFINITION.

WE cannot inquire far into the meaning of proverbs or traditional sayings without discovering that the common understanding of general and abstract names is loose and uncertain. Common speech is a quicksand.

Consider how we acquire our vocabulary, how we pick up the words that we use from our neighbours and from books, and why this is so soon becomes apparent. Theoretically we know the full meaning of a name when we know all the attributes that it connotes, and we are not justified in extending it except to objects that possess all the attributes. This is the logical ideal, but between the *ought to be* of Logic and the *is* of practical life, there is a vast difference. How seldom do we conceive words in their full meaning! And who is to instruct us in the full meaning? It is not as in the exact sciences, where we start with a knowledge of the full meaning. In Geometry, for example, we learn the definitions of the words used, *point, line, parallel,* etc., before we proceed to use them. But in common speech, we learn words first in their application to individual cases. Nobody ever defined *good* to us, or *fair,* or *kind,* or *highly educated.* We hear the words applied to individual objects: we utter them in the same connexion : we extend them to other objects that strike us as like without knowing the precise points of likeness that the convention of common speech includes. The more exact meaning we learn by gradual induction from individual cases. *Ugly, beautiful, good, bad*—we learn the words first as applicable to things and persons : gradually there arises a more or less definite sense of what the objects so designated have in common. The individual's extension of the name proceeds upon what in the objects has most impressed him when he caught the word : this may differ in different individuals ; the usage of neighbours corrects individual eccentricities. The child in arms shouts *Da* at the passing stranger who reminds him of his father : for him at first it is a general name applicable to every man : by degrees he learns that for him it is a singular name.

The mode in which words are learnt and extended may be studied most simply in the nursery. A child, say, has learnt to say *mambro* when it sees its nurse. The nurse works a hand-turned sewing machine, and sings to it as she works. In the street the child sees an organ-grinder singing as he turns his handle : it calls *mambro :* the nurse catches the meaning and the child is overjoyed. The organ-grinder has a monkey : the child has an india-rubber monkey toy : it calls this also *mambro.* The name is extended to a monkey in a picture-book. It has a toy musical box with a handle: this also becomes *mambro*, the word being extended along another line of resemblance. A stroller with a French fiddle comes within the denotation of the word: a towel-rail is also called *mambro* from some fancied resemblance to the fiddle. A very swarthy hunch-back *mambro* frightens the child: this leads to the transference of the word to a terrific coalman with a bag of coals on his back. In a short time the word has become a name for a great variety of objects that have nothing whatever common to all of them, though each is strikingly like in some point to a predecessor in the series. When the application becomes too heterogeneous, the word ceases to be of use as a sign and is gradually abandoned, the most impressive meaning being the last to go. In a child's vocabulary where the word *mambro* had a run of nearly two years, its last use was as an adjective signifying ugly or horrible.

The history of such a word in a child's language is a type of what goes on in the language of men. In the larger history we see similar extensions under similar motives, checked and controlled in the same way by surrounding usage.

It is obvious that to avoid error and confusion, the meaning or connotation of names, the concepts, should somehow be fixed: names cannot otherwise have an identical reference in human intercourse. We may call this ideal fixed concept the **Logical Concept:** or we may call it the **Scientific Concept,** inasmuch as one of the main objects of the sciences is to attain such ideals in different departments of study. But in actual speech we have also the **Personal Concept,** which varies more or less with the individual user, and the **Popular** or **Vernacular Concept**, which, though roughly fixed, varies from social sect to social sect and from generation to generation.

The variations in Popular Concepts may be traced in linguistic history. Words change with things and with the aspects of things, as these change in public interest and importance. As long as the attributes that govern the application of words are simple, sensible attributes, little confusion need arise : the variations are matters of curious research for the philologist, but are logically insignificant. Murray's Dictionary, or such books as Trench's *English Past and Present*, supply endless examples, as many, indeed, as there are words in the language. *Clerk* has almost as many connotations as our typical *mambro :* clerk in holy orders, church clerk, town clerk, clerk of assize, grocer's clerk. In Early English, the word meant " man in a religious order, cleric, clergyman " ; ability to read, write, and keep accounts being a prominent attribute of the class, the word was extended on this simple ground till it has ceased altogether to cover its original field except as a formal designation. But no confusion is caused by the variation, because the property connoted ·is simple.[1] So with any common noun : street, carriage, ship, house, merchant, lawyer, professor. We might be puzzled to give an exact definition of such words,

---

[1] Except, perhaps, in new offices to which the name is extended, such as *Clerk* of School Board. The name, bearing its most simple and common meaning, may cause popular misapprehension of the nature of the duties. Any uncertainty in meaning may be dangerous in practice : elections have been affected by the ambiguity of this word.

to say precisely what they connote in common usage; but the risk of error in the use of them is small.

When we come to words of which the logical concept is a complex relation, an obscure or intangible attribute, the defects of the popular conception and its tendencies to change and confusion, are of the greatest practical importance. Take such words as *Monarchy, tyranny, civil freedom, freedom of contract, landlord, gentleman, prig, culture, education, temperance, generosity.* Not merely should we find it difficult to give an analytic definition of such words : we might be unable to do so, and yet flatter ourselves that we had a clear understanding of their meaning. But let two men begin to discuss any proposition in which any such word is involved, and it will often be found that they take the word in different senses. If the relation expressed is complex, they have different sides or lines of it in their minds; if the meaning is an obscure quality, they are guided in their application of it by different outward signs.

Monarchy, in its original meaning, is applied to a form of government in which the will of one man is supreme, to make laws or break them, to appoint or dismiss officers of state and justice, to determine peace or war, without control of statute or custom. But supreme power is never thus uncontrolled in reality; and the word has been extended to cover governments in which the power of the titular head is controlled in many different modes and degrees. The existence of a head, with the title of King or Emperor, is the simplest and most salient fact : and wherever this exists, the popular concept of a monarchy is realised. The President of the United States has more real power than the Sovereign of Great Britain ; but the

one government is called a Republic and the other
a Monarchy. People discuss the advantages and
disadvantages of monarchy without first deciding
whether they take the word in its etymological sense
of unlimited power, or its popular sense of titular
kingship, or its logical sense of power definitely
limited in certain ways. And often in debate,
monarchy is really a singular term for the government
of Great Britain.

Culture, religious, generous, are names for inward
states or qualities : with most individuals some simple
outward sign directs the application of the word—it
may be manner, or bearing, or routine observances, or
even nothing more significant than the cut of the
clothes or of the hair. Small things undoubtedly are
significant, and we must judge by small things when
we have nothing else to go by : but instead of trying
to get definite conceptions for our moral epithets, and
suspending judgment till we know that the use of the
epithet is justified, the trifling superficial sign becomes
for us practically the whole meaning of the word. We
feel that we must have a judgment of some sort at
once : only simple signs are suited to our impatience.

It was with reference to this state of things that
Hegel formulated his paradox that the true abstract
thinker is the plain man who laughs at philosophy as
what he calls abstract and unpractical. He holds
decided opinions for or against this or the other
abstraction, *freedom, tyranny, revolution, reform, socialism,*
but what these words mean and within what limits the
things signified are desirable or undesirable, he is in
too great a hurry to pause and consider.

The disadvantages of this kind of " abstract " thinking are obvious. The accumulated wisdom of man-

kind is stored in language. Until we have cleared our conceptions, and penetrated to the full meaning of words, that wisdom is a sealed book to us. Wise maxims are interpreted by us hastily in accordance with our own narrow conceptions. All the vocables of a language may be more or less familiar to us, and yet we may not have learnt it as an instrument of thought. Outside the very limited range of names for what we see and use in the daily routine of life, food and clothes and the common occupations of men, words have little meaning for us, and are the vehicles merely of thin preconceptions and raw prejudices.

The remedy for "abstract" thinking is more thinking, and in pursuing this two aims may be specified for the sake of clearness, though they are closely allied, and progress towards both may often be made by one and the same operation. (1) We want to reach a clear and full conception of the meaning of names as used now or at a given time. Let us call this the *Verification of the Meaning*. (2) We want to fix such conceptions, and if necessary readjust their boundaries. This is the province of *Definition*, which cannot be effectually performed without *Scientific Classification* or *Division*.

I.—Verification of the Meaning — Dialectic.

This can only be done by assembling the objects to which the words are applied, and considering what they have in common. To ascertain the actual connotation we must run over the actual denotation. And since in such an operation two or more minds are better than one, discussion or dialectic is both more fruitful and more stimulating than solitary reflection or reading.

The first to practise this process on a memorable scale, and with a distinct method and purpose, was Socrates. To insist upon the necessity of clear conceptions, and to assist by his dialectic procedure in forming them, was his contribution to philosophy.

His plan was to take a common name, profess ignorance of its meaning, and ask his interlocutor whether he would apply it in such and such an instance, producing one after another. According to Xenophon's *Memorabilia* he habitually chose the commonest names, *good*, *unjust*, *fitting*, and so forth, and tried to set men thinking about them, and helped them by his questions to form an intelligent conception of the meaning.

For example, what is the meaning of injustice? Would you say that the man who cheats or deceives is unjust? Suppose a man deceives his enemies, is there any injustice in that? Can the definition be that a man who deceives his friends is unjust? But there are cases where friends are deceived for their own good: are these cases of injustice? A general may inspirit his soldiers by a falsehood. A man may cajole a weapon out of his friend's hand when he sees him about to commit suicide. A father may deceive his son into taking medicine. Would you call these men unjust? By some such process of interrogation we are brought to the definition that a man is unjust who deceives his friends to their hurt.

Observe that in much of his dialectic the aim of Socrates was merely to bring out the meaning lying vague and latent, as it were, in the common mind. His object was simply what we have called the verification of the meaning. And a dialectic that confines itself to the consideration of what is ordinarily meant as distinct from what ought to be meant, may often serve a useful purpose. Disputes about words are not always as idle as is sometimes supposed. Mr. H. Sidgwick truly remarks (*à propos* of the terms of Political Economy) that there is often more profit in seeking a definition than in finding it. Conceptions are not merely cleared but deepened by the process. Mr. Sidgwick's remarks are so happy that I must take leave to quote them : they apply not merely to the verification of ordinary meaning but also to the study of special uses by authorities, and the reasons for those special uses.

" The truth is—as most readers of Plato know, only it is a truth difficult to retain and apply—that what we gain by discussing a definition is often but slightly represented in the superior fitness of the formula that we ultimately adopt; it consists chiefly in the greater clearness and fulness in which the characteristics of the matter to which the formula refers have been brought before the mind in the process of seeking for it. While we are apparently aiming at definitions of terms, our attention should be really fixed on distinctions and relations of fact. These latter are what we are concerned to know, contemplate, and as far as possible arrange and systematise ; and in subjects where we cannot present them to the mind in ordinary fulness by the exercise of the organs of sense, there is no way of surveying them so convenient as that of reflecting on our use of common terms. . . . In comparing different definitions our aim should be far less to decide which we ought to adopt, than to apprehend and duly consider the grounds on which each has commended itself to reflective minds. We shall generally find that each writer has noted some relation, some resemblance or difference, which others have overlooked ; and we shall gain in completeness, and often in precision, of view by following him in his observations, whether or not we follow him in his conclusions." [1]

Mr. Sidgwick's own discussions of *Wealth, Value,* and *Money* are models. A clue is often found to the meaning in examining startlingly discrepant statements connected with the same leading word. Thus we find some authorities declaring that " style" cannot be taught or learnt, while others declare that it can. But on trying to ascertain what they mean by " style," we find that those who say it cannot be taught mean either a certain marked individual character or manner of writing—as in Buffon's saying, *Le style c'est l'homme même*—or a certain felicity and dignity of expression, while those who say style can be taught mean lucid method in the structure of sentences or in the arrangement of a discourse. Again in discussions on the rank of poets, we find different conceptions of what constitutes greatness in poetry lying at the root of the inclusion of this or the other poet among great poets. We find one poet excluded from the first rank of greatness because his poetry was not serious ; another because his poetry was not widely popular ; another because he wrote comparatively little; another because he wrote only songs or odes and never attempted drama or epic. These various opinions point to different conceptions of what constitutes greatness in poets, different connotations of " great poet ". Comparing different opinions concerning " education " we may be led to ask whether it means more than instruction in the details of certain subjects, whether it does not also import the formation of a

---

[1] Sidgwick's *Political Economy*, pp. 52-3. Ed. 1883.

disposition to learn or an interest in learning or
instruction in a certain method of learning.

Historically, dialectic turning on the use of words
preceded the attempt to formulate principles of Definition, and attempts at precise definition led to Division
and Classification, that is to systematic arrangement
of the objects to be defined. Attempt to define any
such word as " education," and you gradually become
sensible of the needs in respect of method that forced
themselves upon mankind in the history of thought.
You soon become aware that you cannot define it by
itself alone ; that you are beset by a swarm of more or
less synonymous words, *instruction, discipline, culture,
training,* and so on ; that these various words represent
distinctions and relations among things more or less
allied ; and that, if each must be fixed to a definite
meaning, this must be done with reference to one
another and to the whole department of things that
they cover.

The first memorable attempts at scientific arrangement were Aristotle's treatises on Ethics and Politics,
which had been the subjects of active dialectic
for at least a century before. That these the most
difficult of all departments to subject to scientific
treatment should have been the first chosen was due
simply to their preponderating interest : " The proper
study of mankind is man ". The systems of what are
known as the Natural Sciences are of modern origin :
the first, that of Botany, dates from Cesalpinus in
the sixteenth century. But the principles on which
Aristotle proceeded in dividing and defining, principles
which have gradually themselves been more precisely
formulated, are principles applicable to all systematic

arrangements for purposes of orderly study. I give them in the precise formulæ which they have gradually assumed in the tradition of Logic. The principles of Division are often given in Formal Logic, and the principles of Classification in Inductive Logic, but there is no valid reason for the separation. The classification of objects in the Natural Sciences, of animals, plants, and stones, with a view to the thorough study of them in form, structure, and function, is more complex than classifications for more limited purposes, and the tendency is to restrict the word classification to these elaborate systems. But really they are only a series of divisions and subdivisions, and the same principles apply to each of the subordinate divisions as well as to the division of the whole department of study.

II.—Principles of Division or Classification and Definition.

Confusion in the boundaries of names arises from confused ideas regarding the resemblances and differences of things. As a protective against this confusion, things must be clearly distinguished in their points of likeness and difference, and this leads to their arrangement in systems, that is, to division and classification. A name is not secure against variation until it has a distinct place in such a system as a symbol for clearly distinguished attributes. Nor must we forget, further, that systems have their day, that the best system attainable is only temporary, and may have to be recast to correspond with changes of things and of man's way of looking at them.

The leading principles of **Division** may be stated as follows:—

I. Every division is made on the ground of differences in some attribute common to all the members of the whole to be divided.

This is merely a way of stating what a logical division is. It is a division of a generic whole or *genus*, an indefinite number of objects thought of together as possessing some common character or attribute. All have this attribute, which is technically called the *fundamentum divisionis*, or generic attribute. But the whole is divisible into smaller groups (*species*), each of which possesses the common character with a difference (*differentia*). Thus, mankind may be divided into White men, Black men, Yellow men, on ground of the differences in the colour of their skins : all have skins of some colour: this is the *fundamentum divisionis:* but each subdivision or species has a different colour: this is the *differentia*. Rectilineal figures are divided into triangles, quadrangles, pentagons, etc., on the ground of differences in the number of angles.

Unless there is a *fund. div., i.e.*, unless the differences are differences in a common character, the division is not a logical division. To divide men into Europeans, opticians, tailors, blondes, brunettes, and dyspeptics is not to make a logical division. This is seen more clearly in connexion with the second condition of a perfect division.

II. In a perfect division, the subdivisions or species are mutually exclusive.

Every object possessing the common character

should be in one or other of the groups, and none should be in more than one.

Confusion between classes, or overlapping, may arise from two causes. It may be due (1) to faulty division, to want of unity in the *fundamentum divisionis;* (2) to the indistinct character of the objects to be defined.

(1) Unless the division is based upon a single ground, unless each species is based upon some mode of the generic character, confusion is almost certain to arise. Suppose the field to be divided, the objects to be classified, are three-sided rectilineal plane figures, each group must be based upon some modification of the three sides. Divide them into equilateral, isosceles, and scalene according as the three sides are all of equal length, or two of equal length, or each of different length, and you have a perfect division. Similarly you can divide them perfectly according to the character of the angles into acute-angled, right-angled and obtuse-angled. But if you do not keep to a single basis, as in dividing them into equilateral, isosceles, scalene, and right-angled, you have a cross-division. The same triangle might be both right-angled and isosceles.

(2) Overlapping, however, may be unavoidable in practice owing to the nature of the objects. There may be objects in which the dividing characters are not distinctly marked, objects that possess the differentiæ of more than one group in a greater or less degree. Things are not always marked off from one another by hard and fast lines. They shade into one another by imperceptible gradations. A clear separation of them may be impossible. In that case you must allow a certain indeterminate margin between

your classes, and sometimes it may be necessary to put an object into more than one class.

To insist that there is no essential difference unless a clear demarcation can be made is a fallacy. A sophistical trick called the *Sorites* or Heap from the classical example of it was based upon this difficulty of drawing sharp lines of definition. Assuming that it is possible to say how many stones constitute a heap, you begin by asking whether three stones form a heap. If your respondent says No, you ask whether four stones form a heap, then five, and so on, and he is puzzled to say when the addition of a single stone makes that a heap which was not a heap before. Or you may begin by asking whether twenty stones form a heap, then nineteen, then eighteen, and so on, the difficulty being to say when what was a heap ceases to be so.

Where the objects classified are mixed states or affections, the products of interacting factors, or differently interlaced or interfused growths from common roots, as in the case of virtues, or emotions, or literary qualities, sharp demarcations are impossible. To distinguish between wit and humour, or humour and pathos, or pathos and sublimity is difficult because the same composition may partake of more than one character. The specific characters cannot be made rigidly exclusive one of another.

Even in the natural sciences, where the individuals are concrete objects of perception, it may be difficult to decide in which of two opposed groups an object should be included. Sydney Smith has commemorated the perplexities of Naturalists over the newly discovered animals and plants of Botany Bay, in especial with the *Ornithorynchus*,—"a quadruped as big as a large cat, with the eyes, colour, and skin of a mole, and the bill and web-feet of a duck—puzzling Dr. Shaw, and rendering the latter half of his life miserable, from his utter inability to determine whether it was a bird or a beast ".

III. The classes in any scheme of division should be of co-ordinate rank.

The classes may be mutually exclusive, and yet the division imperfect, owing to their not being of equal rank. Thus in the ordinary division of the Parts of Speech, parts, that is, of a sentence, Prepositions and Conjunctions are not co-ordinate in respect of function, which is the basis of the division, with Nouns, Adjectives, Verbs, and Adverbs. The preposition is a part of a phrase which serves the same function as an adjective, *e.g.*, *royal* army, army *of the king;* it is thus functionally part of a part, or a particle. So with the conjunction : it also is part of a part, *i.e.*, part of a clause serving the function of adjective or adverb.

IV. The basis of division (*fundamentum divisionis*) should be an attribute admitting of important differences.

The importance of the attribute chosen as basis may vary with the purpose of the division. An attribute that is of no importance in one division, may be important enough to be the basis of another division. Thus in a division of houses according to their architectural attributes, the number of windows or the rent is of little importance ; but if houses are taxed or rated according to the number of windows or the rent, these attributes become important enough to be a basis of division for purposes of taxation or rating. They then admit of important differences.

That the importance is relative to the purpose of the
division should be borne in mind because there is a
tendency to regard attributes that are of importance
in any familiar or pre-eminent division as if they had
an absolute importance. In short, disregard of this
relativity is a fallacy to be guarded against.

In the sciences, the purpose being the attainment
and preservation of knowledge, the objects of study are
divided so as to serve that purpose. Groups must be ,
formed so as to bring together the objects that have
most in common. The question, Who are to be placed
together ? in any arrangement for purposes of study,
receives the same answer for individuals and for classes
that have to be grouped into higher classes, namely,
Those that have most in common. This is what Dr.
Bain happily calls "the golden rule" of scientific
classification : "Of the various groupings of resembling
things, preference is given to such as have the greatest
number of attributes in common". I slightly modify
Dr. Bain's statement : he says "the most numerous
and the most important attributes in common". But
for scientific purposes number of attributes constitutes
importance, as is well recognised by Dr. Fowler when
he says that the test of importance in an attribute proposed as a basis of classification is the number of
other attributes of which it is an index or invariable
accompaniment. Thus in *Zoology* the squirrel, the
rat, and the beaver are classed together as Rodents,
the difference between their teeth and the teeth of
other Mammalia being the basis of division, because
the difference in teeth is accompanied by differences in
many other properties. So the hedge-hog, the shrew-
mouse, and the mole, though very unlike in outward
appearance and habits, are classed together as Insec-

tivora, the difference in what they feed on being accompanied by a number of other differences.

The Principles of **Definition.** The word "definition" as used in Logic shows the usual tendency of words to wander from a strict meaning and become ambiguous. Throughout most of its uses it retains this much of a common signification, the fixing or determining of the boundaries of a class [1] by making clear its constituent attributes. Now in this making clear two processes may be distinguished, a material process and a verbal process. We have (1) the clearing up of the common attributes by a careful examination of the objects included in the class: and we have (2) the statement of these common attributes in language. The rules of definition given by Dr. Bain, who devotes a separate Book in his Logic to the subject of Definition, concern the first of these processes: the rules more commonly given concern mainly the second.

One eminent merit in Dr. Bain's treatment is that it recognises the close connexion between Definition and Classification. His cardinal rules are reduced to two.

---

[1] Some logicians, however, speak of defining a thing, and illustrate this as if by a thing they meant a concrete individual, the realistic treatment of Universals lending itself to such expressions. But though the authority of Aristotle might be claimed for this, it is better to confine the name in strictness to the main process of defining a class. Since, however, the method is the same whether it is an individual or a class that we want to make distinct, there is no harm in the extension of the word definition to both varieties. See Davidson's *Logic of Definition*, chap. ii.

I. *Assemble for comparison representative individuals of the class.*

II. *Assemble for comparison representative individuals of the contrasted class or classes.*

Seeing that the contrasted classes are contrasted on some basis of division, this is in effect to recognise that you cannot clearly define any class except in a scheme of classification. You must have a wide *genus* with its *fundamentum divisionis*, and, within this, *species* distinguished by their several *differentiæ*.

Next, as to the verbal process, rules are commonly laid down mostly of a trifling and obvious character. That " a definition should state neither more nor less than the common attributes of the class," or than the attributes signified by the class-name, is sometimes given as a rule of definition. This is really an explanation of what a definition is, a definition of a definition. And as far as mere statement goes it is not strictly accurate, for when the attributes of a genus are known it is not necessary to give all the attributes of the species, which include the generic attributes as well, but it is sufficient to give the generic name and the differentia. Thus Poetry may be defined as " a Fine Art having metrical language as its instrument ". This is technically known as definition *per genus et differentiam.* This mode of statement is a recognition of the connexion between Definition and Division.

The rule that " a definition should not be a synonymous repetition of the name of the class to be defined," is too obvious to require formal statement. To describe a Viceroy as a man who exercises viceregal functions, may have point as an epigram in the case of a *faineant* viceroy, but it is not a definition.

So with the rule that "a definition should not be couched in ambiguous unfamiliar, or figurative language". To call the camel "the ship of the desert" is a suggestive and luminous description of a property, but it is not a definition. So with the noble description of Faith as "the substance of things hoped for, the evidence of things not seen". But if one wonders why so obvious a "rule" should be laid down, the answer is that it has its historical origin in the caprices of two classes of offenders, mystical philosophers and pompous lexicographers.[1]

That "the definition should be simply convertible with the term for the class defined," so that we may say, for example, either: "Wine is the juice of the grape," or, "The juice of the grape is wine," is an obvious corollary from the nature of definition, but should hardly be dignified with the name of a "rule".

The Principles of **Naming.** Rules have been formulated for the choice of names in scientific definition and classification, but it may be doubted whether such choice can be reduced to precise rule. It is enough to draw attention to certain considerations obvious enough on reflection.

We may take for granted that there should be distinct names for every defining attribute (a *Terminology*) and for every group or class (a *Nomenclature*). What about the selection of the names? Suppose an investigator is struck with likenesses and differences that seem to him important enough to be the basis of a new division, how should he be guided in his choice of names for the new groups that he proposes? Should

---

[1] See Davidson's *Logic of Definition*, chap. iii.

he coin new names, or should he take old names and try to fit them with new definitions?

The balance of advantages is probably in favour of Dr. Whewell's dictum that "in framing scientific terms, the appropriation of old words is preferable to the invention of new ones". Only care must be taken to keep as close as possible to the current meaning of the old word, and not to run counter to strong associations. This is an obvious precept with a view to avoiding confusion. Suppose, for example, that in dividing Governments you take the distribution of political power as your basis of division and come to the conclusion that the most important differences are whether this power is vested in a few or in the majority of the community. You want names to fix this broad division. You decide instead of coining the new word *Pollarchy* to express the opposite of *Oligarchy* to use the old words *Republic* and *Oligarchy*. You would find, as Sir George Cornewall Lewis found, that however carefully you defined the word Republic, a division under which the British Government had to be ranked among Republics would not be generally understood and accepted. Using the word in the sense explained above, Mr. Bagehot maintained that the constitution of Great Britain was more Republican than that of the United States, but his meaning was not taken except by a few.

The difficulty in choosing between new words and old words to express new meanings is hardly felt in the exact sciences. It is at least at a minimum. The innovator may encounter violent prejudice, but, arguing with experts, he can at least make sure of being understood, if his new division is based upon

real and important differences. But in other subjects
the difficulty of transmitting truth or of expressing it
in language suited for precise transmission, is almost
greater than the difficulty of arriving at truth. Between
new names and old names redefined, the possessor of
fresh knowledge, assuming it to be perfectly verified,
is in a quandary. The objects with which he deals
are already named in accordance with loose divisions
resting on strong prejudices. The names in current
use are absolutely incapable of conveying his meaning.
He must redefine them if he is to use them. But in
that case he runs the risk of being misunderstood
from people being too impatient to master his rede-
finition. His right to redefine may even be challenged
without any reference to the facts to be expressed : he
may simply be accused of circulating false linguistic
coin, of debasing the verbal currency. The other
alternative open to him is to coin new words. In
that case he runs the risk of not being read at all.
His contribution to verified knowledge is passed by
as pedantic and unintelligible. There is no simple
rule of safety : between Scylla and Charybdis the
mariner must steer as best he may. Practically the
advantage lies with old words redefined, because
thereby discussion is provoked and discussion clears
the air.

Whether it is best to attempt a formal definition
or to use words in a private, peculiar, or esoteric
sense, and leave this to be gathered by the reader
from the general tenor of your utterances, is a question
of policy outside the limits of Logic. It is for the
logician to expound the method of Definition and the
conditions of its application: how far there are subjects
that do not admit of its application profitably must be

decided on other grounds.   But it is probably true
that no man who declines to be bound by a formal
definition of his terms is capable of carrying them
in a clear unambiguous sense through a heated
controversy.

Chapter II.

THE FIVE PREDICABLES.—VERBAL AND REAL PREDICATION.

We give a separate chapter to this topic out of respect for the space that it occupies in the history of Logic. But except as an exercise in subtle distinction for its own sake, all that falls to be said about the Predicables might be given as a simple appendix to the chapter on Definition.

Primarily, the Five Predicables or Heads of Predicables—Genus, Species, Differentia, Proprium, and Accidens—are not predicables at all, but merely a list or enumeration of terms used in dividing and defining on the basis of attributes. They have no meaning except in connexion with a fixed scheme of division. Given such a scheme, and we can distinguish in it the whole to be divided (the *genus*), the subordinate divisions (the *species*), the attribute or combination of attributes on which each species is constituted (the *differentia*), and other attributes, which belong to some or all of the individuals but are not reckoned for purposes of division and definition (*Propria* and *Accidentia*). The list is not itself a logical division: it is heterogeneous, not homogeneous; the two first are names of classes, the three last of attributes. But corresponding to it we might make a homogeneous division of attributes, as follows:—

Attributes

```
                    |
    ┌───────────────┴───────────────┐
    |                               |
 Defining                      Non-defining
    |                               |
 ┌──┴──────┐                 ┌───────┴────────┐
 |         |                 |                |
Generic  Specific         Proprium        Accidens
        (Differentia)
```

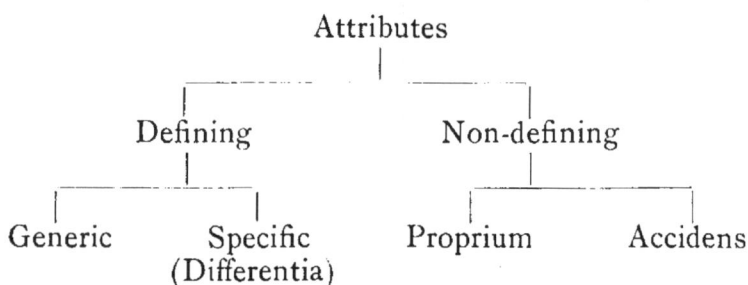

The origin of the title Predicables as applied to these
five terms is curious, and may be worth noting as an
instance of the difficulty of keeping names precise, and
of the confusion arising from forgetting the purpose
of a name. Porphyry in his εἰσαγωγὴ or Introduction
explains the five words (φωναὶ) simply as terms that it is
useful for various purposes to know, expressly mentioning definition and division.   But he casually remarks
that Singular names, " This man," " Socrates," can
be predicated only of one individual, whereas *Genera,
Species, Differentiæ*, etc., are predicable of many.   That
is to say he describes them as Predicables simply by
contradistinction from Singular names.   A name,
however, was wanted for the five terms taken all
together, and since they are not a logical division, but
merely a list of terms used in dividing and defining,
there was no apt general designation for them such
as would occur spontaneously.   Thus it became the
custom to refer to them as the Predicables, a means of
reference to them collectively being desiderated, while
the meaning of this descriptive title was forgotten.

   To call the five divisional elements or *Divisoria*
Predicables is to present them as a division of Predicate Terms on the basis of their relation to the Subject
Term : to suggest that every Predicate Term must be
either a Genus or a Species, or a Differentia, or a

Proprium, or an Accidens of the Subject Term. They are sometimes criticised as such, and it is rightly pointed out that the Predicate is never a species of or with reference to the Subject. But, in truth, the five so-called Predicables were never meant as a division of predicates in relation to the subject : it is only the title that makes this misleading suggestion.

To complete the confusion it so happens that Aristotle used three of the Five terms in what was virtually a division of Predicates inasmuch as it was a division of Problems or Questions. In expounding the methods of Dialectic in the Topica he divided Problems into four classes according to the relation of the Predicate to the Subject. The Predicate must either be simply convertible with the subject or not. If simply convertible, the two must be coextensive, and the Predicate must be either a Proprium or the Definition. If not simply convertible, the Predicate must either be part of the Definition or not. If part of the Definition it must be either a Generic Property or a Differentia (both of which in this connexion Aristotle includes under Genus) : if not part of the Definition, it is an Accident. Aristotle thus arrives at a fourfold division of Problems or Predicates :—γένος (*Genus*, including *Differentia*, διαφορὰ) ; ὅρος (Definition) ; τὸ ἴδιον (*Proprium*) ; and τὸ συμβεβηκὸς (*Accidens*). The object of it was to provide a basis for his systematic exposition ; each of the four kinds admitted of differences in dialectic method. For us it is a matter of simple curiosity and ingenuity. It serves as a monument of how much Greek dialectic turned on Definition, and it corresponds exactly to the division of attributes into Defining and Non-defining given above. It is sometimes said that Aristotle showed a more scientific mind

than Porphyry in making the Predicables four instead
of five. This is true if Porphyry's list had been meant
as a division of attributes : but it was not so meant.

The distinction between **Verbal** or **Analytic** and
Real or **Synthetic** Predication corresponds to the
distinction between Defining and Non-defining attributes, and also has no significance except with
reference to some scheme of Division, scientific and
precise or loose and popular.

When a proposition predicates of a subject something
contained in the full notion, concept, or definition of
the subject term, it is called Verbal, Analytic, or
Explicative : *verbal*, inasmuch as it merely explains
the meaning of a name ; *explicative* for the same
reason ; *analytic*, inasmuch as it unties the bundle of
attributes held together in the concept and pays out
one, or all one by one.

When the attributes of the Predicate are not contained
in the concept of the Subject, the proposition is called
Real, Synthetic, or *Ampliative*, for parallel reasons.

Thus : "A triangle is a three-sided rectilinear
figure" is Verbal or Analytic ; "Triangles have
three angles together equal to two right angles,"
or "Triangles are studied in schools," is Real or
Synthetic.

According to this distinction, **pred**ications of the
whole Definition or of a Generic attribute or of a
Specific attribute are Verbal : predications of Accident
are Real. A nice point is whether Propria are Verbal
or Real. They can hardly be classed with Verbal,
inasmuch as one may know the full meaning of the
name without knowing them : but it might be argued
that they are Analytic, inasmuch as they are implicitly

contained in the defining attributes as being deducible from them.

Observe, however, that the whole distinction is really valid only in relation to some fixed or accepted scheme of classification or division. Otherwise, what is Verbal or Analytic to one man may be Real or Synthetic to another. It might even be argued that every proposition is Analytic to the man who utters it and Synthetic to the man who receives it. We must make some analysis of a whole of thought before paying it out in words : and in the process of apprehending the meaning of what we hear or read we must add the other members of the sentence on to the subject. Whether or not this is super-subtle, it clearly holds good that what is Verbal (in the sense defined) to the learned man of science may be Real to the learner. That the horse has six incisors in each jaw or that the domestic dog has a curly tail, is a Verbal Proposition to the Natural Historian, a mere exposition of defining marks ; but the plain man has a notion of horse or dog into which this defining attribute does not enter, and to him accordingly the proposition is Real.

But what of propositions that the plain man would at once recognise as Verbal ? Charles Lamb, for example, remarks that the statement that "a good name shows the estimation in which a man is held in the world" is a verbal proposition. Where is the fixed scheme of division there ? The answer is that by a fixed scheme of division we do not necessarily mean a scheme that is rigidly, definitely and precisely fixed. To make such schemes is the business of Science. But the ordinary vocabulary of common intercourse as a matter of fact proceeds upon schemes of division, though the names used in common speech are not always scientifically accurate, not always the best that could be devised for the easy acquisition and sure transmission of thorough knowledge. The plain man's vocabulary, though often twisted aside by such causes as we have specified, is roughly moulded on the most marked distinguishing attributes of things. This was practically recognised by Aristotle when he made one of his modes of definition consist in something like what we have called verifying the meaning of a name, ascertaining the attributes that it signifies in common speech or in the speech of sensible men. This is to ascertain the essence, οὐσία, or *Substantia*, of things, the most salient attributes that strike the common eye either at once or after the closer inspection that comes of long companionship, and form the basis of the ordinary vocabulary. " Properly speaking," Mansel says,[1] " All Definition is an inquiry into *Attributes*. Our complex notions of Substances can only be resolved into various Attributes, with the addition of an unknown *substratum :* a something to which we are compelled to regard these attributes as belonging. *Man*, for example, is analysed into Animality, Rationality, and the something which exhibits these phenomena. Pursue the analysis and the result is the same. We have a something corporeal, animated, sensible, rational. An unknown constant must always be added to complete the integration." This " unknown constant" was what Locke called the *Real* Essence, as distinguished from the *Nominal* Essence, or complex of attributes. It

---

[1] Aldrich's Compendium, Appendix, Note C. The reader may be referred to Mansel's Notes A and C for valuable historical notices of the Predicables and Definition.

is upon this nominal essence, upon divisions of things according to attributes, that common speech rests, and if it involves many cross-divisions, this is because the divisions have been made for limited and conflicting purposes.

CHAPTER III.

ARISTOTLE'S CATEGORIES.

In deference to tradition a place must be found in every logical treatise for Aristotle's Categories. No writing of the same length has exercised a tithe of its influence on human thought. It governed scholastic thought and expression for many centuries, being from its shortness and consequent easiness of transcription one of the few books in every educated man's library. It still regulates the subdivisions of Parts of Speech in our grammars. Its universality of acceptance is shown in the fact that the words *category* (κατηγορία) and *predicament*, its Latin translation, have passed into common speech.

The Categories have been much criticised and often condemned as a division, but, strange to say, few have inquired what they originally professed to be a division of, or what was the original author's basis of division. Whether the basis is itself important, is another question : but to call the division imperfect, without reference to the author's intention, is merely confusing, and serves only to illustrate the fact that the same objects may be differently divided on different principles of division. Ramus was right in saying that the Categories had no logical significance, inasmuch as they could not be made a basis for departments of logical method; and Kant and Mill in saying that they had no philosophical significance, inasmuch as they are founded upon no theory of Knowing and Being: but this is to condemn them for not being what they were never intended to be.

The sentence in which Aristotle states the objects to be divided, and his division of them is so brief and bold that bearing in mind the subsequent history of the Categories, one first comes upon it with a certain surprise. He says simply:—

"Of things expressed without syntax (*i.e.*, single words), each signifies either substance, or quantity, or quality, or relation, or place, or time, or disposition (*i.e.*, attitude or internal arrangement), or appurtenance, or action (doing), or suffering (being done to)." [1]

The objects, then, that Aristotle proposed to classify were single words (the *themata simplicia* of the School-men). He explains that by "out of syntax" (ἀνεὺ συμπλοκῆς) he means without reference to truth or falsehood: there can be no declaration of truth or falsehood without a sentence, a combination, or syntax: "man runs" is either true or false, "man" by itself, "runs" by itself, is neither. His division, therefore, was a division of single words according to their dif-ferences of signification, and without reference to the truth or falsehood of their predication. [2]

Signification was thus the basis of division. But

---

[1] τῶν κατὰ μηδεμίαν συμπλοκὴν λεγομένων ἕκαστον ἤτοι οὐσίαν σημαίνει, ἢ ποσὸν, ἢ ποιὸν, ἢ πρός τι, ἢ ποῦ, ἢ ποτὲ, ἢ κεῖσθαι, ἢ ἔχειν, ἢ ποιεῖν, ἢ πάσχειν. (Categ. ii. 6.)

[2] To describe the Categories as a grammatical division, as Mansel does in his instructive Appendix C to Aldrich, is a little misleading without a qualification. They are non-logical inas-

according to what differences? The Categories themselves are so abstract that this question might be
discussed on their bare titles interminably. But often
when abstract terms are doubtful, an author's intention
may be gathered from his examples. And when Aristotle's examples are ranged in a table, certain principles
of subdivision leap to the eyes. Thus :—

much as they have no bearing on any logical purpose. But they
are grammatical only in so far as they are concerned with words.
They are not grammatical in the sense of being concerned with
the function of words in predication. The unit of grammar in
this sense is the sentence, a combination of words in syntax ; and
it is expressly with words out of syntax that Aristotle deals, with
single words not in relation to the other parts of a sentence, but in
relation to the things signified. In any strict definition of the
provinces of Grammar and Logic, the Categories are neither
grammatical nor logical : the grammarians have appropriated
them for the subdivision of certain parts of the sentence, but with
no more right than the logicians. They really form a treatise by
themselves, which is in the main ontological, a discussion of substances and attributes as underlying the forms of common speech.
In saying this I use the word substance in the modern sense : but
it must be remembered that Aristotle's οὐσία, translated substantia,
covered the word as well as the thing signified, and that his
Categories are primarily classes of words. The union between
names and things would seem to have been closer in the Greek
mind than we can now realise. To get at it we must note that
every separate word (τὸ λεγόμενον) is conceived as having a being
or thing (τὸ ὄν) corresponding to it, so that beings or things
(τὰ ὄντα) are coextensive with single words : a being or thing is
whatever receives a separate name. This is clear and simple
enough, but perplexity begins when we try to distinguish between
this nameable being and concrete being, which last is Aristotle's
category of οὐσία, the being signified by a Proper or a Common
as distinguished from an Abstract Noun. As we shall see, it is
relatively to the highest sense of this last kind of being, namely,
the being signified by a Proper name, that he considers the other
kinds of being.

Substance (οὐσία) (*Substantia*)	Man (ἄνθρωπος)	} COMMON NOUN {	Substance
Quantity (ποσὸν) (*Quantitas*)	Five-feet-five (τρίπηχυ)		Permanent
Quality (ποιὸν) (*Qualitas*)	Scholarly (γραμματικὸν)	ADJECTIVE	
Relation (πρός τι) (*Relatio*)	Bigger (μεῖζον)		Attribute
Place (ποῦ) (*Ubi*)	In-the-Lyceum (ἐν Λυκείῳ)	ADVERB	Temporary
Time (ποτὲ) (*Quando*)	Yesterday (χθὲς)		
Disposition (κεῖσθαι) (*Positio*)	Reclines (ἀνάκειται)		
Appurtenance (ἔχειν) (*Habitus*)	Has-shoes-on (ὑποδέδεται)	VERB	Attribute
Action (ποιεῖν) (*Actio*)	Cuts (τέμνει)		
Passion (πάσχειν) (*Passio*)	Is cut (τέμνεται)		

In looking at the examples, our first impression is that Aristotle has fallen into a confusion. He professes' to classify words out of syntax, yet he gives words with the marks of syntax on them. Thus his division is accidentally grammatical, a division of parts of speech, parts of a sentence, into Nouns, Adjectives, Adverbs, and Verbs. And his subdivisions of these parts are still followed in our grammars. But really it is not the grammatical function that he attends to, but the signification: and looking further at the examples, we see what differences of signification he had in his mind. It is differences relative to a concrete individual, differences in the words applied to him according as they signify the substance of him or his attributes, permanent or temporary.

Take any concrete thing, Socrates, this book, this table. It must be some kind of a thing, a man, a book. It must have some size or quantity, six feet high, three inches broad. It must have some quality, white, learned, hard. It must have relations with other things, half this, double that, the son of a father. It must be somewhere, at some time, in some attitude, with some "havings," appendages, appurtenances, or belongings, doing something, or having something done to it. Can you conceive any name (simple or composite) applicable to any object of perception, whose signification does not fall into one or other of these classes? If you cannot, the categories are justified as an exhaustive division of significations. They are a complete list of the most general resemblances among individual things, in other words, of the *summa genera*, the *genera generalissima* of predicates concerning this, that or the other concrete individual. No individual thing is *sui generis:* everything is like other things: the categories are the most general likenesses.

The categories are exhaustive, but do they fulfil another requisite of a good division—are they mutually exclusive? Aristotle himself raised this question, and some of his answers to difficulties are instructive. Particularly his discussion of the distinction between Second Substances or Essences and Qualities. Here he approximates to the modern doctrine of the distinction between Substance and Attribute as set forth in our quotation from Mansel at p. 110. Aristotle's Second Essences (δεύτεραι οὐσίαι) are common nouns or general names, Species and Genera, *man, horse, animal*, as distinguished from Singular names, *this man, this horse*, which he calls First Substances (πρῶται οὐσίαι), essences *par excellence*, to which real existence in the highest sense is attributed. Common nouns are put in the First Category because they are predicated in answer to the question, What is this? But he raises the difficulty whether they may not rather be regarded as being in the Third Category, that of Quality (τὸ ποιόν). When we say, "This is a man," do we not declare what sort of a thing he is? do we not declare his Quality? If Aristotle had gone farther along this line, he would have arrived at the modern point of view that a man is a man in virtue of his possessing certain attributes, that general names are applied in virtue of their connotation. This would have been to make the line of distinction between the First Category and the Third pass between First Essence and Second, ranking the Second Essences with Qualities. But Aristotle did not get out of the difficulty in this way. He solved it by falling back on the differences in common speech. "Man" does not signify the quality simply, as "whiteness" does. "Whiteness" signifies nothing but the quality. That

is to say, there is no separate name in common
speech for the common attributes of man. His
further obscure remark that general names "define
quality round essence" (περὶ οὐσίαν), inasmuch as
they signify what sort a certain essence is, and that
genera make this definition more widely than species,
bore fruit in the mediæval discussions between Realists
and Nominalists by which the signification of general
names was cleared up.

Another difficulty about the mutual exclusiveness of
the Categories was started by Aristotle in connexion
with the Fourth Category, Relation (πρός τι *Ad aliquid,
To something*). Mill remarks that "that could not be
a very comprehensive view of the nature of Relation
which would exclude action, passivity, and local situation
from that Category," and many commentators, from
Simplicius down to Hamilton, have remarked that all
the last six Categories might be included under Relation. This is so far correct that the word Relation is one
of the vaguest and most extensive of words; but the
criticism ignores the strictness with which Aristotle
confined himself in his Categories to the forms of
common speech. It is clear from his examples that in
his Fourth Category he was thinking only of " relation "
as definitely expressed in common speech. In his
meaning, any word is a relative which is joined with
another in a sentence by means of a preposition or
a case-inflection. Thus " disposition " is a relative :
it is the disposition *of* something. This kind of
relation is perfect when the related terms reciprocate
grammatically; thus " master," " servant," since we
can say either " the master of the servant," or " the
servant of the master ". In mediæval logic the term
Relata was confined to these perfect cases, but the

Category had a wider scope with Aristotle. And he expressly raised the question whether a word might not have as much right to be put in another Category as in this. Indeed, he went further than his critics in his suggestions of what Relation might be made to include. Thus: "big" signifies Quality; yet a thing is big with reference to something else, and is so far a Relative. Knowledge must be knowledge of something, and is a relative: why then should we put "knowing" (*i.e.*, learned) in the Category of Quality. "Hope" is a relative, as being the hope *of* a man and the hope of something. Yet we say, "I have hope," and there hope would be in the category of Having, Appurtenance. For the solution of all such difficulties, Aristotle falls back upon the forms of common speech, and decides the place of words in his categories according to them. This was hardly consistent with his proposal to deal with separate words ⸆ut of syntax, if by this was meant anything more than dealing with them without reference to truth or falsehood. He did not and could not succeed in dealing with separate words otherwise than as parts of sentences, owing their signification to their position as parts of a transient plexus of thought. In so far as words have their being in common speech, and it is their being in this sense that Aristotle considers in the Categories, it is a transient being. What being they represent besides is, in the words of Porphyry, a very deep affair, and one that needs other and greater investigation.

Chapter IV.

THE CONTROVERSY ABOUT UNIVERSALS.—DIFFI-
CULTIES CONCERNING THE RELATION OF
GENERAL NAMES TO THOUGHT AND TO
REALITY.

In the opening sentences of his Isagoge, before giving
his simple explanation of the Five Predicables,
Porphyry mentions certain questions concerning
Genera and Species, which he passes over as being
too difficult for the beginner. " Concerning genera and
species," he says, " the question whether they subsist
(*i.e.*, have real substance), or whether they lie in the
mere thoughts only, or whether, granting them to subsist, they are corporeal or incorporeal, or whether they
subsist apart, or in sensible things and cohering round
them—this I shall pass over, such a question being a
very deep affair and one that needs other and greater
investigation."

This passage, written about the end of the third
century, A.D., is a kind of isthmus between Greek
Philosophy and Mediæval: it summarises questions
which had been turned over on every side and most
intricately discussed by Plato and Aristotle and their
successors, and the bald summary became a starting-
point for equally intricate discussions among the
Schoolmen, among whom every conceivable variety of
doctrine found champions. The dispute became known

as the dispute about Universals, and three ultra-
typical forms of doctrine were developed, known
respectively as Realism, Nominalism, and Conceptualism. Undoubtedly the dispute, with all its waste
of ingenuity, had a clearing effect, and we may fairly
try now what Porphyry shrank from, to gather some
simple results for the better understanding of general
names and their relations to thoughts and to things.
The rival schools had each some aspect of the general
name in view, which their exaggeration served to
render more distinct.

What does a general name signify? For logical
purposes it is sufficient to answer—the points of
resemblance as grasped in the mind, fixed by a name
applicable to each of the resembling individuals. This
is the signification of the general name *logically*, its
connotation or concept, the identical element of
objective reference in all uses of a general name.

But other questions may be asked that cannot be so
simply answered. What is this concept in thought?
What is there in our minds corresponding to the
general name when we utter it? How is its signification conceived? What is the signification *psychologically*?

We may ask, further, What is there in nature that
the general name signifies? What is its relation to
reality? What corresponds to it in the real world?
Has the unity that it represents among individuals no
existence except in the mind? Calling this unity, this
one in the many, the Universal (*Universale*, τὸ πᾶν),
what is the Universal *ontologically*?

It was this ontological question that was so hotly
and bewilderingly debated among the Schoolmen.
Before giving the ultra-typical answers to it, it may be

well to note how this question was mixed up with still
other questions of Theology and Cosmogony. Recognising that there is a unity signified by the general
name, we may go on to inquire into the ground of the
unity. Why are things essentially like one another?
How is the unity maintained? How is it continued?
Where does the common pattern come from? The
question of the nature of the Universal thus links itself
with metaphysical theories of the construction of the
world, or even with the Darwinian theory of the origin
of species.

Passing by these remoter questions, we may give
the answers of the three extreme schools to the ontological question, What is a Universal?

The answer of the Ultra-Realists, broadly put, was
that a Universal is a substance having an independent
existence in nature.

Of the Ultra-Nominalists, that the Universal is a
name and nothing else, *vox et præterea nihil;* that
this name is the only unity among the individuals of
a species, all that they have in common.

Of the Ultra-Conceptualists, that the individuals
have more in common than the name, that they have
the name plus the meaning, *vox + significatio,* but that
the Universals, the genera and species, exist only in
the mind.

Now these extreme doctrines, as literally interpreted
by opponents, are so easily refuted and so manifestly
untenable, that it may be doubted whether they were
ever held by any thinker, and therefore I call them
Ultra-Realism, Ultra-Nominalism, and Ultra-Concep-
tualism. They are mere exaggerations or caricatures,
set up by opponents because they can be easily knocked
down.

To the Ultra-Realists, it is sufficient to say that if there existed anywhere a substance having all the common attributes of a species and only these, having none of the attributes peculiar to any of the individuals of that species, corresponding to the general name as an individual corresponds to a Proper or Singular name, it would not be the Universal, the unity pervading the individuals, but only another individual.

To the Ultra-Nominalists, it is sufficient to say that the individuals must have more in common than the name, because the name is not applied arbitrarily, but on some ground. The individuals must have in common that on account of which they receive the common name: to call them by the same name is not to make them of the same species.

To the Ultra-Conceptualists, it is sufficient to say that when we employ a general name, as when we say " Socrates is a man," we do not refer to any passing thought or state of mind, but to certain attributes independent of what is passing in our minds. We cannot make a thing of this or that species by merely thinking of it as such.

The ultra-forms of these doctrines are thus easily shown to be inadequate, yet each of the three, Realism, Nominalism, and Conceptualism, represents a phase of the whole truth.

Thus, take Realism. Although it is not true that there is anything in reality corresponding to the general name such as there is corresponding to the singular name, the general name merely signifying attributes of what the singular name signifies, it does not follow, as the opponents of Ultra-Realism hastily assume, that there is nothing in the real world corresponding to the general name. Three senses may be particularised in which Realism is justified.

(1) The points of resemblance from which the concept is formed are as real as the individuals themselves. It is true in a sense that it is our thought that gives unity to the individuals of a class, that gathers the many into one, and so far the Conceptualists are right. Still we should not gather them into one if they did not resemble one another: that is the reason why we think of them together: and the respects in which they resemble one another are as much independent of us and our thinking as the individuals themselves, as much beyond the power of our thought to change. We must go behind the activity of the mind in unifying to the reason for the unification: and the ground of unity is found in what really exists. We do not confer the unity: we do not make all men or all dogs alike: we find them so. The curly tails in a thousand domestic dogs, which serve to distinguish them from wolves and foxes, are as real as the thousand individual domestic dogs. In this sense the Aristotelian doctrine, *Universalia in re*, expresses a plain truth.

(2) The Platonic doctrine, formulated by the Schoolmen as *Universalia ante rem*, has also a plain validity. Individuals come and go, but the type, the Universal, is more abiding. Men are born and die: man remains throughout. The snows of last year have vanished, but snow is still a reality to be faced. Wisdom does not perish with the wise men of any generation. In this plain sense, at least, it is true that Universals exist before Individuals, have a greater permanence, or, if we like to say so, a higher, as it is a more enduring, reality.

(3) Further, the "idea," concept, or universal, though it cannot be separated from the individual, and whether or not we ascribe to it the separate suprasensual existence of the archetypal forms of Plato's poetical fancy, is a very potent factor in the real world. Ideals of conduct, of manners, of art, of policy, have a traditional life: they do not pass away with the individuals in whom they have existed, in whom they are temporarily materialised: they survive as potent influences from age to age. The "idea" of Chaucer's Man of Law, who always "seemed busier than he was," is still with us. Mediæval conceptions of chivalry still govern conduct. The Universal enters into the Individual, takes possession of him, makes of him its temporary manifestation.

Nevertheless, the Nominalists are right in insisting on the importance of names. What we call the real world is a common object of perception and knowledge to you and me: we cannot arrive at a knowledge of it without some means of communication with one another: our means of communication is language. It may be doubted whether even thinking could go far without symbols with the help of which conceptions may be made definite. A concept cannot be explained without reference to a symbol. There is even a sense in which the Ultra-Nominalist doctrine that the individuals in a class have nothing in common but the name is tenable. Denotability by the same name is the only respect in which those individuals are absolutely identical : in this sense the name alone is common to them, though it is applied in virtue of their resemblance to one another.

Finally, the Conceptualists are right in insisting on the mind's activity in connexion with general names.

Genera and species are not mere arbitrary subjective collections: the union is determined by the characters of the things collected. Still it is with the concept in each man's mind that the name is connected: it is by the activity of thought in recognising likenesses and forming concepts that we are able to master the diversity of our impressions, to introduce unity into the manifold of sense, to reduce our various recollections to order and coherence.

So much for the Ontological question. Now for the **Psychological.** What is in the mind when we employ a general name? What is the Universal psychologically? How is it conceived?

What breeds confusion in these subtle inquiries is the want of fixed unambiguous names for the things to be distinguished. It is only by means of such names that we can hold on to the distinctions, and keep from puzzling ourselves. Now there are three things to be distinguished in this inquiry, which we may call the Concept, the Conception, and the Conceptual or Generic Image. Let us call them by these names, and proceed to explain them.

By the Concept, I understand the meaning of the general name, what the general name signifies: by the Conception, the mental act or state of him who conceives this meaning. The concept of "triangle," *i.e.*, what you and I mean by the word, is not my act of mind or your act of mind when we think or speak of a triangle. The Conception, which is this act, is an event or incident in our mental history, a psychical act or state, a distinct occurrence, a particular fact in time as much as the battle of Waterloo. The concept is the objective reference of the name, which is the same, or at least is understood to be the same, every

time we use it. I make a figure on paper with ink
or on a blackboard with chalk, and recognise or conceive it as a triangle : you also conceive it as such :
we do the same to-morrow : we did the same yesterday :
each act of conception is a different event, but the concept is the same throughout.

Now the psychological question about the Universal
is, What is this conception ? We cannot define it
positively further than by saying that it consists in
realising the meaning of a general name : the act
being unique, we can only make it intelligible by
producing an example of it. But we may define it
negatively by distinguishing it from the conceptual
image. Whenever we conceive anything, "man,"
"horse," there is generally present to our minds an
image of a man or horse, with accidents of size,
colour, position or other categories. But this conceptual image is not the concept, and the mental act
of forming it is not conception.

This distinction between mental picturing or
imaging and the conception of common attributes is
variously expressed. The correlative terms *Intuitive*
and *Symbolical* Thinking, *Presentative* and *Representative*
Knowledge have been employed.[1] But whatever terms

---

[1] The only objection to these terms is that they have slipped
from their moorings in philosophical usage. Thus instead of
Leibnitz's use of Intuitive and Symbolical, which corresponds
to the above distinction between Imaging and Conception, Mr.
Jevons employs the terms to express a distinction among
conceptions proper. We can understand what a chiliagon
means, but we cannot form an image of it in our minds, except
in a very confused and imperfect way; whereas we can form
a distinct image of a triangle. Mr. Jevons would call the
conception of the triangle *Intuitive*, of the chiliagon *Symbolical*.

we use, the distinction itself is vital, and the want of it leads to confusion.

Thus the fact that we cannot form a conceptual image composed solely of common attributes has been used to support the argument of Ultra-Nominalism, that the individuals classed under a common name have nothing in common but the name. What the word "dog" signifies, *i.e.*, the "concept" of dog, is neither big nor little, neither black nor tan, neither here nor there, neither Newfoundland, nor Retriever, nor Terrier, nor Greyhound, nor Pug, nor Bulldog. The concept consists only of the attributes common to all dogs apart from any that are peculiar to any variety or any individual. Now we cannot form any such conceptual image. Our conceptual image is always of some definite size and shape. Therefore, it is argued, we cannot conceive what a dog means, and dogs have nothing in common but the name. This, however, does not follow. The concept is not the conceptual image, and forming the image is not conception. We may even, as in the case of a chiliagon, or thousand-sided figure, conceive the meaning without being able to form any definite image.

How, then, do we ordinarily proceed in conceiving, if we cannot picture the common attributes alone and apart from particulars ? We attend, or strive to attend, only to those aspects of an image which it has in common with the individual things denoted. And if

Again, while Mansel uses the words Presentative and Representative to express our distinction, a more common usage is to call actual Perception Presentative Knowledge, and ideation or recollection in idea Representative.

we want to make our conception definite, we pass in review an indefinite number of the individuals, case after case.

A minor psychological question concerns the nature of the conceptual image. Is it a copy of some particular impression, or a confused blur or blend of many? Possibly neither: possibly it is something like one of Mr. Galton's composite photographs, photographs produced by exposing the same surface to the impressions of a number of different photographs in succession. If the individuals are nearly alike, the result is an image that is not an exact copy of any one of the components and yet is perfectly distinct. Possibly the image that comes into our mind's eye when we hear such a word as "horse" or "man" is of this character, the result of the impressions of a number of similar things, but not identical with any one. As, however, different persons have different conceptual images of the same concept, so we may have different conceptual images at different times. It is only the concept that remains the same.

But how, it may be asked, can the concept remain the same? If the universal or concept psychologically is an intellectual act, repeated every time we conceive, what guarantee have we for the permanence of the concept? Does this theory not do away with all possibility of defining and fixing concepts?

This brings us back to the doctrine already laid down about the truth of Realism. The theory of the concept is not exhausted when it is viewed only psychologically, as a psychic act. If we would understand it fully, we must consider the act in its relations to the real experience of ourselves and others. To fix this act, we give it a separate name,

calling it the conception : and then we must go behind
the activity of the mind to the objects on which it is
exercised.   The element of fixity is found in them.
And here also the truth of Nominalism comes in.
By means of words we enter into communication
with other minds.   It is thus that we discover what
is real, and what is merely personal to ourselves.

PART III.

THE INTERPRETATION OF PROPOSITIONS. —OPPOSITION AND IMMEDIATE INFERENCE.

CHAPTER I.

THEORIES OF PREDICATION.—THEORIES OF JUDGMENT.

WE may now return to the Syllogistic Forms, and the consideration of the compatibility or incompatibility, implication, and interdependence of propositions.

It was to make this consideration clear and simple that what we have called the Syllogistic Form of propositions was devised. When are propositions incompatible? When do they imply one another? When do two imply a third? We have seen in the Introduction how such questions were forced upon Aristotle by the disputative habits of his time. It was to facilitate the answer that he analysed propositions into Subject and Predicate, and viewed the Predicate as a reference to a class: in other words, analysed the Predicate further into a Copula and a Class Term.

But before showing how he exhibited the inter-connexion of propositions on this plan, we may turn aside to consider various so-called Theories of Predication or of Judgment. Strictly speaking, they are not altogether relevant to Logic, that is to say, as a practical science: they are partly logical, partly psychological theories: some of them have no bearing whatever on practice, but are matters of pure scientific curiosity: but historically they are connected with the logical treatment of propositions as having been developed out of this.

The least confusing way of presenting these theories is to state them and examine them both logically and psychologically. The logical question is, Has the view any advantage for logical purposes? Does it help to prevent error, to clear up confusion? Does it lead to firmer conceptions of the truth? The psychological question is, Is this a correct theory of how men actually think when they make propositions? It is a question of *what is* in the one case, and of *what ought to be for a certain purpose* in the other.

Whether we speak of Proposition or of Judgment does not materially affect our answer. A Judgment is the mental act accompanying a Proposition, or that may be expressed in a proposition and cannot be expressed otherwise: we can give no other intelligible definition or description of a judgment. So a proposition can only be defined as the expression of a judgment: unless there is a judgment underneath them, a form of words is not a proposition.

Let us take, then, the different theories in turn. We shall find that they are not really antagonistic, but only different: that each is substantially right from its own point of view: and that they seem to contradict one another only when the point of view is misunderstood.

I. *That the Predicate term may be regarded as a class in or from which the Subject is included or excluded.* Known as the Class-Inclusion, Class-Reference, or Denotative view.

This way of analysing propositions is possible, as we have seen, because every statement implies a general name, and the extension or denotation of a general name is a class defined by the common attribute or attributes. It is useful for syllogistic purposes : certain relations among propositions can be most simply exhibited in this way.

But if this is called a Theory of Predication or Judgment, and taken psychologically as a theory of what is in men's minds whenever they utter a significant Sentence, it is manifestly wrong. When discussed as such, it is very properly rejected. When a man says " P struck Q," he has not necessarily a class of " strikers of Q " definitely in his mind. What he has in his mind is the logical equivalent of this, but it is not this directly. Similarly, Mr. Bradley would be quite justified in speaking of Two Terms and a Copula as a superstition, if it were meant that these analytic elements are present to the mind of an ordinary speaker.

II. *That every Proposition may be regarded as affirming or denying an attribute of a subject.* Known sometimes as the Connotative or the Denotative-Connotative view. This also follows from the implicit presence of a general name in every sentence. But it should not be taken as meaning that the man who says: " Tom came here yesterday," or " James generally sits there," has a clearly analysed Subject and Attribute in his mind.   Otherwise it is as far wrong as the other view.

III.   *That every proposition may be regarded as an equation between two terms.*   Known as the Equational View.

This is obviously not true for common speech or ordinary thought.   But it is a possible way of regarding the analytic components of a proposition, legitimate enough if it serves any purpose.   It is a modification of the Class-Reference analysis, obtained by what is known as Quantification of the Predicate.   In " All S is in P," P is undistributed, and has no symbol of Quantity.   But since the proposition imports that All S is a part of P, *i.e.*, Some P, we may, if we choose, prefix the symbol of Quantity, and then the proposition may be read " All S = Some P ".   And so with the other forms.

Is there any advantage in this ?   Yes : it enables us to subject the formulæ to algebraic manipulation.   But any logical advantage—any help to thinking?   None whatever.   The elaborate syllogistic systems of Boole, De Morgan, and Jevons are not of the slightest use in helping men to reason correctly.   The value ascribed to them is merely an illustration of the Bias of Happy Exercise.   They are beautifully ingenious, but they leave every recorded instance of learned Scholastic trifling miles behind.

IV.   *That every proposition is the expression of a comparison between concepts.*   Sometimes called the Conceptualist View.

" To judge," Hamilton says, " is to recognise the relation of congruence or confliction in which two concepts, two individual things, or a concept and an individual compared together stand to each other."

This way of regarding propositions is permissible or not according to our interpretation of the words "congruence" and "confliction," and the word "concept". If by concept we mean a conceived attribute of a thing, and if by saying that two concepts are congruent or conflicting, we mean that they may or may not cohere in the same thing, and by saying that a concept is congruent or conflicting with an individual that it may or may not belong to that individual, then the theory is a corollary from Aristotle's analysis. Seeing that we must pass through that analysis to reach it, it is obviously not a theory of ordinary thought, but of the thought of a logician performing that analysis.

The precise point of Hamilton's theory was that the logician does not concern himself with the question whether two concepts are or are not as a matter of fact found in the same subject, but only with the question whether they are of such a character that they may be found, or cannot be found, in the same subject. In so far as his theory is sound, it is an abstruse and technical way of saying that we may consider the consistency of propositions without considering whether or not they are true, and that consistency is the peculiar business of syllogistic logic.

V. *That the ultimate subject of every judgment is reality.*

This is the form in which Mr. Bradley and Mr. Bosanquet deny the Ultra-Conceptualist position. The same view is expressed by Mill when he says that "propositions are concerned with things and not with our ideas of them".

The least consideration shows that there is justice in the view thus enounced. Take a number of propositions :—

The streets are wet.
George has blue eyes.
The Earth goes round the Sun.
Two and two make four.

Obviously, in any of these propositions, there is a reference beyond the conceptions in the speaker's mind, viewed merely as incidents in his mental history. They express beliefs about things and the relations among things *in rerum natura :* when any one understands them and gives his assent to them, he never stops to think of the speaker's state of mind, but of what the words represent.   When states of mind are spoken of, as when we say that our ideas are confused, or that a man's conception of duty influences his conduct, those states of mind are viewed as objective facts in the world of realities.   Even when we speak of things that have in a sense no reality, as when we say that a centaur is a combination of man and horse, or that centaurs were fabled to live in the vales of Thessaly, it is not the passing state of mind expressed by the speaker as such that we attend to or think of ; we pass at once to the objective reference of the words.

Psychologically, then, the theory is sound : what is its logical value ?   It is sometimes put forward as if it were inconsistent with the Class-reference theory or the theory that judgment consists in a comparison of concepts.   Historically the origin of its formal statement is its supposed opposition to those theories.   But really it is only a misconception of them that it contradicts.   It is inconsistent with the Class-reference view only if by a class we understand an arbitrary subjective collection, not a collection of things on the ground of common attributes. And it is inconsistent with the Conceptualist theory only if by a concept we understand not the objective reference of a general name, but what we have distinguished as a conception or a conceptual image. The theory that the ultimate subject is reality is assumed in both the other theories, rightly understood. If every proposition is the utterance of a judgment, and every proposition implies a general name, and every general name has a meaning or connotation, and every such meaning is an attribute of things and not a mental state, it is implied that the ultimate subject of every proposition is reality. But we may consider whether or not propositions are consistent without considering whether or not they are true, and it is only their mutual consistency that is considered in the syllogistic formulæ. Thus, while it is perfectly correct to say that every proposition expresses either truth or falsehood, or that the characteristic quality of a judgment is to be true or false, it is none the less correct to say that we may temporarily suspend consideration of truth or falsehood, and that this is done in what is commonly known as Formal Logic.

VI. *That every proposition may be regarded as expressing relations between phenomena.*

Bain follows Mill in treating this as the final import of Predication. But he indicates more accurately the logical value of this view in speaking of it as important for laying out the divisions of Inductive Logic. They differ slightly in their lists of Universal Predicates based upon Import in this sense—Mill's being Resemblance, Coexistence, Simple Sequence, and Causal Sequence, and Bain's being Coexistence, Succession, and Equality or Inequality.

But both lay stress upon Coexistence and Succession, and we shall find that the distinctions between Simple Sequence and Causal Sequence, and between Repeated and Occasional Coexistence, are all-important in the Logic of Investigation.   But for syllogistic purposes the distinctions have no relevance.

CHAPTER II.

THE "OPPOSITION" OF PROPOSITIONS.—THE INTERPRETATION OF "NO".

PROPOSITIONS are technically said to be "opposed" when, having the same terms in Subject and Predicate, they differ in Quantity, or in Quality, or in both.[1]

[1] This is the traditional definition of Opposition from an early period, though the tradition does not start from Aristotle. With him opposition (ἀντικεῖσθαι) meant, as it still means in ordinary speech, incompatibility. The technical meaning of Opposition is based on the diagram (given afterwards in the text) known as the Square of Opposition, and probably originated in a confused apprehension of the reason why it received that name. It was called the Square of Opposition, because it was intended to illustrate the doctrine of Opposition in Aristotle's sense and the ordinary sense of repugnance or incompatibility. What the Square brings out is this. If the four forms A E I O are arranged symmetrically according as they differ in quantity, or quality, or both, it is seen that these differences do not correspond symmetrically to compatibility and incompatibility : that propositions may differ in quantity or in quality without being incompatible, and that they may differ in both (as Contradictories) and be less violently incompatible than when they differ in one only (as Contraries). The original purpose of the diagram was to bring this out, as is done in every exposition of it. Hence it was called the Square of Opposition. But as a descriptive title this is a misnomer : it should have been the Square of Differences in Quantity or Quality. This misnomer has been perpetuated by appropriating Opposition as a common name for difference in Quantity or Quality when the terms are the same and in the same

The practical question from which the technical doctrine has been developed was how to determine the significance of contradiction. What is meant by giving the answer " No " to a proposition put interrogatively ? What is the interpretation of " No " ? What is the respondent committed to thereby ?

" Have all ratepayers a vote ? " If you answer " No," you are bound to admit that some ratepayers have not. O is the **Contradictory** of A. If A is false, O must be true. So if you deny O, you are bound to admit A : one or other must be true : either Some ratepayers have not a vote or All have.

Is it the case that no man can live without sleep ? Deny this, and you commit yourself to maintaining that Some man, one at least, can live without sleep. I is the Contradictory of E ; and *vice versâ*.

Contradictory opposition is distinguished from **Contrary,** the opposition of one Universal to another, of A to E and E to A. There is a natural tendency to meet a strong assertion with the very reverse. Let it be maintained that women are essentially faithless or that " the poor in a lump is bad," and disputants are apt to meet this extreme with another, that constancy is to be found only in women or true virtue only among the poor. Both extremes, both A and E, may be false : the truth may lie between : Some are, Some not.

order, and distinguishing it in this sense from Repugnance or Incompatibility (Tataretus in Summulas, *De Oppositionibus* [1501], Keynes, *The Opposition of Propositions* [1887]). Seeing that there never is occasion to speak of Opposition in the limited sense except in connexion with the Square, there is no real risk of confusion. A common name is certainly wanted in that connexion, if only to say that Opposition (in the limited or diagrammatic sense) does not mean incompatibility.

Logically, the denial of A or E implies only the admission of O or I. You are not committed to the full contrary. But the implication of the Contradictory is absolute ; there is no half-way house where the truth may reside. Hence the name of **Excluded Middle** is applied to the principle that " Of two Contradictories one or other must be true : they cannot both be false ".

While both Contraries may be false, they cannot both be true.

It is sometimes said that in the case of Singular propositions, the Contradictory and the Contrary coincide. A more correct doctrine is that in the case of Singular propositions, the distinction is not needed and does not apply. Put the question " Is Socrates wise ? " or " Is this paper white ? " and the answer " No " admits of only one interpretation, provided the terms remain the same. Socrates may become foolish, or this paper may hereafter be coloured differently, but in either case the subject term is not the same about which the question was asked. Contrary opposition belongs only to general terms taken universally as subjects. Concerning individual subjects an attribute must be either affirmed or denied simply : there is no middle course. Such a proposition as " Socrates is sometimes not wise," is not a true Singular proposition, though it has a Singular term as grammatical subject. Logically, it is a Particular proposition, of which the subject-term is the actions or judgments of Socrates.[1]

---

[1] Cp. Keynes, pt. ii. ch. ii. s. 57. Aristotle laid down the distinction between Contrary and Contradictory to meet another quibble in contradiction, based on taking the Universal as a whole and indivisible subject like an Individual, of which a given predicate must be either affirmed or denied.

Opposition, in the ordinary sense, is the opposition of incompatible propositions, and it was with this only that Aristotle concerned himself. But from an early period in the history of Logic, the word was extended to cover mere differences in Quantity and Quality among the four forms A E I O, which differences have been named and exhibited symmetrically in a diagram known as: The Square of Opposition.

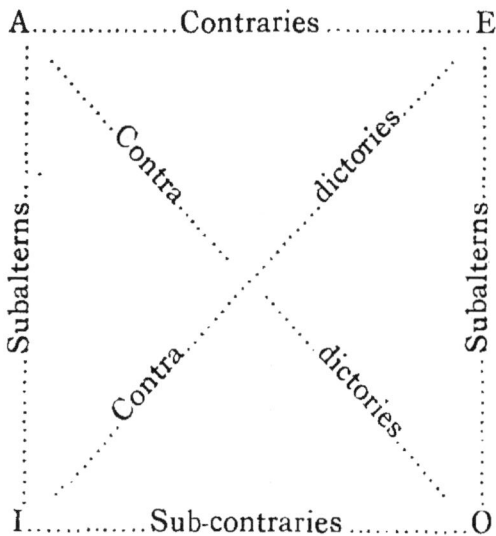

A.............Contraries.............E

I............Sub-contraries...........O

(diagram: Square of Opposition, with Subalterns on the left and right sides, and Contradictories along the diagonals.)

The four forms being placed at the four corners of the Square, and the sides and diagonals representing relations between them thus separated, a very pretty and symmetrical doctrine is the result.

Contradictories, A and O, E and I, differ both in Quantity and in Quality.

Contraries, A and E, differ in Quality but not in Quantity, and are both Universal.

Sub-contraries, I and O, differ in Quality but not in Quantity, and are both Particular.

Subalterns, A and I, E and O, differ in Quantity but not in Quality.

Again, in respect of concurrent truth and falsehood there is a certain symmetry.

Contradictories cannot both be true, nor can they both be false.

Contraries may both be false, but cannot both be true.

Sub-contraries may both be true, but cannot both be false.

Subalterns may both be false and both true. If the Universal is true, its subalternate Particular is true: but the truth of the Particular does not similarly imply the truth of its Subalternating Universal.

This last is another way of saying that the truth of the Contrary involves the truth of the Contradictory, but the truth of the Contradictory does not imply the truth of the Contrary.

There, however, the symmetry ends. The sides and the diagonals of the Square do not symmetrically represent degrees of incompatibility, or opposition in the ordinary sense.

There is no incompatibility between two Sub-contraries or a Subaltern and its Subalternant. Both may be true at the same time. Indeed, as Aristotle remarked of I and O, the truth of the one commonly implies the truth of the other : to say that some of the crew were drowned, implies that some were not, and *vice versâ*. Subaltern and Subalternant also are compatible, and something more. If a man has admitted A or E, he cannot refuse to admit I or O, the Particular of the same Quality. If All poets are irritable, it cannot be denied that some are so; if None is, that Some are not. The admission of the Contrary includes the admission of the Contradictory.

Consideration of Subalterns, however, brings to
light a nice ambiguity in Some. It is only when I is
regarded as the Contradictory of E, that it can properly
be said to be Subalternate to A. In that case the
meaning of Some is " not none," *i.e.*, " Some at least ".
But when Some is taken as the sign of Particular
quantity simply, *i.e.*, as meaning " not all," or " some
at most," I is not Subalternate to A, but opposed to it
in the sense that the truth of the one is incompatible
with the truth of the other.

Again, in the diagram Contrary opposition is represented by a side and Contradictory by the diagonal ;
that is to say, the stronger form of opposition by the
shorter line. The Contrary is more than a denial :
it is a counter-assertion of the very reverse, τὸ ἐνάντιον.
" Are good administrators always good speakers ? "
" On the contrary, they never are." This is a much
stronger opposition, in the ordinary sense, than a
modest contradictory, which is warranted by the
existence of a single exception. If the diagram were
to represent incompatibility accurately, the Contrary
ought to have a longer line than the Contradictory,
and this it seems to have had in the diagram that
Aristotle had in mind (*De Interpret.*, c. 10).

It is only when Opposition is taken to mean merely
difference in Quantity and Quality that there can be
said to be greater opposition between Contradictories
than between Contraries. Contradictories differ both
in Quantity and in Quality : Contraries, in Quality
only.

There is another sense in which the Particular
Contradictory may be said to be a stronger opposite
than the Contrary. It is a stronger position to take
up argumentatively. It is easier to defend than a

Contrary. But this is because it offers a narrower and more limited opposition.

We deal with what is called Immediate Inference in the next chapter. Pending an exact definition of the process, it is obvious that two immediate inferences are open under the above doctrines. (1) Granted the truth of any proposition, you may immediately infer the falsehood of its Contradictory. (2) Granted the truth of any Contrary, you may immediately infer the truth of its Subaltern.[1]

[1] I have said that there is little risk of confusion in using the word Opposition in its technical or limited sense. There is, however, a little. When it is said that these inferences are based on Opposition, or that Opposition is a mode of Immediate Inference, there is confusion of ideas unless it is pointed out that when this is said, it is Opposition in the ordinary sense that is meant. The inferences are really based on the rules of Contrary and Contradictory Opposition ; Contraries cannot both be true, and of Contradictories one or other must be.

Chapter III.

THE IMPLICATION OF PROPOSITIONS.—IMMEDIATE FORMAL INFERENCE.—EDUCTION.

The meaning of Inference generally is a subject of dispute, and to avoid entering upon debatable ground at this stage, instead of attempting to define Inference generally, I will confine myself to defining what is called Formal Inference, about which there is comparatively little difference of opinion.

Formal Inference then is the apprehension of what is implied in a certain datum or admission: the derivation of one proposition, called the **Conclusion,** from one or more given, admitted, or assumed propositions, called the **Premiss** or **Premisses.**

When the conclusion is drawn from one proposition, the inference is said to be **immediate;** when more than one proposition is necessary to the conclusion, the inference is said to be **mediate.**

Given the proposition, " All poets are irritable," we can immediately infer that " Nobody that is not irritable is a poet "; and the one admission implies the other. But we cannot infer immediately that " all poets make bad husbands ". Before we can do this we must have a second proposition conceded, that "All irritable persons make bad husbands". The inference in the second case is called Mediate.[1]

The modes and conditions of valid Mediate Inference constitute Syllogism, which is in effect the reasoning together of separate admissions. With this we shall deal presently. Meantime of Immediate Inference.

To state all the implications of a certain form of proposition, to make explicit all that it implies, is the same thing with showing what immediate inferences from it are legitimate. Formal inference, in short, is the eduction of all that a proposition implies.

Most of the modes of Immediate Inference formulated by logicians are preliminary to the Syllogistic process, and have no other practical application. The most important of them technically is the process known as Conversion, but others have been judged worthy of attention.

ÆQUIPOLLENT OR EQUIVALENT FORMS—OBVERSION.

Æquipollence or Equivalence (Ισοδυναμία) is defined as the perfect agreement in sense of two propositions that differ somehow in expression.[2]

The history of Æquipollence in logical treatises illustrates two tendencies. There is a tendency on the one hand to narrow a theme down to definite and manageable forms. But when a useful exercise is discarded from one place it has a tendency to break out in another under another name. A third tendency

---

[1] I purposely chose disputable propositions to emphasise the fact that Formal Logic has no concern with the truth, but only with the interdependence of its propositions.

[2] Mark Duncan, *Inst. Log.*, ii. 5, 1612.

may also be said to be specially well illustrated—the tendency to change the traditional application of logical terms.

In accordance with the above definition of Æqui-pollence or Equivalence, which corresponds with ordinary acceptation, the term would apply to all cases of "identical meaning under difference of expression". Most examples of the reduction of ordinary speech into syllogistic form would be examples of æquipol-lence ; all, in fact, would be so were it not that ordinary speech loses somewhat in the process, owing to the indefiniteness of the syllogistic symbol for particular quality, Some. And in truth all such transmutations of expression are as much entitled to the dignity of being called Immediate Inferences as most of the processes so entitled.

Dr. Bain uses the word with an approach to this width of application in discussing all that is now most commonly called Immediate Inference under the title of Equivalent Forms. The chief objection to this usage is that the Converse *per accidens* is not strictly equivalent. A debater may want for his argument less than the strict equivalent, and content himself with educing this much from his opponent's admission. (Whether Dr. Bain is right in treating the Minor and Conclusion of a Hypothetical Syllogism as being equivalent to the Major, is not so much a question of naming.)

But in the history of the subject, the traditional usage has been to confine Æquipollence to cases of equivalence between positive and negative forms of expression. "Not all are," is equivalent to "Some are not": "Not none is," to "Some are". In Pre-Aldrichian text-books, Æquipollence corresponds mainly to what it is now customary to call (*e.g.*, Fowler, pt. iii. c. ii., Keynes, pt. ii. c. vii.) Immediate Inference based on Opposition. The denial of any proposition involves the admission of its contradictory. Thus, if the negative particle " Not " is placed before the sign of Quantity, All or Some, in a proposition, the resulting proposition is equivalent to the Contradictory of the original. Not all S is P = Some S is not P. Not any S is P = No S is P. The mediæval logicians tabulated these equivalents, and also the forms resulting from placing the negative particle after, or both before and after, the sign of Quantity. Under the title of Æquipollence, in fact, they considered the interpretation of the negative particle generally. If the negative is placed after the universal sign, it results in the Contrary : if both before and after, in the Subaltern. The statement of these equivalents is a puzzling exercise which no doubt accounts for the prominence given it by Aristotle and the Schoolmen. The latter helped the student with the following Mnemonic line : *Præ Contradic., post Contrar., præ postque Subaltern.*[1]

---

[1] There can be no doubt that in their doctrine of Æquipollents, the Schoolmen were trying to make plain a real difficulty in interpretation, the interpretation of the force of negatives. Their results would have been more obviously useful if they had seen their way to generalising them. Perhaps too they wasted their strength in applying it to the artificial syllogistic forms, which men do not ordinarily encounter except in the manipulation of syllogisms. Their results might have been generalised as follows :—

(1) A " not " placed before the sign of Quantity contradicts the whole proposition. Not " All S is P," not " No S is P," not " Some S is P," not " Some S is not P," are equivalent respectively to contradictories of the propositions thus negated.

(2) A " not " placed after the sign of Quantity affects the

To Æquipollence belonged also the manipulation of the forms known after the *Summulæ* as *Exponibiles,* notably *Exclusive* and *Exceptive propositions*, such as None but barristers are eligible, The virtuous alone are happy. The introduction of a negative particle into these already negative forms makes a very trying problem in interpretation. The æquipollence of the Exponibiles was dropped from text-books long before Aldrich, and it is the custom to laugh at them as extreme examples of frivolous scholastic subtlety : but most modern text-books deal with part of the doctrine of the *Exponibiles* in casual exercises.

Curiously enough, a form left unnamed by the scholastic logicians because too simple and useless, has the name Æquipollent appropriated to it, and to it alone, by Ueberweg, and has been adopted under various names into all recent treatises.

Bain calls it the **Formal Obverse,**[1] and the title of

copula, and amounts to inverting its Quality, thus denying the predicate term of the same quantity of the subject term of which it was originally affirmed, and *vice versâ*.

All S is " not " P = No S is P.
No S is " **not** " P = All S is P.
Some S is " not " P = Some S is not P.
Some S is " not " not P = Some S is P.

(3) If a " not " is placed before as well as after, the resulting forms are obviously equivalent (under Rule 1) to the assertion of the contradictories of the forms on the right (in the illustration of Rule 2).

Not	All S is " not " P	= No S is P	= Some S is P.
Not	No S is " not " P	= All S is P	= Some S is not P.
Not	Some S is " not " P	= Some S is not P	= All S is P.
Not	Some S is " not " not P	= Some S is P	= No S is P.

[1] *Formal* to distinguish it from what he called the *Material Obverse*, about which more presently.

Obversion (which has the advantage of rhyming with **Conversion**) has been adopted by Keynes, Miss Johnson, and others.

Fowler (following Karslake) calls it **Permutation.** The title is not a happy one, having neither rhyme nor reason in its favour, but it is also extensively used.

This immediate inference is a very simple affair to have been honoured with such a choice of terminology. " This road is long : therefore, it is not short," is an easy inference : the second proposition is the Obverse, or Permutation, or Æquipollent, or (in Jevons's title) the Immediate Inference by Privative Conception, of the first.

The inference, such as it is, depends on the Law of Excluded Middle. Either a term P, or its contradictory, not-P, must be true of any given subject, S : hence to affirm P of all or some S, is equivalent to denying not-P of the same : and, similarly, to deny P, is to affirm not-P. Hence the rule of Obversion ; —Substitute for the predicate term its Contrapositive,[1] and change the Quality of the proposition.

> All S is P = No S is not-P.
> No S is P = All S is not-P.
> Some S is P = Some S is not not-P.
> Some S is not P = Some S is not-P.

CONVERSION.

The process takes its name from the interchange of the terms. The Predicate-term becomes the Subject-term, and the Subject-term the Predicate-term.

When propositions are analysed into relations of

---

[1] The mediæval word for the opposite of a term, the word Contradictory being confined to the propositional form.

inclusion or exclusion between terms, the assertion of any such relation between one term and another, implies a Converse relation between the second term and the first. The statement of this implied assertion is technically known as the **Converse** of the original proposition, which may be called the *Convertend.*

Three modes of Conversion are commonly recognised :—(*a*) **Simple Conversion ;** (*b*) **Conversion** *per accidens* or by limitation ; (*c*) **Conversion by Contraposition.**

(*a*) E and I can be simply converted, only the terms being interchanged, and Quantity and Quality remaining the same.

If S is wholly excluded from P, P must be wholly excluded from S. If Some S is contained in P, then Some P must be contained in S.

(*b*) A cannot be simply converted. To know that All S is contained in P, gives you no information about that portion of P which is outside S. It only enables you to assert that Some P is S ; that portion of P, namely, which coincides with S.

O cannot be converted either simply or *per accidens.* Some S is not P does not enable you to make any converse assertion about P. All P may be S, or No P may be S, or Some P may be not S. All the three following diagrams are compatible with Some S being excluded from P.

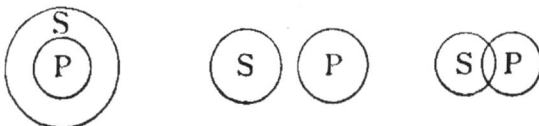

(*c*) Another mode of Conversion, known by mediæval logicians following Boethius as *Conversio per contra-*

positionem terminorum, is useful in some syllogistic manipulations. This Converse is obtained by substituting for the predicate term its Contrapositive or Contradictory, not-P, making the consequent change of Quality, and simply converting. Thus All S is P is converted into the equivalent No not-P is S.[1]

Some have called it " Conversion by Negation," but "negation" is manifestly too wide and common a word to be thus arbitrarily restricted to the process of substituting for one term its opposite.

Others (and this has some mediæval usage in its favour, though not the most intelligent) would call the form All not-P is not-S (the Obverse or Permutation of No not-P is S), the Converse by Contraposition. This is to conform to an imaginary rule that in Conversion the Converse must be of the same Quality with the Convertend. But the essence of Conversion is the interchange of Subject and Predicate : the Quality is not in the definition except by a bungle : it is an accident. No not-P is S, and Some not-P is S are the forms used in Syllogism, and therefore specially named. Unless a form had a use, it was left unnamed, like the Subalternate forms of Syllogism : Nomen habent nullum : nec, si bene colligis, usum.

---

[1] It is to be regretted that a practice has recently crept in of calling this form, for shortness, the Contrapositive simply. By long-established usage, dating from Boethius, the word Contrapositive is a technical name for a terminal form, not-A, and it is still wanted for this use. There is no reason why the propositional form should not be called the Converse by Contraposition, or the Contrapositive Converse, in accordance with traditional usage.

Table of Contrapositive Converses.

	Con. Con.
All S is P	No not-P is S
No S is P	Some not-P is S
Some S is not P	Some not-P is S
Some S is P	None.

When not-P is substituted for P, Some S is P becomes Some S is not not-P, and this form is inconvertible.

Other Forms of Immediate Inference.

I have already spoken of the Immediate Inferences based on the rules of Contradictory and Contrary Opposition (see p. 145).

Another process was observed by Thomson, and named *Immediate Inference by Added Determinants.* If it is granted that " A negro is a fellow-creature," it follows that " A negro in suffering is a fellow-creature in suffering ". But that this does not follow for every attribute[1] is manifest if you take another case :—" A tortoise is an animal : therefore, a fast tortoise is a fast animal ". The form, indeed, holds in cases not worth specifying : and is a mere handle for quibbling. It could not be erected into a general rule unless it were true that whatever distinguishes a species within a class, will equally distinguish it in every class in which the first is included.

Modal Consequence has also been named among the forms of Immediate Inference. By this is meant the inference of the lower degrees of certainty from the

---

[1] *Cf.* Stock, part iii. c. vii. ; Bain, *Deduction*, p. 109.

higher. Thus *must be* is said to imply *may be ;* and *None can be* to imply *None is.*

Dr. Bain includes also *Material Obversion,* the · analogue of *Formal Obversion* applied to a Subject. Thus Peace is beneficial to commerce, implies that War is injurious to commerce. Dr. Bain calls this Material Obversion because it cannot be practised safely without reference to the matter of the proposition. We shall recur to the subject in another chapter.

Chapter IV.

THE COUNTER-IMPLICATION OF PROPOSITIONS.

In discussing the Axioms of Dialectic, I indicated that the propositions of common speech have a certain negative implication, though this does not depend upon any of the so-called Laws of Thought, Identity, Contradiction, and Excluded Middle. Since, however, the counter-implicate is an important guide in the interpretation of propositions, it is desirable to recognise it among the modes of Immediate Inference.

I propose, then, first, to show that people do ordinarily infer at once to a counter-sense ; second, to explain briefly the Law of Thought on which such an inference is justified ; and, third, how this law may be applied in the interpretation of propositions, with a view to making subject and predicate more definite.

Every affirmation about anything is an implicit negation about something else. Every say is a gain-say. That people ordinarily act upon this as a rule of interpretation a little observation is sufficient to show : and we find also that those who object to having their utterances interpreted by this rule often shelter themselves under the name of Logic.

Suppose, for example, that a friend remarks, when the conversation turns on children, that John is a good boy, the natural inference is that the speaker has in his mind another child who is not a good boy. Such an inference would at once be drawn by any actual hearer, and the speaker would protest in vain that he said nothing about anybody but John. Suppose there are two candidates for a school appointment, A and B, and that stress is laid upon the fact that A is an excellent teacher. A's advocate would at once be understood to mean that B was not equally excellent as a teacher.

The fairness of such inferences is generally recognised. A reviewer, for example, of one of Mrs. Oliphant's historical works, after pointing out some small errors, went on to say that to confine himself to censure of small points, was to acknowledge by implication that there were no important points to find fault with.

Yet such negative implications are often repudiated as illogical. It would be more accurate to call them extra-logical. They are not condemned by any logical doctrine : they are simply ignored. They are extra-logical only because they are not legitimated by the Laws of Identity, Contradiction, and Excluded Middle: and the reason why Logic confines itself to those laws is that they are sufficient for Syllogism and its subsidiary processes.

But, though extra-logical, to infer a counter-implicate is not unreasonable : indeed, if Definition, clear vision of things in their exact relations, is our goal rather than Syllogism, a knowledge of the counter-implicate is of the utmost consequence. Such an implicate there must always be under an all-pervading Law of Thought which has not yet been named, but which may be called tentatively the law of Homogeneous Counter-relativity. The title, one hopes, is sufficiently technical-looking : though cumbrous, it is descriptive. The law itself is simple, and may be thus stated and explained.

The Law of Homogeneous Counter-relativity.

> Every positive in thought has a contrapositive, and the positive and contrapositive are of the same kind.

The first clause of our law corresponds with Dr. Bain's law of Discrimination or Relativity : it is, indeed, an expansion and completion of that law. Nothing is known absolutely or in isolation ; the various items of our knowledge are inter-relative; everything is known by distinction from other things. Light is known as the opposite of darkness, poverty of riches, freedom of slavery, in of out; each shade of colour by contrast to other shades.   What Dr. Bain lays stress upon is the element of difference in this inter-relativity.   He bases this law of our knowledge on the fundamental law of our sensibility that change of impression is necessary to consciousness.   A long continuance of any unvaried impression results in insensibility to it.   We have seen instances of this in illustrating the maxim that custom blunts sensibility (p. 74).   Poets have been beforehand with philosophers in formulating this principle.   It is expressed with the greatest precision by Barbour in his poem of " The Bruce," where he insists that men who have never known slavery do not know what freedom is.

> Thus contrar thingis evermare
> Discoverings of t' other are.

Since, then, everything that comes within our consciousness comes as a change or transition from
something else, it results that our knowledge is counter-
relative.   It is in the clash or conflict of impressions
that knowledge emerges : every item of knowledge has
its illuminating foil, by which it is revealed, over against
which it is defined.   Every positive in thought has its
contrapositive.

So much for the element of difference.   But this is
not the whole of the inter-relativity.   The Hegelians
rightly lay stress on the common likeness that connects
the opposed items of knowledge.

"Thought is not only *distinction ;* it is, at the same time,
relation.[1]   If it marks off one thing from another, it, at the
same time, connects one thing with another.   Nor can either of
these functions of thought be separated from the other : as
Aristotle himself said, the knowledge of opposites is one.   A
thing which has nothing to distinguish it is unthinkable, but
equally unthinkable is a thing which is so separated from all
other things as to have no community with them.   If then the

---

[1] It is significant of the unsuitableness of the vague unqualified
word Relativity to express a logical distinction that Dr. Bain calls
his law the Law of Relativity simply, having regard to the relation
of difference, *i.e.*, to Counter-Relativity, while Dr. Caird applies
the name Relativity simply to the relation of likeness, *i.e.*, to Co-
relativity.   It is with a view to taking both forms of relation
into account that I name our law the Law of Homogeneous
Counter-relativity.   The Protagorean Law of Relativity has
regard to yet another relation, the relation of knowledge
to the knowing mind : these other logical laws are of relations
among the various items of knowledge.   Aristotle's category of
Relation is a fourth kind of relation not to be confused with the
others.   "Father—son," "uncle—nephew," "slave—master," are
relata in Aristotle's sense : "father," "uncle" are homogeneous
counter-relatives, varieties of kinship ; so "slave," "freeman" are
counter-relatives in social status.

law of contradiction be taken as asserting the self-identity of
things or thoughts in a sense that excludes their community—in
other words, if it be not taken as limited by another law which
asserts the *relativity* of the things or thoughts distinguished—it
involves a false abstraction. . . . If, then, the world, as an intelligible world, is a world of distinction, differentiation, individuality,
it is equally true that in it as an intelligible world there are no
absolute separations or oppositions, no antagonisms which cannot
be reconciled."[1]

In the penultimate sentence of this quotation Dr.
Caird *differentiates* his theory against a Logical counter-
theory of the Law of Identity, and in the last sentence
against an Ethical counter-theory : but the point here
is that he insists on the relation of likeness among
opposites. Every impression felt is felt as a change
or transition from something else : but it is a variation
of the same impression—the something else, the
contrapositive, is not entirely different. Change
itself is felt as the opposite of sameness, difference
of likeness, and likeness of difference. We do not
differentiate our impression against the whole world,
as it were, but against something nearly akin to it—
upon some common ground. The positive and the
contrapositive are of the same kind.

Let us surprise ourselves in the act of thinking and
we shall find that our thoughts obey this law. We
take note, say, of the colour of the book before us :
we differentiate it against some other colour actually
before us in our field of vision or imagined in our
minds. Let us think of the blackboard as black : the
blackness is defined against the whiteness of the
figures chalked or chalkable upon it, or against the
colour of the adjacent wall. Let us think of a man as

<hr/>

[1] Dr. Caird's *Hegel*, p. 134.

a soldier; the opposite in our minds is not the colour of his hair, or his height, or his birthplace, or his nationality, but some other profession—soldier, sailor, tinker, tailor. It is always by means of some contrapositive that we make the object of our thoughts definite; it is not necessarily always the same opposite, but against whatever opposite it is, they are always homogeneous. One colour is contradistinguished from another colour, one shade from another shade : colour may be contradistinguished from shape, but it is within the common genus of sensible qualities.

A curious confirmation of this law of our thinking has been pointed out by Mr. Carl Abel.[1] In Egyptian hieroglyphics, the oldest extant language, we find, he says, a large number of symbols with two meanings, the one the exact opposite of the other. Thus the same symbol represents *strong* and *weak; above—below; with—without; for—against.* This is what the Hegelians mean by the reconciliation of antagonisms in higher unities. They do not mean that black is white, but only that black and white have something in common—they are both colours.

I have said that this law of Homogeneous Counter-relativity has not been recognised by logicians. This, however, is only to say that it has not been explicitly formulated and named, as not being required for Syllogism; a law so all-pervading could not escape recognition, tacit or express. And accordingly we find that it is practically assumed in Definition : it is really the basis of definition *per genus et differentiam.* When we wish to have a definite conception of anything, to apprehend what it is, we place it in some

[1] See article on Counter-Sense, *Contemporary Review*, April, 1884.

genus and distinguish it from species of the same.   In
fact our law might be called the Law of Specification :
in obeying the logical law of what we ought to do with
a view to clear thinking, we are only doing with
exactness and conscious method what we all do and
cannot help doing with more or less definiteness in our
ordinary thinking.

It is thus seen that logicians conform to this law
when they are not occupied with the narrow considerations proper to Syllogism.   And another unconscious
recognition of it may be found in most logical text-books.
Theoretically the not-A of the Law of Contradiction—
(A is not not-A)—is an infinite term.   It stands for
everything but A.   This is all that needs to be assumed
for Conversion and Syllogism.   But take the examples
given of the Formal Obverse or Permutation, " All men
are fallible ".   Most authorities would give as the
Formal Obverse of this, " No men are infallible ".
But, strictly speaking, " infallible " is of more limited
and definite signification than not-fallible.   Not-fallible,
other than fallible, is brown, black, chair, table, and
every other nameable thing except fallible.   Thus in
Obversion and Conversion by Contraposition, the
homogeneity of the negative term is tacitly assumed ;
it is assumed that A and not-A are of the same kind.

Now to apply this Law of our Thought to the interpretation of propositions.   Whenever a proposition is
uttered we are entitled to infer at once (or *immediately*)
that the speaker has in his mind some counter-proposition, in which what is overtly asserted of the ostensible
subject is covertly denied of another subject.   And we
must know what this counter-proposition, the counter-
implicate is, before we can fully and clearly understand

his meaning. But inasmuch as any positive may have more than one contrapositive, we cannot tell immediately or without some knowledge of the circumstances or context, what the precise counter-implicate is. The peculiar fallacy incident to this mode of interpretation is, knowing that there must be some counter-implicate, to jump rashly or unwarily to the conclusion that it is some definite one.

Dr. Bain applies the term Material Obverse to the form, Not-S is not P, as distinguished from the form S is not not-P, which he calls the Formal Obverse, on the ground that we can infer the Predicate-contrapositive at once from the form, whereas we cannot tell the Subject-contrapositive without an examination of the matter. But in truth we cannot tell either Predicate-contrapositive or Subject-contrapositive as it is in the mind of the speaker from the bare utterance. We can only tell that if he has in his mind a proposition definitely analysed into subject and predicate he must have contrapositives in his mind of both, and that they must be homogeneous. Let a man say, " This book is a quarto ". For all that we know he may mean that it is not a folio or that it is not an octavo: we only know for certain, under the law of Homogeneous Counter-relativity, that he means some definite other size. Under the same law, we know that he has a homogeneous contrapositive of the subject, a subject that admits of the same predicate, some other book in short. What the particular book is we do not know.

It would however be a waste of ingenuity to dwell upon the manipulation of formulæ founded on this law. The practical concern is to know that for the interpretation of a proposition, a knowledge of the counter-implicate, a knowledge of what it is meant to deny, is essential.

The manipulation of formulæ, indeed, has its own special snare. We are apt to look for the counterparts of them in the grammatical forms of common speech. Thus, it might seem to be a fair application of our law to infer from the sentence, "Wheat is dear," that the speaker had in his mind that Oats or Sugar or Shirting or some other commodity is cheap. But this would be a rash conclusion. The speaker may mean this, but he *may* also mean that wheat is dear now as compared with some other time : that is, the Positive subject in his mind may be " Wheat as now," and the Contra-positive " Wheat as then ". So a man may say, "All men are mortal," meaning that the angels never taste death, " angels " being the contrapositive of his subject " men ". Or he may mean merely that mortality is a sad thing, his positive subject being men as they are, and his contrapositive men as he desires them to be. Or his emphasis may be upon the *all*, and he may mean only to deny that some one man in his mind (Mr. Gladstone, for example) is immortal. It would be misleading, therefore, to prescribe propositions as exercises in Material Obversion, if we give that name to the explicit expression of the Contrapositive Subject : it is only from the context that we can tell what this is. The man who wishes to be clearly understood gives us this information, as when the epigrammatist said : " We are all fallible---even the youngest of us ".

But the chief practical value of the law is as a guide in studying the development of opinions. Every doctrine ever put forward has been put forward in opposition to a previous doctrine on the same subject. Until we know what the opposed doctrine is, we cannot be certain of the meaning. We cannot gather it with precision from a mere study of the grammatical or even (in the narrow sense of the word) the logical content of the words used. This is because the framers of doctrines have not always been careful to put them in a clear form of subject and predicate, while their impugners have not moulded their denial exactly on the language of the original. No doubt it would have been more conducive to clearness if they had done so. But they have not, and we must take them as they are. Thus we have seen that the Hegelian doctrine of Relativity is directed against certain other doctrines in Logic and in Ethics; that Ultra-Nominalism is a contradiction of a certain form of Ultra-Realism; and that various theories of Predication each has a backward look at some predecessor.

I quote from Mr. A. B. Walkley a very happy application of this principle of interpretation :—

" It has always been a matter for speculation why so sagacious an observer as Diderot should have formulated the wild paradox that the greatest actor is he who feels his part the least. Mr. Archer's bibliographical research has solved this riddle. Diderot's paradox was a protest against a still wilder one. It seems that a previous eighteenth century writer on the stage, a certain Saint-Albine, had advanced the fantastic propositions that none but a magnanimous man can act magnanimity, that only lovers can do justice to a love scene, and kindred assertions that read like variations on the familiar ' Who drives fat oxen must himself be fat '. Diderot saw the absurdity of this; he saw also the essentially artificial nature of the French tragedy and comedy of his own day; and he hastily took up the position which Mr. Archer has now shown to be untenable."

This instance illustrates another principle that has to be borne in mind in the interpretation of doctrines from their historical context of counter-implication.

This is the tendency that men have to put doctrines in too universal a form, and to oppose universal to universal, that is, to deny with the flat contrary, the very reverse, when the more humble contradictory is all that the truth admits of.   If a name is wanted for this tendency, it might be called the tendency to Over-Contradiction.   Between " All are " and " None are," the sober truth often is that " Some are " and " Some are not," and the process of evolution has often consisted in the substitution of these sober forms for their more violent predecessors.

PART IV.

THE INTERDEPENDENCE OF PROPOSITIONS.—MEDIATE INFERENCE.—SYLLOGISM.

CHAPTER I.

THE SYLLOGISM.

WE have already defined mediate inference as the derivation of a conclusion from more than one proposition. The type or form of a mediate inference fully expressed consists of three propositions so related that one of them is involved or implied in the other two.

> Distraction is exhausting.
> Modern life is full of distraction.
> ∴ Modern life is exhausting.

We say nothing of the truth of these propositions. I purposely choose questionable ones. But do they hang together? If you admit the first two, are you bound in consistency to admit the third? Is the truth of the conclusion a necessary consequence of the truth of the premisses? If so, it is a valid mediate inference from them.

When one of the two premisses is more general than the conclusion, the argument is said to be **Deductive.**
You lead down from the more general to the less general. The general proposition is called the Major Premiss, or Grounding Proposition, or Sumption : the other premiss the Minor, or Applying Proposition, or Subsumption.

> Undue haste makes waste.
> This is a case of undue hasting.
> ∴ It is a case of undue wasting.

We may, and constantly do, apply principles and draw conclusions in this way without making any formal analysis of the propositions.   Indeed we reason mediately and deductively whenever we make any application of previous knowledge, although the process is not expressed in propositions at all and is performed so rapidly that we are not conscious of the steps.

For example, I enter a room, see a book, open it and begin to read.   I want to make a note of something : I look round, see a paper case, open it, take a sheet of paper and a pen, dip the pen in the ink and proceed to write.   In the course of all this, I act upon certain inferences which might be drawn out in the **form** of Syllogisms.   First, in virtue of previous knowledge I recognise what lies before me as a book. The process by which I reach the conclusion, though it passes in a flash, might be analysed and expressed in propositions.

> Whatever presents certain outward appearances,
>   contains readable print.
> This presents such appearances.
> ∴ It contains readable print.

So with the paper case, and the pen, and the ink. I infer from peculiar appearances that what I see contains paper, that the liquid will make a black mark on the white sheet, and so forth.

We are constantly in 'daily life subsuming particulars under known universals in this way. " Whatever has certain visible properties, has certain other properties: this has the visible ones : therefore, it has the others " is a form of reasoning constantly latent in our minds.

The Syllogism may be regarded as the explicit expression of this type of deductive reasoning; that is, as the analysis and formal expression of this every-day process of applying known universals to particular cases. Thus viewed it is simply the analysis of a mental process, as a psychological fact; the analysis of the procedure of all men when they reason from signs; the analysis of the kind of assumptions they make when they apply knowledge to particular cases. The assumptions may be warranted, or they may not : but as a matter of fact the individual who makes the confident inference has such assumptions and subsumptions latent in his mind.

But practically viewed, that is *logically* viewed, if you regard Logic as a practical science, the Syllogism is a contrivance to assist the correct performance of reasoning together or syllogising in difficult cases. It applies not to mental processes but to results of such expressed in words, that is, to propositions. Where the Syllogism comes in as a useful form is when certain propositions are delivered to you *ab extra* as containing a certain conclusion ; and the connexion is not apparent. These propositions are analysed and thrown into a form in which it is at once apparent whether the alleged connexion exists. This form is the Syllogism : it is, in effect, an analysis of given arguments.

It was as a practical engine or organon that it was invented by Aristotle, an organon for the syllogising of admissions in Dialectic. The germ of the invention was the analysis of propositions into terms. The syllogism was conceived by Aristotle as a reasoning together of terms. His prime discovery was that whenever two propositions necessarily contain or imply a conclusion, they have a common term, that is, only three terms between them : that the other two terms which differ in each are the terms of the conclusion ; and that the relation asserted in the conclusion between its two terms is a necessary consequence of their relations with the third term as declared in the premisses.

Such was Aristotle's conception of the Syllogism and such it has remained in Logic. It is still, strictly speaking, a syllogism of terms : of propositions only secondarily and after they have been analysed. The conclusion is conceived analytically as a relation between two terms. In how many ways may this relation be established through a third term? The various moods and figures of the Syllogism give the answer to that question.

The use of the very abstract word " relation " makes the problem appear much more difficult than it really is. The great charm of Aristotle's Syllogism is its simplicity. The assertion of the conclusion is reduced to its simplest possible kind, a relation of inclusion or exclusion, contained or not contained. To show that the one term is or is not contained in the other we have only to find a third which contains the one and is contained or not contained in the other.

The practical difficulties, of course, consist in the reduction of the conclusions and arguments of common speech to definite terms thus simply related. Once they are so reduced, their independence or the opposite is obvious. Therein lies the virtue of the Syllogism.

Before proceeding to show in how many ways two terms may be Syllogised through a third, we must have technical names for the elements.

The third term is called the **Middle** (M) (τὸ μέσον) : the other two the Extremes (ἄκρα).

The **Extremes** are the Subject (S) and the Predicate (P) of the conclusion.

In an affirmative proposition (the normal form) S is contained in P : hence P is called the **Major**[1] term (τὸ μεῖζον), and S the **Minor** (τὸ ἔλαττον), being respectively larger and smaller in extension. All difficulty about the names disappears if we remember that in bestowing them we start from the conclusion. That was the problem (πρόβλημα) or thesis in dialectic, the question in dispute.

The two Premisses, or propositions giving the relations between the two Extremes and the Middle, are named on an equally simple ground.

One of them gives the relation between the Minor Term, S, and the Middle, M. S, All or Some, is or is not in M. This is called the Minor Premiss.

The other gives the relation between the Major

---

[1] Aristotle calls the Major the First (τὸ πρῶτον) and the Minor the Last (τὸ ἔσχατον), probably because that was their order in the conclusion when stated in his most usual form, " P is predicated of S," or " P belongs to S ".

Term and the Middle.   M, All or Some, is or is not in
P.   This is called the Major Premiss.[1]

---

[1] When we speak of the Minor or the Major simply, the
reference is to the terms.   To avoid a confusion into which
beginners are apt to stumble, and at the same time to emphasise
the origin of the names, the Premisses might be spoken of at first
as the Minor's Premiss and the Major's Premiss.   It was only in
the Middle Ages when the origin of the Syllogism had been forgotten, that the idea arose that the terms were called Major and
Minor because they occurred in the Major and the Minor
Premiss respectively.

Chapter II.

FIGURES AND MOODS OF THE SYLLOGISM.

I.—The First Figure.

THE forms (technically called **Moods**, *i.e.*, modes) of the First Figure are founded on the simplest relations with the Middle that will yield or that necessarily involve the disputed relation between the Extremes.

The simplest type is stated by Aristotle as follows: " When three terms are so related that the last (the Minor) is wholly in the Middle, and the Middle wholly either in or not in the first (the Major) there must be a perfect syllogism of the Extremes ".[1]

When the Minor is partly in the Middle, the Syllogism holds equally good. Thus there are four possible ways in which two terms (ὅροι, plane enclosures) may be connected or disconnected through a third. They are usually represented by circles as being the neatest of figures, but any enclosing outline answers the purpose, and the rougher and more irregular it is the more truly will it represent the extension of a word.

---

[1] ῞Οταν οὖν ὅροι τρεῖς οὕτως ἔχωσι πρὸς ἀλλήλους ὥστε τὸν ἔσχατον ἐν ὅλῳ εἶναι τῷ μέσῳ, καὶ τὸν μέσον ἐν ὅλῳ τῷ πρώτῳ ἢ εἶναι ἢ μὴ εἶναι, ἀνάγκη τῶν ἄκρων εἶναι συλλογισμὸν τέλειον. (Anal. Prior., i. 4.)

Conclusion A.
  All M is in P.
  All S is in M.
  All S is in P.

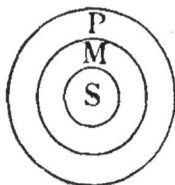

Conclusion E.
  No M is in P.
  All S is in M.
  No S is in P.

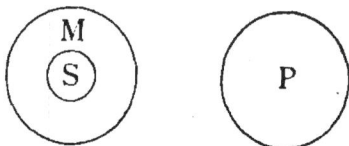

Conclusion I.
  All M is in P.
  Some S is in M.
  Some S is in P.

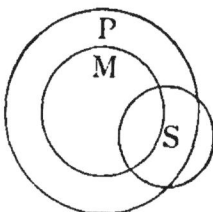

Conclusion O.
  No M is in P.
  Some S is in M.
  Some S is not in P.

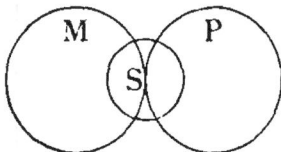

These four forms constitute what are known as the moods of the First Figure of the Syllogism. Seeing that all propositions may be reduced to one or other of the four forms, A, E, I, or O, we have in these premisses abstract types of every possible valid argument from general principles. It is all the same whatever be the matter of the proposition. Whether the subject of debate is mathematical, physical, social, or political, once premisses in these forms are conceded, the conclusion follows irresistibly, *ex vi formæ*, *ex necessitate formæ*. If an argument can be analysed into these forms, and you admit its propositions, you are bound in consistency to admit the conclusion— unless you are prepared to deny that if one thing is in another and that other in a third, the first is in the third, or if one thing is in another and that other wholly outside a third, the first is also outside the third.

This is called the **Axiom of Syllogism.** The most common form of it in Logic is that known as the *Dictum*, or *Regula de Omni et Nullo :* " Whatever is predicated of All or None of a term, is predicated of whatever is contained in that term ". It has been expressed with many little variations, and there has been a good deal of discussion as to the best way of expressing it, the relativity of the word best being often left out of sight. *Best* for what purpose ? Practically that form is the best which best commands general assent, and for this purpose there is little to choose between various ways of expressing it. To make it easy and obvious it is perhaps best to have two separate forms, one for affirmative conclusions and one for negative. Thus: " Whatever is affirmed of all M, is affirmed of whatever is contained in M : and whatever is denied of all M, is denied of whatever is contained in M ". The only advantage of including the two forms in one expression, is compendious neatness. " A part of a part is a part of the whole," is a neat form, it being understood that an individual or a species is part of a genus. " What is said of a whole, is said of every one of its parts," is really a sufficient statement of the principle : the whole being the Middle Term, and the Minor being a part of it, the Major is predicable of the Minor affirmatively or negatively if it is predicable similarly of the Middle.

This Axiom, as the name imports, is indemonstrable. As Aristotle pointed out in the case of the Axiom of Contradiction, it can be vindicated, if challenged, only by reducing the challenger to a practical absurdity. You can no more deny it than you can deny that if a leaf is in a book and the book is in your pocket, the leaf is in your pocket. If you say that you have a sovereign in your purse and your purse is in your pocket, and yet that the sovereign is not in your pocket: will you give me what is in your pocket for the value of the purse?

II.—The Minor Figures of the Syllogism, and their Reduction to the First.

The word Figure ($\sigma\chi\hat{\eta}\mu\alpha$) applies to the form or figure of the premisses, that is, the order of the terms in the statement of the premisses, when the Major Premiss is put first, and the Minor second.

In the First Figure the order is

M P
S M.

But there are three other possible orders or figures, namely:—

Fig. ii.	Fig. iii.	Fig. iv.
PM	MP	PM
SM	MS	MS.

It results from the doctrines of Conversion that valid arguments may be stated in these forms, inasmuch as a proposition in one order of terms may be equivalent to a proposition in another. Thus No

M is in P is convertible with No P is in M : consequently the argument

> No P is in M
> All S is in M,

in the Second Figure is as much valid as when it is stated in the First—

> No M is in P
> All S is in M.

Similarly, since All M is in S is convertible into Some S is in M, the following arguments are equally valid :—

Fig. iii.		Fig. i.
All M is in P		All M is in P
All M is in S	=	Some S is in M.

Using both the above Converses in place of their Convertends, we have—

Fig. iv.		Fig. i.
No P is in M		No M is in P
All M is in S	=	Some S is in M.

It can be demonstrated (we shall see presently how) that altogether there are possible four valid forms or moods of the Second Figure, six of the Third, and five of the Fourth. An ingenious Mnemonic of these various moods and their reduction to the First Figure by the transposition of terms and premisses has come down from the thirteenth century. The first line names the moods of the First, Normal, or Standard Figure.

BArbArA, CE*l*ArE*nt*, DA*r*II, FE*r*IO*que* prioris ;
CE*s*ArE, CA*m*E*str*E*s*, FE*st*I*n*O, BA*r*O*k*O, secundæ ;
Tertia DA*r*A*pt*I, DI*s*A*m*I*s*, DA*t*I*s*I, FE*l*A*pt*O*n*,
BO*k*A*rd*O, FE*r*I*s*O*que*, habet ; quarta insuper addit,
BrA*m*A*nt*IP, CA*m*E*n*E*s*, DI*m*A*r*I*s*, FE*s*A*p*O, F*r*E*s*I*s*O*n*.

The vowels in the names of the Moods indicate the propositions of the Syllogism in the four forms, A E I O.   To write out any Mood at length you have only to remember the Figure, and transcribe the propositions in the order of Major Premiss, Minor Premiss, and Conclusion.   Thus, the Second Figure being $\frac{PM}{SM}$ FE*st*I*n*O is written—

> No P is in M.
> Some S is in M.
> Some S is not in P.

The Fourth Figure being $\frac{PM}{MS}$ DI*m*A*r*I*s* is

> Some P is in M.
> All M is in S.
> Some S is in P.

The initial letter in a Minor Mood indicates that Mood of the First to which it may be reduced.   Thus Festino is reduced to Ferio, and Dimaris to Darii.   In the cases of Baroko and Bokardo, B indicates that you may employ Barbara to bring any impugner to confusion, as shall be afterwards explained.

The letters *s*, *m*, and *p* are also significant.   Placed after a vowel, *s* indicates that the proposition has to be simply converted.   Thus, FE*st*I*n*O :—

> No P is in M.
> Some S is in M.
> Some S is not in P.

Simply convert the Major Premiss, and you get FE*r*IO, of the First.

> No M is in P.
> Some S is in M.
> Some S is not in P.

m (*muta*, or *move*) indicates that the premisses have to be transposed. Thus, in CA*m*E*str*E*s*, you have to transpose the premisses, as well as simply convert the Minor Premiss before reaching the figure of CE*l*A*r*E*nt*.

> All P is in M   _   No M is in S
> No S is in M   All P is in M.

From this it follows in CE*l*A*r*E*nt* that No P is in S, and this simply converted yields No S is in P.

A simple transposition of the premisses in DI*m*A*r*I*s* of the Fourth

> Some P is in M
> All M is in S

yields the premisses of DA*r*II

> All M is in S
> Some P is in M,

but the conclusion Some P is in S has to be simply converted.

Placed after a vowel, *p* indicates that the proposition has to be converted *per accidens*. Thus in FE*l*A*pt*O*n* of the Third (MP, MS)

> No M is in P
> All M is in S
> Some S is not in P

you have to substitute for All M is in S its converse by limitation to get the premisses of FE*r*IO.

Two of the Minor Moods, Baroko of the Second Figure, and Bokardo of the Third, cannot be reduced to the First Figure by the ordinary processes of Conversion and Transposition. It is for dealing with these intractable moods that Contraposition is required. Thus in BA*r*O*k*O of the Second (PM, SM)

> All P is in M.
> Some S is not in M.

Substitute for the Major Premiss its Converse by Contraposition, and for the Minor its Formal Obverse or Permutation, and you have FE*r*IŌ of the First, with not-M as the Middle.

> No not-M is in P.
> Some S is in not-M.
> Some S is not in P.

The processes might be indicated by the Mnemonic FA*cs*O*c*O, with *c* indicating the contraposition of the predicate term or Formal Obversion.

The reduction of BO*k*A*rd*O,

> Some M is not in P
> All M is in S
> Some S is not in P,

is somewhat more intricate. It may be indicated by DO*cs*A*m*O*sc*. You substitute for the Major Premiss its Converse by Contraposition, transpose the Premisses, and you have DA*r*II.

> All M is in S.
> Some not-P is in M.
> Some not-P is in S.

Convert now the conclusion by Contraposition, and you have Some S is not in P.

The author of the Mnemonic apparently did not recognise Contraposition, though it was admitted by Boethius ; and, it being impossible without this to demonstrate the validity of Baroko and Bokardo by showing them to be equivalent with valid moods of the First Figure, he provided for their demonstration by the special process known as *Reductio ad absurdum.* B indicates that Barbara is the medium.

The rationale of the process is this. It is an imaginary opponent that you reduce to an absurdity or self-contradiction. You show that it is impossible with consistency to admit the premisses and at the same time deny the conclusion. For, let this be done ; let it be admitted as in BA*r*O*k*O that,

> All P is in M
> Some S is not in M,

but denied that Some S is not in P. The denial of a proposition implies the admission of its Contradictory. If it is not true that Some S is not in P, it must be true that All S is in P. Take this along with the admission that All P is in M, and you have a syllogism in BA*rb*A*r*A,

> All P is in M
> All S is in P,

yielding the conclusion All S is in M. If then the original conclusion is denied, it follows that All S is in M. But this contradicts the Minor Premiss, which has been admitted to be true. It is thus shown that an opponent cannot admit the premisses and deny the conclusion without contradicting himself.

The same process may be applied to Bokardo.

> Some M is not in P.
> All M is in S.
> Some S is not in P.

Deny the conclusion, and you must admit that All S is in P.   Syllogised in Barbara with All M is in S, this yields the conclusion that All M is in P, the contradictory of the Major Premiss.

The beginner may be reminded that the argument *ad absurdum* is not necessarily confined to Baroko and Bokardo.   It is applied to them simply because they are not reducible by the ordinary processes to the First Figure.   It might be applied with equal effect to other Moods, DI*m*A*r*Is, *e.g.*, of the Third.

> Some M is in P.
> All M is in S.
> Some S is in P.

Let Some S is in P be denied, and No S is in P must be admitted.   But if No S is in P and All M is in S, it follows (in Celarent) that No M is in P, which an opponent cannot hold consistently with his admission that Some M is in P.

The beginner sometimes asks : What is the use of reducing the Minor Figures to the First ?   The reason is that it is only when the relations between the terms are stated in the First Figure that it is at once apparent whether or not the argument is valid under the Axiom or *Dictum de Omni.*   It is then undeniably evident that if the Dictum holds the argument holds.

And if the Moods of the First Figure hold, their equivalents in the other Figures must hold too.

Aristotle recognised only two of the Minor Figures, the Second and Third, and thus had in all only fourteen valid moods.

The recognition of the Fourth Figure is attributed by Averroes to Galen. Averroes himself rejects it on the ground that no arguments expressed naturally, that is, in accordance with common usage, fall into that form. This is a sufficient reason for not spending time upon it, if Logic is conceived as a science that has a bearing upon the actual practice of discussion or discursive thought. And this was probably the reason why Aristotle passed it over.

If however the Syllogism of Terms is to be completed as an abstract doctrine, the Fourth Figure must be noticed as one of the forms of premisses that contain the required relation between the extremes. There is a valid syllogism between the extremes when the relations of the three terms are as stated in certain premisses of the Fourth Figure.

III.—THE SORITES.

A chain of Syllogisms is called a Sorites. Thus :—

> All A is in B.
> All B is in C.
> All C is in D.
> $\vdots$
>
> All X is in Z.
> $\therefore$ All A is in Z.

A Minor Premiss can thus be carried through a

series of Universal Propositions each serving in turn as a Major to yield a conclusion which can be syllogised with the next.   Obviously a Sorites may contain one particular premiss, provided it is the first; and one universal negative premiss, provided it is the last. A particular or a negative at any other point in the chain is an insuperable bar.

CHAPTER III.

THE DEMONSTRATION OF THE SYLLOGISTIC MOODS.
—THE CANONS OF THE SYLLOGISM.

How do we know that the nineteen moods are the only possible forms of valid syllogism ?

Aristotle treated this as being self-evident upon trial and simple inspection of all possible forms in each of his three Figures.

Granted the parity between predication and position in or out of a limited enclosure (term, ὅρος), it is a matter of the simplest possible reasoning. You have three such terms or enclosures, S, P and M ; and you are given the relative positions of two of them to the third as a clue to their relative positions to one another. Is S in or out of P, and is it wholly in or wholly out or partly in or partly out ? You know how each of them lies towards the third : when can you tell from this how S lies towards P ?

We have seen that when M is wholly in or out of P, and S wholly or partly in M, S is wholly or partly in or out of P.

Try any other given positions in the First Figure, and you find that you cannot tell from them how S lies relatively to P. Unless the Major Premiss is Universal, that is, unless M lies wholly in or out of P, you can draw no conclusion, whatever the Minor

Premiss may give.   Given, *e.g.*, All S is in M, it may
be that All S is in P, or that No S is in P, or that
Some S is in P, or that Some S is not in P.

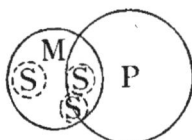

Again, unless the Minor Premiss is affirmative, no
matter what the Major Premiss may be, you can draw
no conclusion.   For if the Minor Premiss is negative,
all that you know is that All S or Some S lies somewhere outside M ; and however M may be situated
relatively to P, that knowledge cannot help towards
knowing how S lies relatively to P.   All S may be P,
or none of it, or part of it.   Given all M is in P ; the
All S (or Some S) which we know to be outside of M
may lie anywhere in P or out of it.

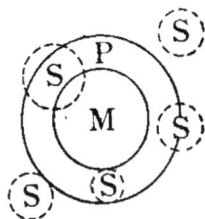

Similarly, in the Second Figure, trial and simple
inspection of all possible conditions shows that there
can be no conclusion unless the Major Premiss is
universal, and one of the premisses negative.

Another and more common way of eliminating the
invalid forms, elaborated in the Middle Ages, is to
formulate principles applicable irrespective of Figure,

and to rule out of each Figure the moods that do not conform to them. These regulative principles are known as The Canons of the Syllogism.

Canon I. In every syllogism there should be three, and not more than three, terms, and the terms must be used throughout in the same sense.

It sometimes happens, owing to the ambiguity of words, that there seem to be three terms when there are really four. An instance of this is seen in the sophism :—

> He who is most hungry eats most.
> He who eats least is most hungry.
> ∴ He who eats least eats most.

This Canon, however, though it points to a real danger of error in the application of the syllogism to actual propositions, is superfluous in the consideration of purely formal implication, it being a primary assumption that terms are univocal, and remain constant through any process of inference.

Under this Canon, Mark Duncan says (*Inst. Log.*, iv. 3, 2), is comprehended another commonly expressed in this form : There should be nothing in the conclusion that was not in the premisses : inasmuch as if there were anything in the conclusion that was in neither of the premisses, there would be four terms in the syllogism.

The rule that in every syllogism there must be three, and only three, propositions, sometimes given as a separate Canon, is only a corollary from Canon I.

Canon II. The Middle Term must be distributed once at least in the Premisses.

The Middle Term must either be wholly in, or wholly out of, one or other of the Extremes before it can be the means of establishing a connexion between them.   If you know only that it is partly in both, you cannot know from that how they lie relatively to one another : and similarly if you know only that it is partly outside both.

The Canon of Distributed Middle is a sort of counter-relative supplement to the *Dictum de Omni*.   Whatever is predicable of a whole distributively is predicable of all its several parts.   If in neither premiss there is a predication about the whole, there is no case for the application of the axiom.

Canon III. No term should be distributed in the conclusion that was not distributed in the premisses.

If an assertion is not made about the whole of a term in the premisses, it cannot be made about the whole of that term in the conclusion without going beyond what has been given.

The breach of this rule in the case of the Major term is technically known as the Illicit Process of the Major : in the case of the Minor term, Illicit Process of the Minor.

Great use is made of this canon in cutting off invalid moods.   It must be remembered that the Predicate term is "distributed" or taken universally in O (Some S is not in P) as well as in E (No S is in P); and that P is never distributed in affirmative propositions.

Canon IV. No conclusion can be drawn from two negative premisses.

Two negative premisses are really tantamount to a declaration that there is no connexion whatever between the Major and the Minor (as quantified in the premisses) and the term common to both premisses ; in short, that this is not a Middle term—that the condition of a valid Syllogism does not exist.

There is an apparent exception to this when the real Middle in an argument is a contrapositive term, not-M. Thus :—

> Nobody who is not thirsty is suffering from fever.
> This person is not thirsty.
> ∴ He is not suffering from fever.

But in such cases it is really the absence of a quality or rather the presence of an opposite quality on which we reason ; and the Minor Premiss is really Affirmative of the form S is in not-M.

Canon V. If one premiss is negative, the conclusion must be negative.

If one premiss is negative, one of the Extremes must be excluded in whole or in part from the Middle term. The other must therefore (under Canon IV.) declare some coincidence between the Middle term and the other extreme ; and the conclusion can only affirm exclusion in whole or in part from the area of this coincidence.

Canon VI. No conclusion can be drawn from two particular premisses.

This is evident upon a comparison of terms in all possible positions, but it can be more easily demonstrated with the help of the preceding canons. The premisses cannot both be particular and yield a conclusion without breaking one or other of those canons.

Suppose both are affirmative, II, the Middle is not distributed in either premiss.

Suppose one affirmative and the other negative, IO, or OI. Then, whatever the Figure may be, that is, whatever the order of the terms, only one term can be distributed, namely, the predicate of O. This (Canon II.) must be the Middle. But in that case there must be Illicit Process of the Major (Canon III.), for one of the premisses being negative, the conclusion is negative (Canon V.), and P its predicate is distributed. Briefly, in a negative mood, both Major and Middle must be distributed, and if both premisses are particular this cannot be.

Canon VII. If one Premiss is particular the conclusion is particular.

This canon is sometimes combined with what we have given as Canon V., in a single rule: " The conclusion follows the weaker premiss ".

It can most compendiously be demonstrated with the help of the preceding canons.

Suppose both premisses affirmative, then, if one is particular, only one term can be distributed in the premisses, namely, the subject of the Universal affirmative premiss. By Canon II., this must be the Middle, and the Minor, being undistributed in the Premisses, cannot be distributed in the conclusion. That is, the conclusion cannot be Universal—must be particular.

Suppose one Premiss negative, the other affirmative. One premiss being negative, the conclusion must be negative, and P must be distributed in the conclusion. Before, then, the conclusion can be universal, all three terms, S, M, and P, must, by Canons II. and III., be distributed in the premisses. But whatever the Figure of the premisses, only two terms can be distributed. For if one of the Premisses be O, the other must be A, and if one of them is E, the other must be I. Hence the conclusion must be particular, otherwise there will be illicit process of the Minor, or of the Major, or of the Middle.

The argument may be more briefly put as follows:

In an affirmative mood, with one premiss particular, only one term can be distributed in the premisses, and this cannot be the Minor without leaving the Middle undistributed. In a negative mood, with one premiss particular, only two terms can be distributed, and the Minor cannot be one of them without leaving either the Middle or the Major undistributed.

Armed with these canons, we can quickly determine, given any combination of three propositions in one of the Figures, whether it is or is not a valid Syllogism.

Observe that though these canons hold for all the Figures, the Figure must be known, in all combinations containing A or O, before we can settle a question of validity by Canons II. and III., because the distribution of terms in A and O depends on their order in predication.

Take AEE. In Fig. I.—

All M is in P.
No S is in M
No S is in P—

the conclusion is invalid as involving an illicit process of the Major. P is distributed in the conclusion and not in the premisses.

In Fig. II. AEE—

All P is in M
No S is in M
No S is in P—

the conclusion is valid (Camestres).

In Fig. III. AEE—

> All M is in P
> No M is in S
> No S is in P—

the conclusion is invalid, there being illicit process of the Major.

In Fig. IV. AEE is valid (Camenes).

Take EIO. A little reflection shows that this combination is valid in all the Figures if in any, the distribution of the terms in both cases not being affected by their order in predication.   Both E and I are simply convertible.   That the combination is valid is quickly seen if we remember that in negative moods both Major and Middle must be distributed, and that this is done by E.

EIE is invalid, because you cannot have a universal conclusion with one premiss particular.

AII is valid in Fig. I. or Fig. III., and invalid in Figs. II. and IV., because M is the subject of A in I. and III. and predicate in II. and IV.

OAO is valid only in Fig. III., because only in that Figure would this combination of premisses distribute both M and P.

Simple exercises of this kind may be multiplied till all possible combinations are exhausted, and it is seen that only the recognised moods stand the test.

If a more systematic way of demonstrating the valid moods is desired, the simplest method is to deduce from the Canons special rules for each Figure. Aristotle arrived at these special rules by simple inspection, but it is easier to deduce them.

I. In the First Figure, the Major Premiss must be Universal, and the Minor Premiss affirmative.

To make this evident by the Canons, we bear in mind the Scheme or Figure—

M in P

S in M—

and try the alternatives of Affirmative Moods and Negative Moods. Obviously in an affirmative mood the Middle is undistributed unless the Major Premiss is Universal. In a negative mood, (1) If the Major Premiss is O, the Minor must be affirmative, and M is undistributed; (2) if the Major Premiss is I, M may be distributed by a negative Minor Premiss, but in that case there would be an illicit process of the Major —P being distributed in the conclusion (Canon V.) and not in the Premisses. Thus the Major Premiss can neither be O nor I, and must therefore be either A or E, *i.e.*, must be Universal.

That the Minor must be affirmative is evident, for if it were negative, the conclusion must be negative (Canon V.) and the Major Premiss must be affirmative (Canon IV.), and this would involve illicit process of the Major, P being distributed in the conclusion and not in the Premisses.

These two special rules leave only four possible valid forms in the First Figure. There are sixteen possible combinations of premisses, each of the four types of proposition being combinable with itself and with each of the others.

AA	EA	IA	OA
AE	EE	IE	OE
AI	EI	II	OI
AO	EO	IO	OO

Special Rule I. wipes out the columns on the right, with the particular major premisses; and AE, EE, AO, and EO are rejected by Special Rule II., leaving BA*rb*A*r*A, CE*l*A*r*E*nt*, DA*r*II and FE*r*IO.

II. In the Second Figure, only Negative Moods are possible, and the Major Premiss must be universal.

Only Negative moods are possible, for unless one premiss is negative, M being the predicate term in both—

$$P \text{ in } M$$
$$S \text{ in } M—$$

is undistributed.

Only negative moods being possible, there will be illicit process of the Major unless the Major Premiss is universal, P being its subject term.

These special rules reject AA and AI, and the two columns on the right.

To get rid of EE and EO, we must call in the general Canon IV.; which leaves us with EA, AE, EI, and AO — CE*s*A*r*E, CA*m*E*str*E*s*, FE*st*I*n*O, BA*r*O*k*O.

III. In the Third Figure, the Minor Premiss must be affirmative.

Otherwise, the conclusion would be negative, and the Major Premiss affirmative, and there would be illicit process of the Major, P being the predicate term in the Major Premiss.

$$M \text{ in } P$$
$$M \text{ in } S.$$

This cuts off AE, EE, IE, OE, AO, EO, IO, OO,—the second and fourth rows in the above list.

II and OI are inadmissible by Canon VI.; which

leaves AÅ, IA, AI, EA, OA, EI—DA*r*A*pt*I, DI*s*A*m*I*s*, DA*t*I*s*I, FE*l*A*pt*O*n*, BO*k*A*rd*O, FE*r*I*s*O—three affirmative moods and three negative.

IV. The Fourth Figure is fenced by three special rules. (1) In negative moods, the Major Premiss is universal. (2) If the Minor is negative, both premisses are universal. (3) If the Major is affirmative, the Minor is universal.

(1) Otherwise, the Figure being

P in M
M in S,

there would be illicit process of the Major.

(2) The Major must be universal by special rule (1), and if the Minor were not also universal, the Middle would be undistributed.

(3) Otherwise M would be undistributed.

Rule (1) cuts off the right-hand column, OA, OE, OI, and OO; also IE and IO.

Rule (2) cuts off AO, EO.

Rule (3) cuts off AI, II.

EE goes by general Canon IV.; and we are left with AA, AE, IA, EA, EI—B*r*A*m*A*nt*I*p*, CA*m*E*n*E*s*, DI*m*A*r*I*s*, FE*s*A*p*O, F*r*E*s*I*s*O*n*.

CHAPTER IV.

THE ANALYSIS OF ARGUMENTS INTO SYLLOGISTIC FORMS.

TURNING given arguments into syllogistic form is apt to seem as trivial and useless as it is easy and mechanical. In most cases the necessity of the conclusion is as apparent in the plain speech form as in the artificial logical form. The justification of such exercises is that they give familiarity with the instrument, serving at the same time as simple exercises in ratiocination : what further uses may be made of the instrument once it is mastered, we shall consider as we proceed.

I.—FIRST FIGURE.

Given the following argument to be put into Syllogistic form : " No war is long popular : for every war increases taxation ; and the popularity of anything that touches the pocket is short-lived ".

The simplest method is to begin with the conclusion —" No war is long popular "—No S is P—then to examine the argument to see whether it yields premisses of the necessary form. Keeping the form in mind, Celarent of Fig. I.—

> No M is P
> All S is M
> No S is P—

we see at once that " Every war increases taxation " is
of the form All S is M. Does the other sentence yield
the Major Premiss No M is P, when M represents the
increasing of taxation, *i.e.*, a class bounded by that
attribute ? We see that the last sentence of the argument is equivalent to saying that " Nothing that
increases taxation is long popular " ; and this with the
Minor yields the conclusion in Celarent.

> Nothing that increases taxation is long popular.
> Every war increases taxation.
> No war is long popular.

Observe, now, what in effect we have done in thus
reducing the argument to the First Figure. In effect,
a general principle being alleged as justifying a certain
conclusion, we have put that principle into such a form
that it has the same predicate with the conclusion.
All that we have then to do in order to inspect the
validity of the argument is to see whether the subject
of the conclusion is contained in the subject of the
general principle. Is war one of the things that
increase taxation ? Is it one of that class ? If so,
then it cannot long be popular, long popularity being
an attribute that cannot be affirmed of any of that
class.

Reducing to the first figure, then, amounts simply
to making the predication of the proposition alleged
as ground uniform with the conclusion based upon it.
The minor premiss or applying proposition amounts to
saying that the subject of the conclusion is contained in
the subject of the general principle. Is the subject of
the conclusion contained in the subject of the general
principle when the two have identical predicates ? If

so, the argument falls at once under the *Dictum de Omni et Nullo.*

Two things may be noted concerning an argument thus simplified.

1. It is not necessary, in order to bring an argument under the *dictum de omni*, to reduce the predicate to the form of an extensive term. In whatever form, abstract or concrete, the predication is made of the middle term, it is applicable in the same form to that which is contained in the middle term.

2. The quantity of the Minor Term does not require special attention, inasmuch as the argument does not turn upon it. In whatever quantity it is contained in the Middle, in that quantity is the predicate of the Middle predicable of it.

These two points being borne in mind, the attention may be concentrated on the Middle Term and its relations with the extremes.

That the predicate may be left unanalysed without affecting the simplicity of the argument or in any way obscuring the exhibition of its turning-point, has an important bearing on the reduction of Modals. The modality may be treated as part of the predicate without in any way obscuring what it is the design of the syllogism to make clear. We have only to bear in mind that however the predicate may be qualified in the premisses, the same qualification must be transferred to the conclusion. Otherwise we should have the fallacy of Four Terms, *quaternio terminorum.*

To raise the question : What is the proper form for a Modal of Possibility, A or I ? is to clear up in an important respect our conceptions of the Universal proposition, " Victories may be gained by accident ".

Should this be expressed as A or I ? Is the predicate applicable to All victories or only to Some ? Obviously the meaning is that of any victory it may be true that it was gained by accident, and if we treat the " mode " as part of the predicate term " things that may be gained by accident," the form of the proposition is All S is in P.

But, it may be asked, does not the proposition that victories may be gained by accident rest, as a matter of fact, on the belief that some victories have been gained in this way ? And is not, therefore, the proper form of proposition Some S is P ?

This, however, is a misunderstanding. What we are concerned with is the formal analysis of propositions as given. And Some victories have been gained by accident is not the formal analysis of Victories may be gained by accident. The two propositions do not give the same meaning in different forms : the meaning as well as the form is different. The one is a statement of a matter of fact : the other of an inference founded on it. The full significance of the Modal proper may be stated thus : In view of the fact that some victories have been gained by accident, we are entitled to say of any victory, in the absence of certain knowledge, that it may be one of them.

A general proposition, in short, is a proposition about a genus, taken universally.

II.—Second Figure.

For testing arguments from general principles, the First Figure is the simplest and best form of analysis.

But there is one common class of arguments that fall naturally, as ordinarily expressed, into the Second

Figure, namely, negative conclusions from the absence of distinctive signs or symptoms, or necessary conditions.

Thirst, for example, is one of the symptoms of fever : if a patient is not thirsty, you can conclude at once that his illness is not fever, and the argument, fully expressed, is in the Second Figure.

> All fever-stricken patients are thirsty.
> This patient is not thirsty.
> ∴. He is not fever-stricken.

Arguments of this type are extremely common. Armed with the general principle that ill-doers are ill-dreaders, we argue from a man's being unsuspicious that he is not guilty. The negative diagnosis of the physician, as when he argues from the absence of sore throat or the absence of a white speck in the throat that the case before him is not one of scarlatina or diphtheria, follows this type : and from its utility in making such arguments explicit, the Second Figure may be called the Figure of Negative Diagnosis.

It is to be observed, however, that the character of the argument is best disclosed when the Major Premiss is expressed by its Converse by Contraposition. It is really from the absence of a symptom that the physician concludes ; as, for example : " No patient that has not a sore throat is suffering from scarlatina ". And the argument thus expressed is in the First Figure. Thus the reduction of Baroko to the First Figure by contraposition of the Middle is vindicated as a really useful process. The real Middle is a contra-positive term, and the form corresponds more closely to the reasoning when the argument is put in the First Figure.

The truth is that if the positive term or sign or necessary condition is prominent as the basis of the argument, there is considerable risk of fallacy. Sore throat being one of the symptoms of scarlatina, the physician is apt on finding this symptom present to jump to a positive conclusion. This is equivalent technically to drawing a positive conclusion from premisses of the Second Figure.

> All scarlatina patients have sore throat.
> This patient has sore throat.

A positive conclusion here is technically known as a Non-Sequitur (Doesn't follow). So with arguments from the presence of a necessary condition which is only one of many. Given that it is impossible to pass without working at the subject, or that it is impossible to be a good marksman without having a steady hand, we are apt to argue that given also the presence of this condition, a conclusion is implicated. But really the premisses given are only two affirmatives of the Second Figure.

"It is impossible to pass without working at the subject."

This, put into the form No not-M is P, is to say that "None who have not worked can pass". This is equivalent, as the converse by contraposition, with —

> All capable of passing have worked at the subject.

But though Q has worked at the subject, it does not follow that he is capable of passing. Technically the middle is undistributed. On the other hand, if he has not worked at the subject, it follows that he is not capable of passing. We can draw a conclusion at once from the absence of the necessary condition, though none can be drawn from its presence alone.

THIRD FIGURE.

Arguments are sometimes advanced in the form of the Third Figure. For instance : Killing is not always murder : for tyrannicide is not murder, and yet it is undoubtedly killing. Or again : Unpleasant things are sometimes salutary : for afflictions are sometimes so, and no affliction can be called pleasant.

These arguments, when analysed into terms, are, respectively, Felapton and Disamis.

> No tyrannicide is murder ;
> All tyrannicide is killing ;
> Some killing is not murder.

> Some afflictions are salutary things ;
> All afflictions are unpleasant things ;
> Some unpleasant things are salutary things.

The syllogistic form cannot in such cases pretend to be a simplification of the argument. The argument would be equally unmistakable if advanced in this form : Some S is not P, for example, M. Some killing is not murder, *e.g.*, tyrannicide. Some unpleasant things are salutary, *e.g.*, some afflictions.

There is really no "deduction" in the third figure, no leading down from general to particular. The middle term is only an example of the minor. It is the syllogism of Contradictory Examples.

In actual debate examples are produced to disprove a universal assertion, affirmative or negative. Suppose it is maintained that every wise man has a keen sense of humour. You doubt this : you produce an instance of the opposite, say Milton. The force of your contradictory instance is not increased by exhibiting the argument in syllogistic form : the point is not made clearer.

The Third Figure was perhaps of some use in Yes and No Dialectic. When you had to get everything essential to your conclusion definitely admitted, it was useful to know that the production of an example to refute a generality involved the admission of two propositions. You must extract from your opponent both that Milton was a wise man, and that Milton had not a keen sense of humour, before you could drive him from the position that all wise men possess that quality.

Examples for Analysis.

Scarlet flowers have no fragrance : this flower has no fragrance : does it follow that this flower is of a scarlet colour ?

Interest in the subject is an indispensable condition of learning easily : Z is interested in the subject : he is bound, therefore, to learn easily.

It is impossible to be a good shot without having a steady hand : John has a steady hand : he is capable, therefore, of becoming a good shot.

Some victories have been won by accident ; for example, Maiwand.

Intemperance is more disgraceful than cowardice, because people have more opportunities of acquiring control of their bodily appetites.

" Some men are not fools, yet all men are fallible." What follows ?

" Some men allow that their memory is not good : every man believes in his own judgment." What is the conclusion, and in what Figure and Mood may the argument be expressed ?

" An honest man's the noblest work of God : Z is an honest man " : therefore, he is—what ?

Examine the logical connexion between the following

" exclamation " and " answer ": " But I hear some one exclaiming that wickedness is not easily concealed. To which I answer, Nothing great is easy."

" If the attention is actively aroused, sleep becomes impossible : hence the sleeplessness of anxiety, for anxiety is a strained attention upon an impending disaster."

" To follow truth can never be a subject of regret; free inquiry does lead a man to regret the days of his childish faith; therefore it is not following truth."—*J. H. Newman.*

He would not take the crown: Therefore 'tis certain he was not ambitious.

As he was valiant, I honour him; as he was ambitious, I slew him.

The Utopians learned the language of the Greeks with more readiness because they were originally of the same race with them.

Nothing which is cruel can be expedient, for cruelty is most revolting to the nature of man.

" The fifth century saw the foundation of the Frank dominion in Gaul, and the first establishment of the German races in Britain. The former was effected in a single long reign, by the energy of one great ruling tribe, which had already modified its traditional usages, and now, by the adoption of the language and religion of the conquered, prepared the way for a permanent amalgamation with them." In the second of the above sentences a general proposition is assumed. Show in syllogistic form how the last proposition in the sentence depends upon it.

" I do not mean to contend that active benevolence may not hinder a man's advancement in the world : for advancement greatly depends upon a reputation for excellence in some one thing of which the world perceives that it has present need : and an obvious attention to other things, though perhaps not incompatible with the excellence itself, may easily prevent a person from obtaining a reputation for it." Pick out the propositions here given as interdependent. Examine whether the principle alleged is sufficiently general to necessitate a conclusion. In what form would it be so ?

Chapter V.

ENTHYMEMES.

There is a certain variety in the use of the word Enthymeme among logicians. In the narrowest sense, it is a valid formal syllogism, with one premiss suppressed. In the widest sense it is simply an argument, valid or invalid, formal in expression or informal, with only one premiss put forward or hinted at, the other being held in the mind (ἐν θυμῷ). This last is the Aristotelian sense.

It is only among formal logicians of the straitest sect that the narrowest sense prevails. Hamilton divides Enthymemes into three classes according as it is the Major Premiss, the Minor Premiss, or the Conclusion that is suppressed. Thus, a full syllogism being :—

> All liars are cowards :
> Caius is a liar :
> ∴ Caius is a coward :—

this may be enthymematically expressed in three ways.

I. Enthymeme of the First Order (*Major understood*).

> Caius is a coward ; for Caius is a liar.

II. Enthymeme of the Second Order (*Minor understood*).

> Caius is a coward ; for all liars are cowards.

III. Enthymeme of the Third Order (*Conclusion understood*).

> All liars are cowards, and Caius is a liar.

The Third Order is a contribution of Hamilton's own. It is superfluous, inasmuch as the conclusion is never suppressed except as a rhetorical figure of speech. Hamilton confines the word Enthymeme to valid arguments, in pursuance of his view that Pure Logic has no concern with invalid arguments.

Aristotle used Enthymeme in the wider sense of an elliptically expressed argument. There has been some doubt as to the meaning of his definition, but that disappears on consideration of his examples. He defines an Enthymeme (Prior Analyt., ii. 27) as "a syllogism from probabilities or signs" (συλλογισμὸς ἐξ εἰκότων ἢ σημείων). The word syllogism in this connexion is a little puzzling. But it is plain from the examples he gives that he meant here by syllogism not even a correct reasoning, much less a reasoning in the explicit form of three terms and three propositions. He used syllogism, in fact, in the same loose sense in which we use the words reasoning and argument, applying without distinction of good and bad.

The sign, he says, is taken in three ways, in as many ways as there are Syllogistic Figures.

(1) A sign interpreted in the First Figure is conclusive. Thus: "This person has been drowned, for he has froth in the trachea". Taken in the First Figure with "All who have froth in the trachea have been drowned" as major premiss, this argument is valid. The sign is conclusive.

(2) "This patient is fever-stricken, for he is thirsty." Assumed that "All fever-stricken patients are thirsty,"

this is an argument in the Second Figure, but it is not a valid argument. Thirst is a sign or symptom of fever, but not a conclusive sign, because it is indicative of other ailments also. Yet the argument has a certain probability.

(3) " Wise men are earnest (σπουδαῖοι), for Pittacus is earnest." Here the suppressed premiss is that " Pittacus is wise ". Fully expressed, the argument is in the Third Figure :—

> Pittacus is earnest.
> Pittacus is wise.
> ∴ Wise men are earnest.

Here again the argument is inconclusive and yet it has a certain probability. The coincidence of wisdom with earnestness in one notable example lends a certain air of probability to the general statement.

Such are Aristotle's examples or strict parallels to them. The examples illustrate also what he says in his *Rhetoric* as to the advantages of enthymemes. For purposes of persuasion enthymemes are better than explicit syllogisms, because any inconclusiveness there may be in the argument is more likely to pass un-detected. As we shall see, one main use of the Syllogism is to force tacit assumptions into light and so make their true connexion or want of connexion apparent. In Logic enthymemes are recognised only to be shown up : the elliptical expression is a cover for fallacy, which it is the business of the logician to strip off.

In Aristotle's examples one of the premisses is expressed. But often the arguments of common speech are even less explicit than this. A general principle is vaguely hinted at : a subject is referred to a class the attributes of which are assumed to be definitely known. Thus :—

> He was too ambitious to be scrupulous in his choice of means.
> He was too impulsive not to have made many blunders.

Each of these sentences contains a conclusion and an enthymematic argument in support of it. The hearer is understood to have in his mind a definite idea of the degree of ambition at which a man ceases to be scrupulous, or the degree of impulsiveness that is incompatible with accuracy.

One form of enthymeme is so common in modern rhetoric as to deserve a distinctive name. It may be called the **Enthymeme of the Abstractly Denominated Principle.** A conclusion is declared to be at variance with the principles of Political Economy, or contrary to the doctrine of Evolution, or inconsistent with Heredity, or a violation of the sacred principle of Freedom of Contract. It is assumed that the hearer is familiar with the principles referred to. As a safeguard against fallacy, it may be well to make the principle explicit in a proposition uniform with the conclusion.

CHAPTER VI.

THE UTILITY OF THE SYLLOGISM.

THE main use of the Syllogism is in dealing with incompletely expressed or elliptical arguments from general principles. This may be called Enthymematic argument, understanding by Enthymeme an argument with only one premiss put forward or hinted at, the other being held in the mind. In order to test whether such reasoning is sound or unsound, it is of advantage to make the argument explicit in Syllogistic form.

There have been heaps and mazes of discussion about the use of the Syllogism, much of it being profitable as a warning against the neglect of Formal Logic. Again and again it has been demonstrated that the Syllogism is useless for certain purposes, and from this it has been concluded that the Syllogism is of no use at all.

The inventor of the Syllogism had a definite practical purpose, to get at the simplest, most convincing, undeniable and irresistible way of putting admitted or self-evident propositions so that their implication should be apparent. His ambition was to furnish a method for the Yes and No Dialectician, and the expounder of science from self-evident principles. A question being put up for discussion, it was an advantage to analyse it, and formulate the necessary premisses: you could then better direct your interrogations or guard your answers. The analysis is similarly useful when you want to construct an argument from self-evident principles.

All that the Syllogism could show was the consistency of the premisses with the conclusion. The conclusion could not go beyond the premisses, because the questioner could not go beyond the admissions of the respondent. There is indeed an advance, but not an advance upon the two premisses taken together. There is an advance upon any one of them, and this advance is made with the help of the other. Both must be admitted: a respondent may admit one without being committed to the conclusion. Let him admit both and he cannot without self-contradiction deny the conclusion. That is all.

Dialectic of the Yes and No kind is no longer practised. Does any analogous use for the Syllogism remain? Is there a place for it as a safeguard against error in modern debate? As a matter of fact it is probably more useful now than it was for its original purpose, inasmuch as modern discussion, aiming at literary grace and spurning exact formality as smacking of scholasticism and pedantry, is much more flabby and confused. In the old dialectic play there was generally a clear question proposed. The interrogative form forced this much on the disputants. The modern debater of the unpedantic, unscholastic school is not so fettered, and may often be seen galloping wildly about without any game in sight or scent, his maxim being to—

Spur boldly on, and dash through thick and thin,
Through sense and nonsense, never out nor in.

Now the syllogistic analysis may often be of some use in helping us to keep a clear head in the face of a confused argument. There is a brilliant defence of the syllogism as an analysis of arguments in the *Westminster Review* for January, 1828. The article was a notice of Whately's Logic : it was written by J. S. Mill. For some reason it has never been reprinted, but it puts the utility of the Syllogism on clearer ground than Mill afterwards sought for it.

Can a fallacy in argument be detected at once ? Is common-sense sufficient ? Common-sense would require some inspection. How would it proceed ? Does common-sense inspect the argument in a lump or piecemeal ? All at once or step by step ? It analyses. How ? First, it separates out the propositions which contribute to the conclusion from those which do not, the essential from the irrelevant. Then it states explicitly all that may have been assumed tacitly. Finally, it enumerates the propositions in order.

Some such procedure as this would be adopted by common-sense in analysing an argument. But when common-sense has done this, it has exhibited the argument in a series of syllogisms.

Such is Mill's early defence of the Syllogism. It is weak only in one point, in failing to represent how common-sense would arrive at the peculiar syllogistic form. It is the peculiar form of logical analysis that is the distinction of the syllogism. When you have disentangled the relevant propositions you have not necessarily put them in this form. The arguments given in text-books to be cast into syllogistic form, consist only as a rule of relevant propositions, but they are not yet formal syllogisms. But common-sense had only one other step to make to reach the distinctive form. It had only to ask after analysing the argument, Is there any form of statement specially suitable for exhibiting the connexion between a conclusion and the general principle on which it is alleged to depend?   Ask yourself the question, and you will soon see that there would be an obvious advantage in making the conclusion and the general principle uniform, in stating them with the same predicate. But when you do this, as I have already shown (p. 197) you state the argument in the First Figure of the Syllogism.

It must, however, be admitted that it is chiefly for exhibiting, or forcing into light, tacit or lurking assumptions that the Syllogistic form is of use. Unless identity of meaning is disguised or distorted by puzzling difference of language, there is no special illuminative virtue in the Syllogism. The argument in a Euclidean demonstration would not be made clearer by being cast into formal Syllogisms.

Again, when the subject matter is simple, the Syllogistic form is not really required for protection against error.   In such enthymemes as the following for example :—

She must be clever : she is so uncompromisingly ugly.
Romeo must be in love : for is he not seventeen?

it is plain to the average intelligence without any knowledge of Syllogism that the argument takes for granted a general proposition and what the general proposition is.

Another thing is plain to the average intelligence, perhaps plainer than to a proficient in the use of the

Syllogism. Clearly we cannot infer with certainty that a woman is clever because she is ugly, unless it is the case that all ugly women are clever. But a Syllogiser, seeing that no certain conclusion can be drawn except upon this condition, is apt to dismiss the argument as altogether worthless. This may be specified as an error incident to the practice of the Syllogism, that it inclines us to look for necessarily conclusive premisses, and to deny all weight to anything short of this. Now in ordinary life it is comparatively seldom that such premisses can be found. We are obliged to proceed on maxims that are not of universal scope, and which lend only a more or less strong colour of probability to cases that can be brought under them. " A little learning is a dangerous thing ; " " Haste makes waste ; " " Slowness of speech is a sign of depth of thought ; " " Vivacity is a sign of shallowness : " such are the " endoxes " or commonplaces of popular knowledge that men bring to bear in daily life. They are not true for all cases, but some of them are true for most or for a good many, and they may be applied with a certain probability though they are not rigidly conclusive. The plain man's danger is that he apply them unthinkingly as universals : the formal logician's danger is that, seeing them to be inapplicable as universals, he dismisses them as being void of all argumentative force.

It helps to fix the limits of Formal Logic to remember that it lies outside its bounds to determine the degree of probability attaching to the application of approximate truths, such as are the staple of arguments in ordinary affairs. Formal Logic, we may repeat, is not concerned with degrees of truth or falsehood, probability or improbability. It merely shows the interdependency of certain arguments, the consistency of conclusion with premisses.

This, however, is a function that might easily be underrated. Its value is more indirect than direct. In showing what is required for a certain conclusion, it puts us on the road to a more exact estimate of the premisses alleged, a sounder judgment of their worth. Well begun is half done: in undertaking the examination of any argument from authority, a formal syllogism is a good beginning.

CHAPTER VII.

CONDITIONAL ARGUMENTS.—HYPOTHETICAL SYLLOGISM, DISJUNCTIVE SYLLOGISM, AND DILEMMA.

THE justification of including these forms of argument in Logic is simply that they are sometimes used in debate, and that confusion may arise unless the precise meaning of the premisses employed is understood. Aristotle did not include them as now given in his exposition of the Syllogism, probably because they have no connexion with the mode of reasoning together to which he appropriated the title. The fallacies connected with them are of such a simple kind that to discuss as a question of method the precise place they should occupy in a logical treatise is a waste of ingenuity.[1]

I.—HYPOTHETICAL SYLLOGISMS.

If A is B, C is D
    A is B   MODUS PONENS.
∴ C is D

If A is B, C is D
    C is not D   MODUS TOLLENS.
∴ A is not B

---

[1] For the history of Hypothetical Syllogism see Mansel's *Aldrich*, Appendix I.

A so-called Hypothetical Syllogism is thus seen to be a Syllogism in which the major premiss is a **Hypothetical Proposition,** that is to say, a complex proposition in which two propositions are given as so related that the truth of one follows necessarily from the truth of the other.

Two propositions so related are technically called the **Antecedent** or Reason, and the **Consequent.**

The meaning and implication of the form, If A is B, C is D, is expressed in what is known as the **Law of Reason and Consequent :—**

" *When two propositions are related as Reason and Consequent, the truth of the Consequent follows from the truth of the Antecedent, and the falsehood of the Antecedent, from the falsehood of the Consequent*".

If A is B, C is D, implies that If C is not D, A is not B. If this subject is educative, it quickens the wits ; if it does not quicken the wits, it is not educative.

Admitted, then, that the law of Reason and Consequent holds between two propositions—that If A is B, C is D : admitted also the Antecedent, the truth of the Consequent follows. This is the **Modus Ponens** or Positive Mode, where you reach a conclusion by obtaining the admission of the Antecedent. Admit the Antecedent and the truth of the Consequent follows.

With the same Major Premiss, you may also, under the Law of Reason and Consequent reach a conclusion by obtaining the denial of the Consequent. This is the **Modus Tollens** or Negative Mode. Deny the Consequent and one is bound to deny the Antecedent.

But to guard against the fallacy technically known as **Fallacia Consequentis,** we must observe what the relation of Reason and Consequent does not imply.

The truth of the Consequent does not involve the truth of the Antecedent, and the falsehood of the Antecedent does not involve the falsehood of the Consequent.

" If the harbour is frozen, the ships cannot come in." If the harbour is not frozen, it does not follow that the ships can come in : they may be excluded by other causes. And so, though they cannot come in, it does not follow that the harbour is frozen.

Questions Connected with Hypothetical Syllogisms.

(1) *Are they properly called Syllogisms?* This is purely a question of Method and Definition. If we want a separate technical name for forms of argument in which two terms are reasoned together by means of a third, the Hypothetical Syllogism, not being in such a form, is not properly so called. The fact is that for the purposes of the Hypothetical Argument, we do not require an analysis into terms at all : it is superfluous : we are concerned only with the affirmation or denial of the constituent propositions as wholes.

But if we extend the word Syllogism to cover all arguments in which two propositions necessarily involve a third, the Hypothetical Argument is on this understanding properly enough called a Syllogism.

(2) *Is the inference in the Hypothetical Syllogism Mediate or Immediate?*

To answer this question we have to consider whether the Conclusion can be drawn from either of the two premisses without the help of the other. If it is possible immediately, it must be educible directly either from the Major Premiss or from the Minor.

(*a*) Some logicians argue as if the Conclusion were immediately possible from the Major Premiss. The Minor Premiss and the Conclusion, they urge, are simply equivalent to the Major Premiss. But this is a misunderstanding. " If A is B, C is D," is not equivalent to " A is B, *therefore* C is D ". " If the harbour is frozen, the ships cannot come in " is not to say that " the harbour is frozen, and therefore," etc. The Major Premiss merely affirms the existence of the relation of Reason and Consequent between the two propositions. But we cannot thereupon assert the Conclusion unless the Minor Premiss is also conceded : that is, the inference of the Conclusion is Mediate, as being from two premisses and not from one alone.

(*b*) Similarly with Hamilton's contention that the Conclusion is inferrible immediately from the Minor Premiss, inasmuch as the Consequent is involved in the Reason. True, the Consequent is involved in the Reason : but we cannot infer from " A is B " to " C is D," unless it is conceded that the relation of Reason and Consequent holds between them ; that is, unless the Major Premiss is conceded as well as the Minor.

(3) *Can Hypothetical Syllogisms be reduced to the Categorical Form ?*

To oppose Hypothetical Syllogisms to Categorical is misleading, unless we take note of the precise difference between them. It is only in the form of the Major Premiss that they differ : Minor Premiss and Conclusion are categorical in both. And the meaning of a Hypothetical Major Premiss (unless it is a mere arbitrary convention between two disputants, to the effect that the Consequent will be admitted if the Antecedent is proved, or that the Antecedent will be relinquished if the Consequent is disproved), can always be put in the form of a general proposition, from which, with the Minor Premiss as applying proposition, a conclusion identical with the original can be drawn in regular Categorical form.

Thus :—

> If the harbour is frozen, the ships cannot come in.
> The harbour is frozen.
> ∴ The ships cannot come in.

This is a Hypothetical Syllogism, *Modus Ponens.* Express the Hypothetical Major in the form of the general proposition which it implies, and you reach a conclusion (in *Barbara*) which is only grammatically different from the original.

> All frozen harbours exclude ships.
> The harbour is frozen.
> ∴ It excludes ships.

Again, take an example of the *Modus Tollens*—

> If rain has fallen, the streets are wet.
> The streets are not wet.
> ∴ Rain has not fallen.

This is reducible, by formulating the underlying proposition, to *Camestres* or *Baroko* of the Second Figure.

> All streets rained upon are wet.
> The streets are not wet.
> ∴ They are not streets rained upon.

Hypothetical Syllogisms are thus reducible, by merely grammatical change,[1] or by the statement of

---

[1] It may be argued that the change is not merely grammatical, and that the implication of a general proposition in a hypothetical and *vice versâ* is a strictly logical concern. At any rate such an implication exists, whether it is the function of the Grammarian or the Logician to expound it.

self-evident implications, to the Categorical form. And, similarly, any Categorical Syllogism may be reduced to the Hypothetical form. Thus :—

> All men are mortal.
> Socrates is a man.
> ∴ Socrates is mortal.

This argument is not different, except in the expression of the Major and the Conclusion, from the following :—

> If Socrates is a man, death will overtake him.
> Socrates is a man.
> ∴ Death will overtake him.

The advantage of the Hypothetical form in argument is that it is simpler. It was much used in Mediæval Disputation, and is still more popular than the Categorical Syllogism. Perhaps the prominence given to Hypothetical Syllogisms as syllogisms in Post-Renaissance text-books is due to the use of them in the formal disputations of graduands in the Universities. It was the custom for the Disputant to expound his argument in this form :—

> If so and so is the case, such and such follows.
> So and so is the case.
> ∴ Such and such follows.

To which the Respondent would reply: *Accipio antecedentem, nego consequentiam*, and argue accordingly. Petrus Hispanus does not give the Hypothetical Syllogism as a Syllogism: he merely explains the true law of Reason and Consequent in connexion with the Fallacia Consequentis in the section on Fallacies. (*Summulæ. Tractatus Sextus.*)

II.—DISJUNCTIVE SYLLOGISMS.

A Disjunctive Syllogism is a syllogism in which the Major Premiss is a **Disjunctive Proposition,** *i.e.,* one in which two propositions are declared to be mutually incompatible. It is of the form Either A is B, or C is D.[1]

If the disjunction between the alternatives is really complete, the form implies four hypothetical propositions :—

> (1) If A is B, C is not D.
> (2) If A is not B, C is D.
> (3) If C is D, A is not B.
> (4) If C is not D, A is B.

Suppose then that an antagonist has granted you a Disjunctive Proposition, you can, using this as a Major Premiss, extract from him four different Conclusions, if you can get him also to admit the requisite Minors. The Mode of two of these is technically called **Modus Ponendo Tollens,** the mode that denies the one alternative by granting the other—A is B, *therefore* C is not D ; C is D, *therefore* A is not B. The other Mode is also twice open, the **Modus Tollendo Ponens**—A is not B, *therefore* C is D ; C is not D, *therefore* A is B.

Fallacy is sometimes committed through the Disjunctive form owing to the fact that in common speech there is a tendency to use it in place of a mere

---

[1] Some logicians prefer the form Either A is, or B is. But the two alternatives are propositions, and if " A is " represents a proposition, the " is " is not the Syllogistic copula. If this is understood it does not matter : the analysis of the alternative propositions is unessential.

hypothetical, when there are not really two incompatible alternatives.   Thus it may be said " Either the witness is perjured, or the prisoner is guilty," when the meaning merely is that if the witness is not perjured the prisoner is guilty.   But really there is not a valid disjunction and a correct use of the disjunctive form, unless four hypotheticals are implied, that is, unless the concession of either involves the denial of the other, and the denial of either the concession of the other.   Now the prisoner may be guilty and yet the witness be perjured ; so that two of the four hypotheticals, namely—

If the witness is perjured, the prisoner is not guilty.

If the prisoner is guilty, the witness is not perjured— do not necessarily hold.   If, then, we would guard against fallacy, we must always make sure before assenting to a disjunctive proposition that there is really a complete disjunction or mutual incompatibility between the alternatives.

III.—The Dilemma.

A Dilemma is a combination of Hypothetical and Disjunctive propositions.

The word has passed into common speech, and its ordinary use is a clue to the logical structure.   We are said to be in a dilemma when we have only two courses open to us and both of them are attended by unpleasant consequences.   In argument we are in this position when we are shut into a choice between two admissions, and either admission leads to a conclusion which we do not like.   The statement of the alternatives as the consequences hypothetically of certain conditions is the major premiss. of the dilemma : once we admit that the relations of Antecedent and Consequent are as stated, we are in a trap, if trap it is : we are on the horns of the dilemma, ready to be tossed from one to the other.

For example :—

> If A is B, A is C, and if A is not B, A is D. But A either is or is not B. Therefore, A either is C or is D.
>
> If A acted of his own motive, he is a knave; if A did not act of his own motive, he is a catspaw. But A either acted of his own motive or he did not. Thereupon A is either a knave or a catspaw.

This is an example of the *Constructive* Dilemma, the form of it corresponding to the common use of the word as a choice between equally unpleasant alternatives. The standard example is the dilemma in which the custodians of the Alexandrian Library are said to have been put by the Caliph Omar in 640 A.D.

> If your books are in conformity with the Koran, they are superfluous; if they are at variance with it, they are pernicious. But they must either be in conformity with the Koran or at variance with it. Therefore they are either superfluous or pernicious.

Where caution has to be exercised is in accepting the clauses of the Major. We must make sure that the asserted relations of Reason and Consequent really hold. It is there that fallacy is apt to creep in and hide its head. The Alexandrian Librarians were rash in accepting the first clause of the conqueror's Major : it does not follow that the books are superfluous unless the doctrines of the Koran are not merely sound but contain all that is worth knowing. The propounder of the dilemma covertly assumes this. It is in the facility that it affords for what is technically known as

Petitio Principii that the Dilemma is a useful instrument for the Sophist. We shall illustrate it further under that head.

What is known as the *Destructive* Dilemma is of a somewhat different form. It proceeds upon the denial of the Consequent as involving the denial of the Antecedent. In the Major you obtain the admission that if a certain thing holds, it must be followed by one or other of two consequences. You then prove by way of Minor that neither of the alternatives is true. The conclusion is that the antecedent is false.

We had an example of this in discussing whether the inference in the Hypothetical Syllogism is Immediate. Our argument was in this form :—

> If the inference is immediate, it must be drawn either from the Major alone or from the Minor alone. But it cannot be drawn from the Major alone, neither can it be drawn from the Minor alone. Therefore, it is not immediate.

In this form of Dilemma, which is often serviceable for clearness of exposition, we must as in the other make sure of the truth of the Major : we must take care that the alternatives are really the only two open. Otherwise the imposing form of the argument is a convenient mask for sophistry. Zeno's famous dilemma, directed to prove that motion is impossible, covers a *petitio principii.*

> If a body moves, it must move either where it is or where it is not. But a body cannot move where it is : neither can it move where it is not. Conclusion, it cannot move at all, *i.e.*, Motion is impossible.

The conclusion is irresistible if we admit the Major, because the Major covertly assumes the point to be proved. In truth, *if* a body moves, it moves neither where it is nor where it is not, but from where it is to where it is not. Motion consists in change of place: the Major assumes that the place is unchanged, that is, that there is no motion.

Chapter VIII.

FALLACIES IN DEDUCTIVE ARGUMENT.— PETITIO PRINCIPII AND IGNORATIO ELENCHI.

The traditional treatment of Fallacies in Logic follows Aristotle's special treatise Περὶ σοφιστικῶν ἐλέγχων— Concerning Sophistical Refutations—Pretended Disproofs—Argumentative Tricks.

Regarding Logic as in the main a protection against Fallacies, I have been going on the plan of taking each fallacy in connexion with its special safeguard, and in accordance with that plan propose to deal here with the two great types of fallacy in deductive argument. Both of them were recognised and named by Aristotle : but before explaining them it is worth while to indicate Aristotle's plan as a whole. Some of his Argumentative Tricks were really peculiar to Yes-and-No Dialectic in its most sportive forms : but his leading types, both Inductive and Deductive, are permanent, and his plan as a whole has historical interest. Young readers would miss them from Logic : they appeal to the average argumentative boy.

He divides Fallacies broadly into Verbal Fallacies (παρὰ τὴν λέξιν, *in dictione*), and Non-Verbal Fallacies (ἔξω τῆς λέξεως, *extra dictionem*).

The first class are mere Verbal Quibbles, and hardly deserve serious treatment, still less minute subdivision. The world was young when time was spent upon them. Aristotle names six varieties, but they all turn on ambiguity of word or structure, and some of them, being dependent on Greek syntax, cannot easily be paralleled in another tongue.

(1) Ambiguity of word (ὁμωνυμία). As if one were to argue: "All cold can be expelled by heat: John's illness is a cold: therefore it can be expelled by heat". Or: "Some afflictions are cheering, for afflictions are sometimes light, and light is always cheering". The serious confusion of ambiguous words is met by Definition, as explained at length in pt. ii. c. i.

(2) *Ambiguity of structure* (ἀμφιβολία).

"What he was beaten with was what I saw him beaten with: what I saw him beaten with was my eye: therefore, what he was beaten with was my eye."

"How do you do?" "Do? Do what?" "I mean, how do you feel?" "How do I feel? With my fingers, of course; but I can see very well." "No, no; I mean, how do you find yourself?" "Then why did you not say so? I never exactly noticed, but I will tell you next time I lose myself."

(3) *Illicit conjunction* (σύνθεσις).

Socrates is good. Socrates is a musician. Therefore Socrates is a good musician.

(4) *Illicit disjunction* (διαίρεσις).

Socrates is a good musician. Therefore he is a good man.

(5) *Ambiguity of pronunciation* (προσῳδία, *fallacia accentus*).

Analogies to words that differ only in accent, such as οὖ and οὔ, may be found in differences of pronunciation. "Hair very thick, sir," said a barber to a customer, whose hair was bushy, but beginning to turn grey. "Yes, I daresay. But I would rather have it thick than thin." " Ah, too thick to-day, sir." " But I don't want to dye it." " Excuse me, sir, I mean the hair of the hatmosphere, t-o-d-a-y, to-day."

" He said, saddle me the ass. And they saddled *him.*"

(6) *Ambiguity of inflexion* (σχῆμα τῆς λέξεως, *Figura dictionis*).

This is not easy to make intelligible in English. The idea is that a termination may be ambiguously interpreted, a neuter participle, *e.g.*, taken for an active. Thus: " George is ailing". " Doing what, did you say? Ailing? What is he ailing? Ginger-aleing?"

Non-Verbal Fallacies, or Fallacies in thought, are a more important division. Aristotle distinguishes seven.

Of these, three are comparatively unimportant and trifling. One of them, known to the Schoolmen as *Fallacia Plurium Interrogationum*, was peculiar to Interrogative disputation. It is the trick of putting more than one question as one, so that a simple Yes commits the respondent to something implied. " Have you left off beating your father?" If you answer Yes, that implies that you have been in the habit of beating him. " Has the practice of excessive drinking ceased in your part of the country?" Such questions were unfair when the Respondent could answer only Yes or No. The modern disputant who demands a plain answer Yes or No, is sometimes guilty of this trick.

Two others, the fallacies known as *A dicto simpliciter ad dictum secundum quid*, and *A dicto secundum quid ad dictum simpliciter*, are as common in modern dialectic as they were in ancient. The trick, conscious or unconscious, consists in getting assent to a statement with a qualification and proceeding to argue as if it had been conceded without qualification, and *vice versâ.* For example, it being admitted that culture is good, a disputant goes on to argue as if the admission applied to some sort of culture in special, scientific, æsthetic, philosophical or moral. The fallacy was also known as *Fallacia Accidentis.* Proving that the Syllogism is useless for a certain purpose, and then claiming to have proved that it is useless for any purpose is another example. Getting a limited admission and then extending it indefinitely is perhaps the more common of the two forms. It is common enough to deserve a shorter name.

The *Fallacia Consequentis,* or *Non-Sequitur,* which consists specially in ignoring the possibility of a plurality of causes, has already been partly explained in connexion with the Hypothetical Syllogism, and will be explained further in the Logic of Induction.

Post hoc ergo proper hoc is a purely Inductive Fallacy, and will be explained in connexion with the Experimental Methods.

There remain the two typical Deductive Fallacies, **Petitio Principii** (Surreptitious Assumption) and **Ignoratio Elenchi** (Irrelevant Argument) about which we must speak more at length.

The phrase of which Petitio Principii or Begging the Question is a translation—τὸ ἐν ἀρχῇ αἰτεῖσθαι—was applied by Aristotle to an argumentative trick in debate by Question and Answer. The trick consisted in taking for granted a proposition necessary to the refutation without having obtained the admission of it. Another expression for the same thing—τὸ ἐν ἀρχῇ λαμβάνειν—taking the principle for granted—is more descriptive.

Generally speaking, Aristotle says, Begging the

Question consists in not demonstrating the theorem. It would be in accordance with this general description to extend the name to all cases of tacitly or covertly, unwittingly to oneself or to one's opponent, assuming any premiss necessary to the conclusion. It is the fallacy of Surreptitious Assumption, and all cases of Enthymematic or Elliptical argument, where the unexpressed links in the chain of argument are not fully understood, are examples of it. By contrast, the articulate and explicit Syllogism is an *Expositio Principii*. The only remedy for covert assumptions is to force them into the light.[1]

Ignoratio Elenchi, ignoring the refutation (τοῦ ἐλέγχου ἄγνοια), is simply arguing beside the point, distracting the attention by irrelevant considerations. It often succeeds by proving some other conclusion which is not the one in dispute, but has a superficial resemblance to it, or is more or less remotely connected with it.

It is easier to explain what these fallacies consist in than to illustrate them convincingly. It is chiefly in long arguments that the mischief is done. "A Fallacy," says Whately, " which when stated barely in a few sentences would not deceive a child, may deceive half the world if diluted in a quarto volume." Very rarely is a series of propositions put before us in regular form and order, all bearing on a definite point. A certain conclusion is in dispute, not very definitely formulated perhaps, and a mixed host of considerations are tumbled out before us. If we were perfectly clear-

---

[1] Cp. Mr. Sidgwick's instructive treatise on Fallacies, International Scientific Series, p. 199.

headed persons, capable of protracted concentration of attention, incapable of bewilderment, always on the alert, never in a hurry, never over-excited, absolutely without prejudice, we should keep our attention fixed upon two things while listening to an argument, the point to be proved, and the necessary premisses. We should hold the point clearly in our minds, and watch indefatigably for the corroborating propositions. But none of us being capable of this, all of us being subject to bewilderment by a rapid whirl of statements, and all of us biased more or less for or against a conclusion, the sophist has facilities for doing two things—taking for granted that he has stated the required premisses (*petitio principii*), and proving to perfect demonstration something which is not the point in dispute, but which we are willing to mistake for it (*ignoratio elenchi*).

It is chiefly in the heat of argument that either Petitio or Ignoratio succeeds. When a fallacy continues to perplex us in cold blood, it must have in its favour either some deeply-rooted prejudice or some peculiar intricacy in the language used, or some abstruseness in the matter. If we are not familiar with the matter of the argument, and have but a vague hold of the words employed, we are, of course, much more easily imposed upon.

The famous Sophisms of antiquity show the fascination exercised over us by proving something, no matter how irrelevant. If certain steps in an argument are sound, we seem to be fascinated by them so that we cannot apply our minds to the error, just as our senses are fascinated by an expert juggler. We have seen how plausibly Zeno's argument against the possibility of motion hides a Petitio : the Fatalist Dilemma is another example of the same sort.

> If it is fated that you die, you will die whether you
> call in a doctor or not, and if it is fated that you will
> recover, you will recover whether you call in a doctor
> or not.   But it must be fated either that you die or
> that you recover.   *Therefore*, you will either die or
> recover whether you call in a doctor or not.

Here it is tacitly assumed in the Major Premiss that
the calling in of a doctor cannot be a link in the fated
chain of events.   In the statement of both the alternative conditions, it is assumed that Fate does not act
through doctors, and the conclusion is merely a
repetition of this assumption, a verbal proposition
after an imposing show of argument.   " If Fate does
not act through doctors, you will die whether you call
in a doctor or not."

The fallacy in this case is probably aided by our
veneration for the grand abstraction of Fate and the
awful idea of Death, which absorbs our attention and
takes it away from the artful *Petitio.*

The Sophism of Achilles and the Tortoise is the
most triumphant of examples of *Ignoratio Elenchi.*

The point that the Sophism undertakes to prove is
that Achilles can never overtake a Tortoise once it
has a certain start : what it really proves, and proves
indisputably, is that he cannot overtake the Tortoise
within a certain space or time.

For simplicity of exposition, let us assume that the
Tortoise has 100 yards start and that Achilles runs ten
times as fast.   Then, clearly, Achilles will not come
up with it at the end of 100 yards, for while he has run
100, the Tortoise has run 10 ; nor at the end of 110, for
then the Tortoise has run 1 more ; nor at the end of 111,
for then the Tortoise has run $\frac{1}{10}$ more ; nor at the end
of $111\frac{1}{10}$, for then the Tortoise has gained $\frac{1}{100}$ more.

So while Achilles runs this $\frac{1}{100}$, the Tortoise runs $\frac{1}{1000}$; while he runs the $\frac{1}{1000}$, it runs $\frac{1}{10000}$. Thus it would seem that the Tortoise must always keep ahead: he can never overtake it.

But the conclusion is only a confusion of ideas: all that is really proved is that Achilles will not overtake the Tortoise while running

$$100 + 10 + 1 + \tfrac{1}{10} + \tfrac{1}{100} + \tfrac{1}{1000} + \tfrac{1}{10000}, \text{ etc.}$$

That is, that he will not overtake it till he has completed the sum of this series, $111\frac{1}{9}$ yards. To prove this is an *ignoratio elenchi;* what the Sophist undertakes to prove is that Achilles will never overtake it, and he really proves that Achilles passes it between the 111th and 112th yards.

The exposure of this sophism is an example also of the value of a technical term. All attempts to expose it without using the term *Ignoratio Elenchi* or something equivalent to it, succeed only in bewildering the student. It is customary to say that the root of the fallacy lies in assuming that the sum of an infinite series is equal to infinity. This profound error may be implied: but if any assumption so hard to understand were really required, the fallacy would have little force with the generality.

It has often been argued that the Syllogism involves a *petitio principii*, because the Major Premiss contains the Conclusion, and would not be true unless the Conclusion were true. But this is really an *Ignoratio Elenchi.* The fact adduced, that the Major Premiss contains the Conclusion, is indisputable ; but this does not prove the Syllogism guilty of Petitio. *Petitio principii* is an argumentative trick, a conscious or unconscious act of deception, a covert assumption, and the Syllogism, so far from favouring this, is an *expositio principii*, an explicit statement of premisses such that, if they are true, the conclusion is true.   The Syllogism merely shows the interdependence of premisses and conclusion; its only tacit assumption is the *Dictum de Omni*.

If, indeed, an opponent challenges the truth of the conclusion, and you adduce premisses necessarily containing it as a refutation, that is an *ignoratio elenchi* unless your opponent admits those premisses.   If he admits them and denies the conclusion, you convict him of inconsistency, but you do not prove the truth of the conclusion.   Suppose a man to take up the position: " I am not mortal, for I have procured the *elixir vitæ* ".   You do not disprove this by saying, " All men are mortal, and you are a man".   In denying that he is mortal, he denies that all men are mortal. Whatever is sufficient evidence that he is not mortal, is sufficient evidence that all men are not mortal. Perhaps it might be said that in arguing, " All men are mortal, and you are a man," it is not so much *ignoratio elenchi* as *petitio principii* that you commit. But be it always remembered that you may commit both fallacies at once.   You may both argue beside the point and beg the question in the course of one and the same argument.

CHAPTER IX

FORMAL OR ARISTOTELIAN INDUCTION.—INDUCTIVE ARGUMENT.

THE distinction commonly drawn between Deduction and Induction is that Deduction is reasoning from general to particular, and Induction reasoning from particular to general.

But it is really only as modes of argumentation that the two processes can be thus clearly and fixedly opposed. The word Induction is used in a much wider sense when it is the title of a treatise on the Methods of Scientific Investigation. It is then used to cover all the processes employed in man's search into the system of reality; and in this search deduction is employed as well as induction in the narrow sense.

We may call Induction in the narrow sense Formal Induction or Inductive Argument, or we may simply call it Aristotelian Induction inasmuch as it was the steps of Inductive argument that Aristotle formulated, and for which he determined the conditions of validity.

Let us contrast it with Deductive argument. In this the questioner's procedure is to procure the admission of a general proposition with a view to forcing the admission of a particular conclusion which is in dispute. In Inductive argument, on the other hand, it is a general proposition that is in dispute, and the procedure is to obtain the admission of particular cases with a view to forcing the admission of this general proposition.

Let the question be whether All horned animals ruminate. You engage to make an opponent admit this. How do you proceed? You ask him whether he admits it about the various species. Does the ox ruminate? The sheep? The goat? And so on. The bringing in of the various particulars is the induction (ἐπαγωγή).

When is this inductive argument complete? When is the opponent bound to admit that all horned animals ruminate? Obviously, when he has admitted it about every one. He must admit that he has admitted it about every one, in other words, that the particulars enumerated constitute the whole, before he can be held bound in consistency to admit it about the whole.

The condition of the validity of this argument is ultimately the same with that of Deductive argument, the identity for purposes of predication of a generic whole with the sum of its constituent parts. The Axiom of Inductive Argument is, *What is predicated of every one of the parts is predicable of the whole.* This is the simple converse of the Axiom of Deductive argument, the *Dictum de Omni,* " What is predicated of the whole is predicable about every one of the parts ". The Axiom is simply convertible because for purposes of predication generic whole and specific or individual parts taken all together are identical.

Practically in inductive argument an opponent is worsted when he cannot produce an instance to the contrary. Suppose he admits the predicate in question to be true of this, that and the other, but denies that this, that and the other constitute the whole class in question, he is defeated in common judgment if he cannot instance a member of the class about which the predicate does not hold. Hence this mode of induction became technically known as *Inductio per enumerationem simplicem ubi non reperitur instantia contradictoria.* When this phrase is applied to a generalisation of fact, Nature or Experience is put figuratively in the position of a Respondent unable to contradict the inquirer.

Such in plain language is the whole doctrine of Inductive Argument. Aristotle's Inductive Syllogism is, in effect, an expression of this simple doctrine tortuously in terms of the Deductive Syllogism. The great master was so enamoured of his prime invention that he desired to impress its form upon everything : otherwise, there was no reason for expressing the process of Induction syllogistically. Here is his description of the Inductive Syllogism :—

" Induction, then, and the Inductive Syllogism, consists in syllogising one extreme with the middle through the other extreme. For example, if B is middle to A and C, to prove through C that A belongs to B." [1]

This may be interpreted as follows : Suppose a general proposition is in dispute, and that you wish to make it good by obtaining severally the admission of all the particulars that it sums up. The type of a general proposition in Syllogistic terminology is the Major Premiss, All M is P. What is the type of the particulars that it sums up ? Obviously, the Conclusion, S is P. This particular is contained in the Major Premiss, All M is P ; its truth is accepted as

---

[1] ἐπαγωγὴ μὲν οὖν ἐστὶ καὶ ὁ ἐξ ἐπαγωγῆς συλλογισμὸς τὸ διὰ τοῦ ἑτέρου θἄτερον ἄκρον τῷ μέσῳ συλλογίσασθαι · Οἶον εἰ τῶν Α Γ μέσον τὸ Β, διὰ τοῦ Γ δεῖξαι τὸ Α τῷ Β ὑπάρχον. (An. Prior., ii. 23.)

contained in the truth of All M is P. S is one of the
parts of the generic whole M ; one of the individuals or
species contained in the class M.   If you wish, then,
to establish P of All M by Induction, you must establish P of all the parts, species, or individuals contained
in M, that is, of all possible S*s*. you must make good
that this, that and the other S is P, and also that this,
that and the other S constitute the whole of M.
You are then entitled to conclude that All M is P : you
have syllogised one Extreme with the Middle through
the other Extreme.   The formal statement of these
premisses and conclusion is the Inductive Syllogism.

> This, that and the other S is P, *Major.*
> This, that and the other S is all M, *Minor.*
> ∴ All M is P, *Conclusion.*
> This, that and the other magnet (*i.e.*, magnets indivi-
>   dually) attract iron.
> This, that and the other magnet (*i.e.*, the individuals
>   separately admitted) are all magnets.
> ∴ All magnets attract iron.

This, that and the other S being simply convertible
with All M, you have only to make this conversion
and you have a syllogism in Barbara where this, that
and the other S figures as the Middle Term.

The practical value of this tortuous expression is not
obvious.   Mediæval logicians shortened it into what
was known as the Inductive Enthymeme : " This,
that and the other, therefore all," an obvious conclusion when this, that and the other constitute all.   It
is merely an evidence of the great master's intoxication
with his grand invention.   It is a proof also that
Aristotle really looked at Induction from the point of
view of Interrogative Dialectic.   His question was,

When is a Respondent bound to admit a general conclusion? And his answer was, When he has admitted a certain number of particulars, and cannot deny that those particulars constitute the whole whose predicate is in dispute. He was not concerned primarily with the analysis of the steps of an inquirer generalising from Nature.

BOOK II.

INDUCTIVE LOGIC, OR THE LOGIC OF SCIENCE.

INTRODUCTION.

PERHAPS the simplest way of disentangling the leading features of the departments of Logic is to take them in relation to historical circumstances. These features are writ large, as it were, in history. If we recognise that all bodies of doctrine have their origin in practical needs, we may conceive different ages as controlled each by a distinctive spirit, which issues its mandate to the men of the age, assigning to them their distinctive work.

The mandate issued to the age of Plato and Aristotle was *Bring your beliefs into harmony one with another*. The Aristotelian Logic was framed in response to this order : its main aim was to devise instruments for making clear the coherence, the concatenation, the mutual implication of current beliefs.

The mandate of the Mediæval Spirit was *Bring your beliefs into harmony with dogma*. The mediæval logic was contracted from Aristotle's under this impulse. Induction as conceived by him was neglected, allowed to dwindle, almost to disappear from Logic. Greater prominence was given to Deduction.

Then as Dogmatic Authority became aggressive, and the Church through its officials claimed to pronounce on matters outside Theology, a new spirit was roused, the mandate of which was, *Bring your beliefs into harmony with facts*. It was under this impulse that a body of methodical doctrine vaguely called Induction gradually originated.

In dealing with the genesis of the Old Logic, we began with Aristotle. None can dispute his title to be called its founder. But who was the founder of the New Logic? In what circumstances did it originate?

The credit of founding Induction is usually given to Francis Bacon, Lord Verulam. That great man claimed it for himself in calling his treatise on the Interpretation of Nature the *Novum Organum.* The claim is generally conceded. Reid's account of the matter represents the current belief since Bacon's own time.

> "After man had laboured in the search of truth near two thousand years by the help of Syllogisms, [Lord] Bacon proposed the method of INDUCTION as a more effectual engine for that purpose. His *Novum Organum* gave a new turn to the thoughts and labours of the inquisitive, more remarkable and more useful than that which the *Organon* of Aristotle had given before, and may be considered as a second grand era in the progress of human nature. . . . Most arts have been reduced to rules after they had been brought to a considerable degree of perfection by the natural sagacity of artists; and the rules have been drawn from the best examples of the art that had been before exhibited; but the art of philosophical induction was delineated by [Lord] Bacon in a very ample manner before the world had seen any tolerable example of it." [1]

There is a radical misconception here, which, for reasons that I hope to make plain, imperatively needs

[1] Hamilton's *Reid,* p. 712.

to be cleared up. It obscures the very essence of " philosophical induction ".

There are three ways in which movement in any direction may be helped forward, Exhortation, Example, and Precept. Exhortation : a man may exhort to the practice of an art and thereby give a stimulus. Example : he may practise the art himself, and show by example how a thing should be done. Precept : he may formulate a clear method, and so make plain how to do it. Let us see what was Bacon's achievement in each of those three ways.

Undoubtedly Bacon's powerful eloquence and high political position contributed much to make the study of Nature fashionable. He was high in place and great in intellect, one of the commanding personalities of his time. Taking "all knowledge for his province," though study was really but his recreation, he sketched out a plan of universal conquest with a clearness and confidence that made the mob eager to range themselves under his leadership. He was the magnificent demagogue of science. There had been champions of " Induction " before him, but they had been comparatively obscure and tongue-tied.

While, however, we admit to the full the great services of this mighty advocate in making an " Inductive " method popular, we should not forget that he had pioneers even in hortatory leadership. His happiest watchword, the Interpretation of Nature, as distinguished from the Interpretation of Authoritative Books, was not of his invention. If we read Whewell's *History of the Inductive Sciences*, we shall find that many before him had aspired to " give a new turn to the labours of the inquisitive," and in particular to substitute inquisition for disquisition.

One might compile from Whewell a long catalogue of eminent men before Bacon who held that the study of Nature was the proper work of the inquisitive: Leonardo da Vinci (1452-1519), one of the wonders of mankind for versatility, a miracle of excellence in many things, painter, sculptor, engineer, architect, astronomer, and physicist; Copernicus (1473-1543), the author of the Heliocentric theory; Telesius (1508-1588), a theoretical reformer, whose *De Rerum Natura* (1565) anticipated not a little of the *Novum Organum ;* Cesalpinus (1520-1603), the Botanist; Gilbert (1540-1603), the investigator of Magnetism. By all these men experiment and observation were advocated as the only way of really increasing knowledge. They all derided mere book-learning. The conception of the world of sense as the original MS. of which systems of philosophy are but copies, was a familiar image with them. So also was Bacon's epigrammatic retort to those who wish to rest on the wisdom of the ancients, that antiquity is the youth of the world and that we are the true ancients. "We are older," said Giordano Bruno, "and have lived longer than our predecessors."

This last argument, indeed, is much older than the sixteenth century. It was used by the Doctor Mirabilis of the thirteenth, the Franciscan Friar, Roger Bacon (1214-1292). "The later men are, the more enlightened they are; and wise men now are ignorant of much the world will some day know." The truth is that if you are in search of a Father for Inductive Philosophy, the mediæval friar has better claims than his more illustrious namesake. His enthusiasm for the advancement of learning was not less nobly ambitious and far-reaching, and he was himself an ardent experimenter and inventor. His

Opus Majus—an eloquent outline of his projects for a new learning, addressed in 1265 to Pope Clement IV., through whom he offered to give to the Church the empire of the world as Aristotle had given it to Alexander—was almost incredibly bold, comprehensive and sagacious. Fixing upon Authority, Custom, Popular Opinion, and the Pride of Supposed Knowledge, as the four causes of human ignorance, he urged a direct critical study of the Scriptures, and after an acute illustration of the usefulness of Grammar and Mathematics (widely interpreted), concluded with Experimental Science as the great source of human knowledge. I have already quoted (p. 15) the Friar's distinction between the two modes of Knowing, Argument and Experience, wherein he laid down that it is only experience that makes us feel certain. It were better, he cried in his impatience, to burn Aristotle and make a fresh start than to accept his conclusions without inquiry.

> Experimental Science, the sole mistress of Specu-lative Science, has three great Prerogatives among other parts of Knowledge. First, she tests by experi-ment the noblest conclusions of all other sciences. Next, she discovers respecting the notions which other sciences deal with, magnificent truths to which these sciences can by no means attain. Her third dignity is that she by her own power and without respect to other sciences investigates the secret of Nature.

So far, then, as Exhortation goes, King James's great lawyer and statesman was not in advance of Pope Clement's friar. Their first principle was the same. It is only by facts that theories can be tested. Man must not impose his own preconceptions (*anticipationes mentis*) on nature. Man is only the

interpreter of nature.   Both were also at one in holding
that the secrets of nature could not be discovered by
discussion, but only by observation and experiment.

Francis Bacon, however, went beyond all his predecessors in furnishing an elaborate Method for the
interpretation of Nature.   When he protested against
the intellect's being left to itself (*intellectus sibi permissus*),
he meant more than speculation left unchecked by
study of the facts.   He meant also that the interpreter
must have a method.   As man, he says, cannot move
rocks by the mere strength of his hands without
instruments, so he cannot penetrate to the secrets of
Nature by mere strength of his intellect without
instruments.   These instruments he undertakes to
provide in his Inductive Method or *Novum Organum*.
And it is important to understand precisely what his
methods were, because it is on the ground of them that
he is called the founder of Inductive Philosophy, and
because this has created a misapprehension of the
methods actually followed by men of science.

Ingenious, penetrating, wide-ranging, happy in
nomenclature, the *Novum Organum* is a wonderful
monument of the author's subtle wit and restless
energy ; but, beyond giving a general impulse to
testing speculative fancies by close comparison with
facts, it did nothing for science.   His method—with
its Tables of Preliminary Muster for the Intellect
(*tabulæ comparentiæ primæ instantiarum ad intellectum*,
facts collected and methodically arranged for the intellect to work upon) ; its Elimination upon first inspection
of obviously accidental concomitants (*Rejectio sive
Exclusiva naturarum*) ; its Provisional Hypothesis
(*Vindemiatio Prima sive Interpretatio Inchoata*) ; its
advance to a true Induction or final Interpretation by

examination of special instances (he enumerates twenty-seven, $3 \times 3 \times 3$, *Prerogativas Instantiarum*, trying to show the special value of each for the inquirer)[1]—was beautifully regular and imposing, but it was only a vain show of a method. It was rendered so chiefly by the end or aim that Bacon proposed for the inquirer. In this he was not in advance of his age; on the contrary, he was probably behind Roger Bacon, and certainly far behind such patient and concentrated thinkers as Copernicus, Gilbert, and Galileo—no discredit to the grandeur of his intellect when we remember that science was only his recreation, the indulgence of his leisure from Law and State.

In effect, his method came to this. Collect as many instances as you can of the effect to be investigated, and the absence of it where you would expect it, arrange them methodically, then put aside guesses at the cause which are obviously unsuitable, then draw up a probable explanation, then proceed to make this exact by further comparison with instances. It is when we consider what he directed the inquirer to search for that we see why so orderly a method was little likely to be fruitful.

He starts from the principle that the ultimate object of all knowledge is use, practice (*scimus ut operemur*). We want to know how Nature produces things that we may produce them for ourselves, if we can. The inquirer's first aim, therefore, should be to find out how the qualities of bodies are produced, to discover the *formæ* or formal causes of each quality. An

---

[1] The *Novum Organum* was never completed. Of the nine heads of special aids to the intellect in the final interpretation he completed only the first, the list of Prerogative Instances.

example shows what he meant by this. Gold is a crowd or conjugation of various qualities or "natures"; it is yellow, it has a certain weight, it is malleable or ductile to a certain degree, it is not volatile (loses nothing under fire), it can be melted, it is soluble.   If we knew the *forma* or formal cause of each of those qualities, we could make gold, provided the causes were within our control.   The first object, then, of the investigator of Nature is to discover such *formæ*, in order to be able to effect the transformation of bodies. It may be desirable also to know the *latens processus*, any steps not apparent to the senses by which a body grows from its first germs or rudiments, and the *schematismus* or ultimate inner constitution of the body. But the discovery of the *formæ* of the constituent qualities (*naturæ singulæ*), heat, colour, density or rarity, sweetness, saltness, and so forth, is the grand object of the Interpreter of Nature ; and it is for this that Bacon prescribed his method.

The *Sylva Sylvarum*, or Natural History, a miscellaneous collection of facts and fictions, observations and traditions, with guesses at the explanation · of them, affords us a measure of Bacon's own advancement as an interpreter of Nature.   It was a posthumous work, and the editor, his secretary, tells us that he often said that if he had considered his reputation he would have withheld it from the world, because it was not digested according to his own method : yet he persuaded himself that the causes therein assigned were far more certain than those rendered by others, "not for any excellence of his own wit, but in respect of his continual conversation with Nature and Experience," and mankind might stay upon them till true Axioms were more fully discovered.   When, however, we examine the causes assigned, we find that in practice Bacon could not carry out his own precepts: that he did not attempt to creep up to an explanation by slow and patient ascent, but jumped to the highest generalisations: and that his explanatory notions were taken not from nature, but from the ordinary traditions of mediæval physical science. He deceived himself, in short, in thinking that he could throw aside tradition and start afresh from observation.

For example. He is struck by the phenomenon of bubbles on water: "It seemeth somewhat strange that the air should rise so swiftly, while it is in the water, and when it cometh to the top should be stayed by so weak a cover as that of the bubble is". The swift ascent of the air he explains as a "motion of percussion," the water descending and forcing up the air, and not a "motion of levity" in the air itself. "The cause of the enclosure of the bubble is for that the appetite to resist separation or discontinuance, which is strong in solids, is also in liquors, though fainter and weaker." "The same reason is of the roundness of the bubble, as well for the skin of water as for the air within. For the air likewise avoideth discontinuance, and therefore casteth itself into a round figure. And for the stop and arrest of the air a little while, it showeth that the air of itself hath little or no appetite of ascending."[1] These notions were not taken direct from the facts: they descended from Aristotle. He differs from Aristotle, however, in his explanation of the colours of birds' feathers. "Aristotle giveth the cause vainly" that birds are more in the beams of the sun than beasts. "But that is

[1] *Sylva Sylvarum*, Century 1, 24.

manifestly untrue; for cattle are more in the sun than birds, that live commonly in the woods or in some covert. The true cause is that the excrementitious moisture of living creatures, which maketh as well the feathers in birds as the hair in beasts, passeth in birds through a finer and more delicate strainer than it doth in beasts. For feathers pass through quills, and hair through skin." It is an instance of percolation or filtering: other effects of the same cause being the gums of trees, which are but a fine passage or straining of the juice through the wood and bark, and Cornish Diamonds and Rock Rubies, which are in like manner " fine exudations of stone ".[1]

These examples of Bacon's Inductions are taken from the *Sylva* at random. But the example which best of all illustrates his attitude as a scientific investigator is the remark he makes in the *Novum Organum* about the Copernican theory. Elsewhere he says that there is nothing to choose between it and the Ptolemaic; and in the *Novum Organum* (lib. ii. 5) he remarks that " no one can hope to terminate the question whether in diurnal motion it is really the earth or the sky that rotates, unless he shall first have comprehended the nature of spontaneous rotation". That is, we must first find out the *forma* or formal cause of spontaneous rotation. This is a veritable *instantia crucis*, as fixing Bacon's place in the mediæval and not in the new world of scientific speculation.

Bacon, in short, in the practice of induction did not advance an inch beyond Aristotle. Rather he retrograded, inasmuch as he failed to draw so clear a line between the respective spheres of Inductive collection

---

[1] *Sylva Sylvarum*, Century 1, 5.

of facts and Explanation. There are two sources of general propositions, according to Aristotle, Induction and Nous. By Induction he meant the generalisation of facts open to sense, the summation of observed particulars, the *inductio per enumerationem simplicem* of the schoolmen. By Nous he meant the Reason or Speculative Faculty, as exercised with trained sagacity by experts. Thus by Induction we gather that all horned animals ruminate. The explanation of this is furnished by the Nous, and the explanation that commended itself to the trained sagacity of his time was that Nature having but a limited amount of hard material and having spent this on the horns, had none left for teeth, and so provided four stomachs by way of compensation. Bacon's guesses at causes are on the same scientific level with this, only he rather confused matters by speaking of them as if they were inductions from fact, instead of being merely fancies superinduced upon fact. His theory of interpretation, it is true, was so far an advance that he insisted on the necessity of verifying every hypothesis by further appeal to facts, though in practice he himself exercised no such patience and never realised the conditions of verification. Against this, again, must be set the fact that by calling his method induction, and laying so much stress on the collection of facts, he fostered, and, indeed, fixed in the public mind the erroneous idea that the whole work of science consists in observation. The goal of science, as Herschel said, is Explanation, though every explanation must be made to conform to fact, and explanation is only another term for attaining to higher generalisations, higher unities.

The truth is that Induction, if that is the name we use for scientific method, is not, as Reid conceived, an exception to the usual rule of arts in being the invention of one man. Bacon neither invented nor practised it. It was perfected gradually in the practice of men of science. The birthplace of it as a conscious method was in the discussions of the Royal Society of London, as the birthplace of the Aristotelian Logic was in the discussions of the Athenian schools. Its first great triumph was Newton's law of Gravitation. If we are to name it after its first illustrious practitioner, we must call it the Newtonian method, not the Baconian. Newton really stands to the Scientific Method of Explanation as Aristotle stands to the Method of Dialectic and Deduction. He partly made it explicit in his *Regulæ Philosophandi* (1685). Locke, his friend and fellow-member of the Royal Society, who applied the method to the facts of Mind in his *Essay Concerning Human Understanding* (1691), made it still further explicit in the Fourth Book of that famous work.

It was, however, a century and a half later that an attempt was first made to incorporate scientific method with Logic under the name of Induction, and add it as a new wing to the old Aristotelian building. This was the work of John Stuart Mill, whose System of Logic, Deductive and Inductive, was first published in 1843.

The genesis of Mill's System of Logic, as of other things, throws light upon its character. And in inquiries into the genesis of anything that man makes we may profitably follow Aristotle's division of causes. The Efficient Cause is the man himself, but we have also to find out the Final Cause, his object or purpose in making the thing, the Material Cause, the sources of his material, and the Formal Cause, the reason why he shaped it as he did. In the case of Mill's system we have to ask: What first moved him to formulate the methods of scientific investigation ? Whence did he derive his materials ? Why did he give his scientific method the form of a supplement to the old Aristotelian Logic ? We cannot absolutely separate the three inquiries, but motive, matter and form each had a traceable influence on the leading features of his System.

First, then, as to his motive. It is a mistake to suppose that Mill's object was to frame an organon that might assist men of science as ordinarily understood in making discoveries. Bacon, his secretary tells us, was wont to complain that he should be forced to be a Workman and a Labourer in science when he thought he deserved to be an Architect in this building. And men of science have sometimes rebuked Mill for his presumption in that, not being himself an investigator in any department of exact science, he should volunteer to teach them their business. But Mill was really guilty of no such presumption. His object, on the contrary, was to learn their method with a view to its application to subjects that had not yet undergone scientific treatment. Briefly stated, his purpose was to go to the practical workers in the exact sciences, Astronomy, Chemistry, Heat, Light, Electricity, Molar and Molecular Physics ; ascertain, not so much how they made their discoveries as how they assured themselves and others that their conclusions were sound ; and having ascertained their tests of truth and principles of proof, to formulate these tests so that they might be applied to propositions outside the range of the exact sciences, propositions in Politics, Ethics, History, Psychology. More particularly he studied how scientific men verify, and when they accept as proved, propositions of causation, explanations of the causes of things.   In effect, his survey of scientific method was designed to lead up to the Sixth Book in his System, the Logic of the Moral Sciences.   There are multitudes of floating endoxes or current opinions concerning man and his concerns, assigning causes for the conduct and character of individuals and of communities.   Mill showed himself quite aware that the same modes of investigation may not be practicable, and that it may not be possible, though men are always ready to assign causes with confidence, to ascertain causes with the same degree of certainty :   but at least the conditions of exact verification should be the same, and it is necessary to see what they are in order to see how far they can be realised.

That such was Mill's design in the main is apparent on internal evidence, and it was the internal evidence that first struck me.   But there is external evidence as well.   We may first adduce some essays on the Spirit of the Age, published in the *Examiner* in 1831, essays which drew from Carlyle the exclamation, " Here is a new Mystic ! "   These essays have never been republished, but they contain Mill's first public expression of the need for a method in social inquiries.   He starts from the Platonic idea that no state can be stable in which the judgment of the wisest in political affairs is not supreme.   He foresees danger in the prevalent anarchy of opinion.   How is it to be averted ?   How are men to be brought to accept loyally the judgment of the expert in public affairs ?   They accept at once and without question the decisions of the specially skilled in the physical sciences.   Why is this ?   For one reason, because there is complete agreement among experts.   And why is there this complete agreement? Because all accept the same tests of truth, the same conditions of proof. Is it not possible to obtain among political investigators similar unanimity as to their methods of arriving at conclusions, so as to secure similar respect for their authority?

We need not stop to ask whether this was a vain dream, and whether it must not always be the case that to ensure confidence in a political or moral adviser more is needed than faith in his special knowledge and trained sagacity. Our point is that in 1831 Mill was in search of a method of reasoning in social questions. Opportunely soon after, early in 1832, was published Herschel's *Discourse on the Study of Natural Philosophy*, the first attempt by an eminent man of science to make the methods of science explicit. Mill reviewed this book in the *Examiner*, and there returns more definitely to the quest on which he was bent. "The uncertainty," he says, "that hangs over the very elements of moral and social philosophy proves that the means of arriving at the truth in those sciences are not yet properly understood. And whither can mankind so advantageously turn, in order to learn the proper means and to form their minds to the proper habits, as to that branch of knowledge in which by universal acknowledgment the greatest number of truths have been ascertained and the greatest possible degree of certainty arrived at?"

We learn from Mill himself that he made an attempt about this time, while his mind was full of Herschel's Discourse, to connect a scientific method with the body of the Old Logic. But he could not make the junction to his satisfaction, and abandoned the attempt in despair. A little later, in 1837, upon the appearance of Whewell's *History of the Inductive Sciences*, he renewed it, and this time with happier results. Whewell's *Philosophy of the Inductive Sciences* was published in 1840, but by that time Mill's system was definitely shaped.

It was, then, to Herschel and Whewell, but especially to the former, that Mill owed the raw materials of his Inductive Method. But why did he desire to concatenate this with the old Logic? Probably because he considered that this also had its uses for the student of society, the political thinker. He had inherited a respect for the old Logic from his father. But it was the point at which he sought to connect the new material with the old, the point of junction between the two, that determined the form of his system. We find the explanation of this in the history of the old Logic. It so happened that Whately's Logic was in the ascendant, and Whately's treatment of Induction gives the key to Mill's.

Towards the end of the first quarter of this century there was a great revival of the study of Logic at Oxford. The study had become mechanical, Aldrich's Compendium, an intelligent but exceedingly brief abstract of the Scholastic Logic, being the text-book beyond which no tutor cared to go. The man who seems to have given new life to the study was a tutor who subsequently became Bishop of Llandaff, Edward Copleston. The first public fruits of the revival begun by him was Whately's article on Logic in the *Encyclopædia Metropolitana*, published as a separate book in 1827. Curiously enough, one of Whately's most active collaborators in the work was John Henry Newman, so that the common room of Oriel, which Mr. Froude describes as the centre from which emanated the High Church Movement, may also be said to have been the centre from which emanated the movement that culminated in the revolution of Logic.

The publication of Whately's Logic made a great stir. It was reviewed by Mill, then a young man of twenty-one, in the *Westminster Review* (1828), and by Hamilton, then forty-five years of age, in the *Edinburgh* (1833). There can be no doubt that it awakened Mill's interest in the subject. A society formed for the discussion of philosophical questions, and called the Speculative Society, met at Grote's house in 1825, and for some years following. Of this society young Mill was a member, and their continuous topic in 1827 was Logic, Whately's treatise being used as a sort of text-book.

It is remarkable that Mill's review of Whately, the outcome of these discussions, says very little about Induction. At that stage Mill's chief concern seems to have been to uphold the usefulness of Deductive Logic, and he even goes so far as to scoff at its eighteenth century detractors and their ambition to supersede it with a system of Induction. The most striking feature of the article is the brilliant defence of the Syllogism as an analysis of arguments to which I have already referred. He does not deny that an Inductive Logic might be useful as a supplement, but apparently he had not then formed the design of supplying such a supplement. When, however, that design seriously entered his mind, consequent upon the felt need of a method for social investigations, it was Whately's conception of Induction that he fell back upon. Historically viewed, his System of Logic was an attempt to connect the practical conditions of proof set forth in Herschel's discourse with the theoretic view of Induction propounded in Whately's. The tag by which he sought to attach the new material to the old system was the Inductive Enthymeme of the Schoolmen as interpreted by Whately.

Whately's interpretation—or misinterpretation—of this Enthymeme, and the conception of Induction underlying it, since it became Mill's ruling conception of Induction, and virtually the formative principle of his system, deserves particular attention.

"This, that and the other horned animal, ox, sheep, goat, ruminate; *therefore*, all horned animals ruminate."

The traditional view of this Enthymeme I have given in my chapter on Formal Induction (p. 238). It is that a Minor Premiss is suppressed : " This, that and the other constitute the whole class ". This is the form of the Minor in Aristotle's Inductive Syllogism.

But, Whately argued, how do we know that this, that and the other—the individuals we have examined —constitute the whole class ?   Do we not assume that what belongs to the individuals examined belongs to the whole class ? This tacit assumption, he contended, is really at the bottom of the Enthymeme, and its proper completion is to take this as the Major Premiss, with the enumeration of individuals as the Minor. Thus :—

> What belongs to the individuals examined belongs to the whole class.
> The property of ruminating belongs to the individuals examined, ox, sheep, goat, etc.
> *Therefore*, it belongs to all.

In answer to this, Hamilton repeated the traditional view, treating Whately's view merely as an instance of the prevailing ignorance of the history of Logic. He pointed out besides that Whately's Major was the postulate of a different kind of inference from that contemplated in Aristotle's Inductive Syllogism, Material as distinguished from Formal inference. This is un.leniable if we take this syllogism purely as an argumentative syllogism. The " all " of the conclusion simply covers the individuals enumerated and admitted to be " all " in the Minor Premiss. If a disputant admits the cases produced to be all and can produce none to the contrary, he is bound to admit the conclusion. Now the inference contemplated by Whately was not inference from an admission to what it implies, but inference from a series of observations to all of a like kind, observed and unobserved.

It is not worth while discussing what historical justification Whately had for his view of Induction. It is at least arguable that the word had come to mean, if it did not mean with Aristotle himself, more than a mere summation of particulars in a general statement. Even Aristotle's respondent in the concession of his Minor admitted that the individuals enumerated constituted all in the truly general sense, not merely all observed but all beyond the range of observation. The point, however, is insignificant. What really signifies is that while Hamilton, after drawing the line between Formal Induction and Material, fell back and entrenched himself within that line, Mill caught up Whately's conception of Induction, pushed forward, and made it the basis of his System of Logic.

In Mill's definition, the mere summation of particulars, *Inductio per enumerationem simplicem ubi non reperitur instantia contradictoria*, is Induction improperly so called. The only process worthy of the name is

Material Induction, inference to the unobserved. Here only is there an advance from the known to the unknown, a veritable " inductive hazard ".

Starting then with this conception of inference to the unobserved as the only true inference, and with an empirical law — a generality extended from observed cases to unobserved—as the type of such inference, Mill saw his way to connecting a new Logic with the old. We must examine this junction carefully, and the brilliant and plausible arguments by which he supported it; we shall find that, biased by this desire to connect the new with the old, he gave a misleading dialectic setting to his propositions, and, in effect, confused the principles of Argumentative conclusion on the one hand and of Scientific Observation and Inference on the other. The conception of Inference which he adopted from Whately was too narrow on both sides for the uses to which he put it. Be it understood that in the central methods both of Syllogistic and of Science, Mill was substantially in accord with tradition; it is in his mode of junction, and the light thereby thrown upon the ends and aims of both, that he is most open to criticism.

As regards the relation between Deduction and Induction, Mill's chief proposition was the brilliant paradox that all inference is at bottom Inductive, that Deduction is only a partial and accidental stage in a process the whole of which may be called Induction. An opinion was abroad—fostered by the apparently exclusive devotion of Logic to Deduction—that all inference is essentially Deductive. Not so, answered Mill, meeting this extreme with another : all inference is essentially Inductive. He arrives at this through the conception that Induction is a generalisation from observed particulars, while Deduction is merely the extension of the generalisation to a new case, a new particular. The example that he used will make his meaning plain.

Take a common Syllogism :—

> All men are mortal.
> Socrates is a man.
> Socrates is mortal.

" The proposition," Mill says, " that Socrates is mortal is evidently an inference. It is got at as a conclusion from something else. But do we in reality conclude it from the proposition, All men are mortal ? " He answers that this cannot be, because if it is not true that Socrates is mortal it cannot be true that all men are mortal. It is clear that our belief in the mortality of Socrates must rest on the same ground as our belief in the mortality of men in general. He goes on to ask whence we derive our knowledge of the general truth, and answers : " Of course from observation. Now all which man can observe are individual cases. . . . A general truth is but an aggregate of particular truths. But a general proposition is not merely a compendious form for recording a number of particular facts. . . . It is also a process of inference. From instances which we have observed we feel warranted in concluding that what we have found true in those instances, holds in all similar ones, past, present, and future. We then record all that we have observed together with what we infer from our observations, in one concise expression." A general proposition is thus at once a summary of particular facts and a memorandum of our right to infer from them. And when we make a deduction we are, as it were, interpreting this memorandum. But it is upon the particular facts that the inference really rests, and Mill contends that we might if we chose infer to the particular conclusion at once without going through the form of a general inference. Thus Mill seeks to make good his point that all inference is essentially Inductive, and that it is only for convenience that the word Induction has been confined to the general induction, while the word Deduction is applied to the process of interpreting our memorandum.

Clear and consecutive as this argument is, it is fundamentally confusing. It confuses the nature of Syllogistic conclusion or Deduction, and at the same time gives a partial and incomplete account of the ground of Material inference.

The root of the first confusion lies in raising the question of the ground of material inference in connexion with the Syllogism. As regards the usefulness of the Syllogism, this is an IGNORATIO ELENCHI. That the Major and the conclusion rest upon the same ground as matters of belief is indisputable : but it is irrelevant. In so far as " Socrates is mortal " is an inference from facts, it is not the conclusion of a Syllogism. This is implicitly and with unconscious inconsistency recognised by Mill when he represents Deduction as the interpretation of a memorandum. To represent Deduction as the interpretation of a memorandum—a very happy way of putting it and quite in accordance with Roger Bacon's view—is really inconsistent with regarding Deduction as an occasional step in the process of Induction. If Deduction is the interpretation of a memorandum, it is no part of the process of inference from facts. The conditions of correct interpretation as laid down in Syllogism are one thing, and the methods of correct inference from facts, the methods of science that he was in search of, are another.

Let us emphasise this view of Deduction as the interpretation of a memorandum. It corresponds exactly with the view that I have taken in discussing the utility of the Syllogism. Suppose we want to know whether a particular conclusion is consistent with our memorandum, what have we to look to ? We have to put our memorandum into such a form that it is at once apparent whether or not it covers our particular case. The Syllogism aspires to be such a form. That is the end and aim of it. It does not enable us to judge whether the memorandum is a legitimate memorandum or not. It only makes clear that if the memorandum is legitimate, so is the conclusion. How to make clear and consistent memoranda of our beliefs in words is a sufficiently complete description of the main purpose of Deductive Logic.

Instead, then, of trying to present Deduction and Induction as parts of the same process, which he was led to do by his desire to connect the new and the old, Mill ought rather, in consistency as well as in the interests of clear system, to have drawn a line of separation between the two as having really different ends, the conditions of correct conclusion from accepted generalities on the one hand, and the conditions of correct inference from facts on the other. Whether the first should be called inference at all is a question of naming that ought to have been considered by itself. We may refuse to call it inference, but we only confuse ourselves and others if we do not acknowledge that in so doing we are breaking with traditional usage. Perhaps the best way in the interests of clearness is to compromise with tradition by calling the one Formal Inference and the other Material Inference.

It is with the latter that the Physical Sciences are mainly concerned, and it was the conditions and methods of its correct performance that Mill desired to systematise in his Inductive Logic. We have next to see how his statement of the grounds of Material Inference was affected by his connexion of Deduction and Induction. Here also we shall find a reason for a clearer separation between the two departments of Logic.

In his antagonism to a supposed doctrine that all reasoning is from general to particular, Mill maintained *simpliciter* that all reasoning is from particulars to particulars. Now this is true only *secundum quid*, and although in the course of his argument Mill introduced the necessary qualifications, the unqualified thesis was confusing. It is perfectly true that we may infer—we can hardly be said to reason—from observed particulars to unobserved. We may even infer, and infer correctly, from a single case. The village matron, called in to prescribe for a neighbour's sick child, infers that what cured her own child will cure the neighbour's, and prescribes accordingly. And she may be right. But it is also true that she may be wrong, and that no fallacy is more common than reasoning from particulars to particulars without the requisite precautions. This is the moral of one of the fables of Camerarius. Two donkeys were travelling in the same caravan, the one laden with salt, the other with hay. The one laden with salt stumbled in crossing a stream, his panniers dipped in the stream, the salt melted, and his burden was lightened. When they came to another stream, the donkey that was laden with hay dipped his panniers in the water, expecting a similar result. Mill's illustrations of correct inference from particulars to particulars were really irrelevant. What we are concerned with in considering the grounds of Inference, is the condition of correct inference, and no inference to an unobserved case is sound unless it is of a like kind with the observed case or cases on which it is founded, that is to say, unless we are entitled to make a general proposition. We need not go through the form of making a general proposition, but if a general proposition for all particulars of a certain description is not legitimate, no more is the particular inference. Mill, of course, did not deny this, he was only betrayed by the turn of his polemic into an unqualified form of statement that seemed to ignore it.

But this was not the worst defect of Mill's attempt at a junction of old and new through Whately's conception of Induction. A more serious defect was due to the insufficiency of this conception to represent all the modes of scientific inference. When a certain attribute has been found in a certain connexion in this, that, and the other, to the extent of all observed instances, we infer that it will be found in all, that the connexion that has obtained within the range of our actual experience has obtained beyond that range and will obtain in the future. Call this an observed uniformity of nature : we hold ourselves justified in expecting that the observed uniformities of nature will continue. Such an observed uniformity—that All animals have a nervous system, that All animals die, that Quinine cures ague—is also called an Empirical Law.

But while we are justified in extending an empirical law beyond the limits within which it has been observed to hold good, it is a mistake to suppose that the main work of science is the collection of empirical laws, and that the only scientific inference is the inference from the observed prevalence of an empirical law to its continuance.   With science the collection of empirical laws is only a preliminary: " the goal of science," in Herschel's phrase, " is explanation ".   In giving such prominence to empirical laws in his theory, Mill confined Induction to a narrower scope than science ascribes to it.   Science aims at reaching " the causes of things ": it tries to penetrate behind observed uniformities to the explanation of them.   In fact, as long as a science consists only of observed uniformities, as long as it is in the empirical stage, it is a science only by courtesy.   Astronomy was in this stage before the discovery of the Law of Gravitation.   Medicine is merely empirical as long as its practice rests upon such generalisations as that Quinine cures ague, without knowing why.   It is true that this explanation may consist only in the discovery of a higher or deeper uniformity, a more recondite law of connexion : the point is that these deeper laws are not always open to observation, and that the method of reaching them is not merely observing and recording.

In the body of his Inductive Logic, Mill gave a sufficient account of the Method of Explanation as practised in scientific inquiry.   It was only his mode of approaching the subject that was confusing, and made it appear as if the proper work of science were merely extending observed generalities, as when we conclude that all men will die because all men have died, or that all horned animals ruminate because all hitherto observed have had this attribute.   A minor source of confusion incident to the same controversy was his refusing the title of Induction proper to a mere summary of particulars. He seemed thereby to cast a slight upon the mere summation of particulars. And yet, according to his theory, it was those particulars that were the basis of the Induction properly so called. That all men will die is an inference from the observation summed up in the proposition that all men have died. If we refuse the name of Induction to the general proposition of fact, what are we to call it? The truth is that the reason why the word Induction is applied indifferently to the general proposition of fact and the general proposition applicable to all time is that, once we are sure of the facts, the transition to the inference is so simple an affair that it has not been found necessary in practice to distinguish them by different names.

Our criticism of Mill would itself mislead if it were taken to mean that the methods of science which he formulated are not the methods of science or that his system of those methods is substantially incomplete. His Inductive Logic as a system of scientific method was a great achievement in organisation, a veritable *Novum Organum* of knowledge. What kept him substantially right was that the methods which he systematised were taken from the practice of men of science. Our criticism amounts only to this, that in correlating the new system with the old he went upon a wrong track. For more than two centuries Deduction had been opposed to Induction, the *ars disserendi* to the *ars inveniendi*. In trying to reconcile them and bring them under one roof, Mill drew the bonds too tight. In stating the terms of the union between the two partners, he did not separate their spheres of work with sufficient distinctness.

Mill's theory of Deduction and Induction and the voluminous criticism to which in its turn it has been subjected have undoubtedly been of great service in clearing up the foundations of reasoning.   But the moral of it is that if we are to make the methods of Science a part of Logic, and to name this department Induction, it is better to discard altogether the questions of General and Particular which are pertinent to Syllogism, and to recognise the new department simply as being concerned with a different kind of inference, inference from facts to what lies beyond them, inference from the observed to the unobserved.

That this is the general aim and proper work of Science is evident from its history.   Get at the secrets of Nature by the study of Nature, penetrate to what is unknown and unexperienced by help of what is known and has been experienced, was the cry of the early reformers of Science.   Thus only, in Roger Bacon's phrase, could certainty—assured, well grounded, rational belief—be reached.   This doctrine, like every other, can be understood only by what it was intended to deny.   The way of reaching certainty that Roger Bacon repudiated was argument, discussion, dialectic. This " concludes a question but does not make us feel certain, or acquiesce in the contemplation of truth that is not also found in Experience ".   Argument is not necessarily useless ; the proposition combated is only that by it alone—by discussion that does not go beyond accepted theories or conceptions — rational belief about the unknown cannot be reached.   The proposition affirmed is that to this end the conclusions of argument must be tested by experience.

Observation of facts then is a cardinal part of the method of Science.   The facts on which our inferences

are based, by which our conclusions are tested, must
be accurate. But in thus laying emphasis on the
necessity of accurate observation, we must beware of
rushing to the opposite extreme, and supposing that
observation alone is enough. Observation, the accurate use of the senses (by which we must understand
inner as well as outer sense), is not the whole work of
Science. We may stare at facts every minute of our
waking day without being a whit the wiser unless we
exert our intellects to build upon them or under them.
To make our examination fruitful, we must have
conceptions, theories, speculations, to bring to the test.
The comparison of these with the facts is the inductive
verification of them. Science has to exercise its
ingenuity both in making hypotheses and in contriving
occasions for testing them by observation. These
contrived occasions are its artificial experiments, which
have come to be called experiments simply by contrast
with conclusive observations for which Nature herself
furnishes the occasion. The observations of Science
are not passive observations. The word experiment
simply means trial, and every experiment, natural or
artificial, is the trial of a hypothesis. In the language
of Leonardo da Vinci, " Theory is the general, Experiments are the soldiers ".

Observation and Inference go hand in hand in the
work of Science, but with a view to a methodical
exposition of its methods, we may divide them broadly
into Methods of Observation and Methods of Inference.
There are errors specially incident to Observation, and
errors specially incident to Inference. How to observe
correctly and how to make correct inferences from our
observations are the two objects of our study in Inductive Logic : we study the examples of Science because

they have been successful in accomplishing those objects.

That all inference to the unobserved is founded on facts, on the data of experience, need not be postulated. It is enough to say that Inductive Logic is concerned with inference in so far as it is founded on the data of experience. But inasmuch as all the data of experience are not of equal value as bases of inference, it is well to begin with an analysis of them, if we wish to take a comprehensive survey of the various modes of inference and the conditions of their validity.

CHAPTER I.

THE DATA OF EXPERIENCE AS GROUNDS OF INFERENCE OR RATIONAL BELIEF.

IF we examine any of the facts or particulars on which an inference to the unobserved is founded, we shall find that they are not isolated individuals or attributes, separate objects of perception or thought, but relations among things and their qualities, constituents, or ingredients.

Take the "particular" from which Mill's village matron inferred, the fact on which she based her expectation of a cure for her neighbour's child. It is a relation between things. We have the first child's ailment, the administration of the drug, and the recovery, a series of events in sequence. This observed sequence is the fact from which she is said to infer, the datum of experience. She expects this sequence to be repeated in the case of her neighbour's child.

Similarly we shall find that, in all cases where we infer, the facts are complex, are not mere isolated things, but relations among things—using the word thing in its widest sense—relations which we expect to find repeated, or believe to have occurred before, or to be occurring now beyond the range of our observation. These relations, which we may call coincidences or conjunctions, are the data of experience from which we start in our beliefs or inferences about the unexperienced.

The problem of Inductive Logic being to determine when or on what conditions such beliefs are rational, we may begin by distinguishing the data of coincidence or conjunction accordingly. There are certain coincidences that we expect to find repeated beyond the occasions on which we have observed them, and others that we do not expect to find repeated. If it is a sound basis of inference that we are in search of, it is evidently to these first, the coincidences that we are assured of finding again, that we must direct our study. Let us see whether they can be specified.

(1) If there is no causal connexion between A and B, using these as symbols for the members of a coincidence—the objects that are presented together— we do not expect the coincidence to be repeated. If A and B are connected as cause and effect, we expect the effect to recur in company with the cause. We expect that when the cause reappears in similar circumstances, the effect also will reappear.

You are hit, *e.g.*, by a snowball, and the blow is followed by a feeling of pain. The sun, we shall say, was shining at the moment of the impact of the snowball on your body. The sunshine preceded your feeling of pain as well as the blow. But you do not expect the pain to recur next time that the sun shines. You do expect it to recur next time you are hit by a snowball.

The taking of food and a certain feeling of strength are causally connected. If we go without food, we are not surprised when faintness or weariness supervenes.

Suppose that when our village matron administered her remedy to her own child, a dog stood by the bedside and barked. The barking in that case would precede the cure. Now, if the matron were what we should call a superstitious person, and believed that this concomitant had a certain efficacy, that the dog's barking and the cure were causally connected, she would take the dog with her when she went to cure her neighbour's child. Otherwise she would not. She would say that the barking was an accidental, casual, fortuitous coincidence, and would build no expectation upon it.

These illustrations may serve to remind us of the familiar fact that the causal nexus is at least one of the things that we depend on in our inferences to the unobserved. To a simple sequence we attach no importance, but a causal sequence or consequence that has been observed is a mainstay of inference.

Whether the causal sequence holds or not as a matter of fact, we depend upon it if we believe in it as a matter of fact. But unless it does hold as a matter of fact, it is valueless as a guide to the unknown, and our belief is irrational. Clearly, therefore, if rational belief is what we aim at, it is of importance that we should make sure of cause and effect as matter of fact in the sequence of events.

One large department of Inductive Logic, the so-called Experimental Methods, is designed to help us in thus making sure, *i.e.*, in ascertaining causal sequence as a matter of fact. It is assumed that by careful observation of the circumstances, we can distinguish between mere simple sequence and causal sequence or consequence, and methods are recommended of observing with the proper precautions against error.

Observe that these methods, though called Inductive, are not concerned with arriving at general propositions.

The principle we go upon is simply this, that if it can be ascertained as matter of fact that a certain thing is related to another as cause and effect, we may count upon the same relation as holding in unobserved Nature, on the general ground that like causes produce like effects in like circumstances.

Observe, also, that I deliberately speak of the causal relation as a relation among phenomena. Whether this use of the words cause and effect is philosophically justifiable, is a question that will be raised and partly discussed later on. Here I simply follow the common usage, in accordance with which objects of perception, *e.g.*, the administration of a drug and the recovery of a patient, are spoken of as cause and effect. Such observable sequences are causal sequences in the ordinary sense, and it is part of the work of Science to observe them. I do not deny that the *true* cause, or the cause that science aims ultimately at discovering, is to be found in the latent constitution or composition of the things concerned. Only that, as we shall see more precisely, is a cause of another description. Meantime, let us take the word to cover what it undoubtedly covers in ordinary speech, the perceptible antecedent of a perceptible consequent.

Strictly speaking, as we shall find, Science has only one method of directly observing when events are in causal sequence. But there are various indirect methods, which shall be described in some sort of order.

For the practical purposes of life, a single ascertained causal sequence is of little value as a basis of inference, because we can infer only to its repetition in identical circumstances. Suppose our village matron had been able to ascertain as a matter of fact—a feat as we shall find not to be achieved by direct observation—that the drug did cure her child, this knowledge by itself would have been practically valueless, because the only legitimate inference would have been that an exactly similar dose would have the same effect in exactly similar circumstances. But, as we shall find, though practically valueless, a single ascertained causal sequence is of supreme value in testing scientific speculations as to the underlying causes.

(2) We have next to see whether there are any other rational expectations based on observed facts. We may lay down as a principle the following :—

If a conjunction or coincidence has constantly been repeated within our experience, we expect it to recur and believe that it has recurred outside our experience.

How far such expectations are rational, and with what degrees of confidence they should be entertained, are the questions for the Logic of Inference, but we may first note that we do as a matter of habit found expectations on repeated coincidence, and indeed guide our daily life in this way. If we meet a man repeatedly in the street at a certain hour, we go out expecting to meet him : it is a shock to our expectations, a surprise, when we do not. If we are walking along a road and find poles set up at regular intervals, we continue our walk expecting to find a pole coincident with the end of each interval.

What Mill calls the uniformities of Nature, the uniformities expressed in general propositions, are from the point of view of the observer, examples of repeated coincidence. Birth, growth, decay, death, are not isolated or variable coincidences with organised being : all are born, all grow, all decay, and all die. These uniformities constitute the order of Nature : the coincidences observed are not occasional, occurring once in a way or only now and then ; they turn up again and again. Trees are among the uniformities on the varied face of Nature : certain relations between the soil and the plant, between trunk, branches, and leaves are common to them. For us who observe, each particular tree that comes under our observation is a repetition of the coincidence. And so with animals : in each we find certain tissues, certain organs, conjoined on an invariable plan.

Technically these uniformities have been divided into uniformities of Sequence and uniformities of Coexistence. Thus the repeated alternation of day and night is a uniformity of Sequence : the invariable conjunction of inertia with weight is a uniformity of Coexistence. But the distinction is really immaterial to Logic. What Logic is concerned with is the observation of the facts and the validity of any inference based on them : and in these respects it makes no difference whether the uniformity that we observe and found upon is one of Sequence or of Coexistence.

It was exclusively to such inferences, inferences from observed facts of repeated coincidence, that Mill confined himself in his theory of Induction, though not in his exposition of the methods. These are the inferences for which we must postulate what he calls the Uniformity of Nature. Every induction, he says, following Whately, may be thrown into the form of a Syllogism, in which the principle of the Uniformity of Nature is the Major Premiss, standing to the inference in the relation in which the Major Premiss of a Syllogism stands to the conclusion. If we express this abstractly denominated principle in propositional form, and take it in connexion with Mill's other saying that the course of Nature is not a uniformity but uniformities, we shall find, I think, that this postulated Major Premiss amounts to an assumption that the observed Uniformities of Nature continue. Mill's Inductive Syllogism thus made explicit would be something like this :—

> All the observed uniformities of Nature continue.
> That all men have died is an observed uniformity.
> *Therefore*, it continues; *i.e.*, all men will die and did die before the beginning of record.

There is no doubt that this is a perfectly sound postulate. Like all ultimate postulates it is indemonstrable; Mill's derivation of it from Experience did not amount to a demonstration. It is simply an assumption on which we act. If any man cares to deny it, there is no argument that we can turn against him. We can only convict him of practical inconsistency, by showing that he acts upon this assumption himself every minute of his waking day. If we do not believe in the continuance of observed uniformities, why do we turn our eyes to the window expecting to find it in its accustomed order of place ? Why do we not look for it in another wall ? Why do we dip our pens in ink, and expect the application of them to white paper to be followed by a black mark ?

The principle is sound, but is it our only postulate in inference to the unobserved, and does the continuance of empirical laws represent all that Science assumes in its inferences ? Mill was not satisfied about this question. He pointed out a difficulty which a mere belief in empirical continuity does not solve. Why do we believe more confidently in some uniformities than in others ? Why would a reported breach of one be regarded with more incredulity than that of another? Suppose a traveller to return from a strange country and report that he had met men with heads growing beneath their shoulders, why would this be pronounced more incredible than a report that he had seen a grey crow? All crows hitherto observed have been black, and in all men hitherto observed the heads have been above the shoulders: if the mere continuity of observed uniformities is all that we go upon in our inferences, a breach of the one uniformity should be just as improbable as a breach of the other, neither more nor less. Mill admitted the difficulty, and remarked that whoever could solve it would have solved the problem of Induction. Now it seems to me that this particular difficulty may be solved, and yet leave another behind. It may be solved within the limits of the principle of empirical — meaning by that observational — continuity. The uniform blackness of the crow is an exception within a wider uniformity: the colour of animals is generally variable. Hence we are not so much surprised at the reported appearance of a grey crow: it is in accordance with the more general law. On the other hand, the uniform position of the head relative to other parts of the body is a uniformity as wide as the animal kingdom: it is a coincidence repeated as often as animals have been repeated, and merely on the principle that uniformities continue, it has an absolutely uncontradicted series in its favour.

But is this principle really all that we assume? Do we not also assume that behind the observed fact of uniformity, there is a cause for it, a cause that does not appear on the surface of the observation, but must be sought outside of its range? And do not the various degrees of confidence with which we expect a repetition of the coincidence, depend upon the extent of our knowledge of the producing causes and the mode of their operation ? At bottom our belief in the continuance of the observed uniformities rests on a belief in the continuance of the producing causes, and till we know what these are our belief has an inferior warrant : there is less reason for our confidence.

To go back to the illustrations with which we started. If we have met a man every day for months at a certain place at a certain hour, it is reasonable to expect to meet him there to-morrow, even if our knowledge does not go beyond the observed facts of repeated coincidence. But if we know also what brings him there, and that this cause continues, we have a stronger reason for our expectation. And so with the case of poles at regular intervals on a road. If we know why they are placed there, and the range of the .purpose, we expect their recurrence more confidently within the limits of that purpose. This further knowledge is a warrant for stronger confidence, because if we know the producing causes, we are in a better position for knowing whether anything is likely to defeat the coincidence. A uniformity is said to be explained when its cause is known, and an inference from an explained uniformity is always more certain than an inference from a uniformity that is merely empirical in the sense of being simply observed.

Now, the special work of Science is to explain, in the sense of discovering the causes at work beneath what lies open to observation. In so doing it follows a certain method, and obeys certain conditions of satisfactory explanation. Its explanations are inferences from facts, inasmuch as it is conformity with observed facts, with outward signs of underlying causal nexus, that is the justification of them. But they are not inferences from facts in the sense above described as empirical inference. In its explanations also Science postulates a principle that may be called the Uniformity of Nature. But this principle is not merely that observed uniformities continue. It may be expressed rather as an assumption that the underlying causes are uniform in their operation, that as they have acted beneath the recorded experiences of mankind, so they have acted before and will continue to act.

The foregoing considerations indicate a plan for a roughly systematic arrangement of the methods of Induction. Seeing that all inference from the data of experience presupposes causal connexion among the data from which we infer, all efforts at establishing sound bases of inference, or rational ground for expectation fall, broadly speaking, under two heads: (1) Methods of ascertaining causal connexion among phenomena as a matter of fact, that is, Methods of Observation; and (2) Methods of ascertaining what the causal connexion is, that is, Methods of Explanation.

These constitute the body of Inductive Logic. But there is a preliminary and a pendant. Without raising the question of causal connexion, we are liable to certain errors in ascertaining in what sequence and with what circumstances events really occurred. These tendencies to error deserve to be pointed out by way of warning, and this I shall attempt in a separate chapter on observation of facts of simple sequence. This is preliminary to the special methods of observing causal sequence. Then, by way of pendant, I shall consider two modes of empirical inference from data in which the causal connexion has not been ascertained or explained—Inference from approximate generalisations to particular cases, and Inference from Analogy.

Most of these methods in one form or another were included by Mill in his system of Inductive Logic, and the great merit of his work was that he did include them, though at some sacrifice of consistency with his introductory theory. With regard to the kind of empirical inference which that theory, following the lead of Whately, took as the type of all inference, Logic has really little to say. It was this probably that was in Mill's mind when he said that there is no Logic of Observation, ignoring the fact that the Experimental Methods are really methods of observation, as well as the Methods of Eliminating Chance by calculation of Probability. There is no method of observing uniformities except simply observing them. Nor indeed is there any "method" of inferring from them : we can only point out that in every particular inference from them we assume or postulate their continuance generally. As regards their observation, we may point out further that a special fallacy is incident to it, the fallacy of ignoring exceptions. If we are prepossessed or prejudiced in favour of a uniformity, we are apt to observe only the favourable instances, and to be blind to cases where the supposed invariable coincidence does not occur. Thus, as Bacon remarked among his *Idola*, we are apt to remember when our dreams come true, and to forget when they do not. Suppose we take up the notion that a new moon on a Saturday is invariably followed by twenty days of unsettled weather, one or two or a few cases in which this notably holds good are apt to be borne in mind, while cases where the weather is neither conspicuously good nor bad are apt to be overlooked. But when a warning has been given against this besetting fallacy, Logic has nothing further to say about empirical uniformities, except that we may infer from them with some degree of reasonable probability, and that if we want ground for a more certain inference we should try to explain them.

Chapter II

ASCERTAINMENT OF SIMPLE FACTS IN THEIR ORDER.
—PERSONAL OBSERVATION.—HEARSAY EVIDENCE
—METHOD OF TESTING TRADITIONAL EVIDENCE.

ALL beliefs as to simple matter of fact must rest ultimately on observation. But, of course, we believe many things to have happened that we have never seen. As Chaucer says :—

> But God forbedë but men shouldë 'lieve
> Wel morë thing than men han seen with eye.
> Man shall not weenen everything a lie
> But if himself it seeth or elsë doth.

For the great bulk of matters of fact that we believe we are necessarily dependent on the observations of others. And if we are to apply scientific method to the ascertainment of this, we must know what errors we are liable to in our recollections of what we have ourselves witnessed, and what errors are apt to arise in the tradition of what purports to be the evidence of eye-witnesses.

I.—PERSONAL OBSERVATION.

It is hard to convince anybody that he cannot trust implicitly to his memory of what he has himself seen.

We are ready enough to believe that others may be deceived: but not our own senses.   Seeing is believing. It is well, however, that we should realise that all observation is fallible, even our own.

Three great besetting fallacies or tendencies to error may be specified :—

1. Liability to have the attention fastened on special incidents, and so diverted from other parts of the occurrence.

2. Liability to confuse and transpose the sequence of events.

3. Liability to substitute inference for fact.

It is upon the first of these weaknesses in man as an observing machine that jugglers chiefly depend on working their marvels.   Sleight of hand counts for much, but diverting the spectator's eyes for a good deal more.   That is why they have music played and patter incessantly as they operate.   Their patter is not purposeless : it is calculated to turn our eyes away from the movements of their nimble hands.

It must be borne in mind that in any field of vision there are many objects, and that in any rapid succession of incidents much more passes before the eyes than the memory can retain in its exact order.   It is of course in moments of excitement and hurry, when our observation is distracted, that we are most subject to fallacious illusions of memory.   Unconsciously we make a coherent picture of what we have seen, and very often it happens that the sequence of events is not what actually passed, but what we were prejudiced in favour of seeing.   Hence the unlikelihood of finding exact agreement among the witnesses of any exciting occurrence, a quarrel, a railway accident, a collision at sea, the incidents of a battle.

" It commonly happens," says Mr. Kinglake,[1] " that incidents occurring in a battle are told by the most truthful bystanders with differences more or less wide." In the attack on the Great Redoubt in the Battle of the Alma, a young officer, Anstruther, rushed forward and planted the colours of the Royal Welsh—but where ? Some distinctly remembered seeing him dig the butt-end of the flagstaff into the parapet : others as distinctly remembered seeing him fall several paces before he reached it. Similarly with the incidents of the death of the Prince Imperial near the Italezi Hills in the Zulu War. He was out as a volunteer with a reconnoitring party. They had off-saddled at a kraal and were resting, when a band of Zulus crept up through the long grass, and suddenly opened fire and made a rush forward. Our scouts at once took horse, as a recon-noitring party was bound to do, and scampered off, but the Prince was overtaken and killed. At the Court-Martial which ensued, the five troopers gave the most conflicting accounts of particulars which an unskilled investigator would think could not possibly have been mistaken by eye-witnesses of the same event. One said that the Prince had given the order to mount before the Zulus fired : another that he gave the order directly after : a third was positive that he never gave the order at all, but that it was given after the surprise by the officer in command. One said that he saw the Prince vault into the saddle as he gave the order : another that his horse bolted as he laid hold of the saddle, and that he ran alongside trying to get up.

The evidence before any Court of Inquiry into an exciting occurrence is almost certain to reveal similar

---

[1] *The Invasion of the Crimea*, iii. 124.

discrepancies.   But what we find it hard to realise is
that we ourselves can possibly be mistaken in what
we have a distinct and positive recollection of having
seen.   It once happened to myself in a London street
to see a drunken woman thrown under a cab by her
husband.   Two cabs were running along, a four-
wheeler and a hansom : the woman staggered almost
under the first, and was thrown under the second.   As
it happened the case never got beyond the police
station to which the parties were conveyed after
fierce opposition from some neighbours, who sympa-
thised entirely with the man.   The woman herself,
when her wounds were dressed, acknowledged the
justice of her punishment, and refused to charge her
husband.   I was all the more willing to acquiesce in
this because I found that while I had the most distinct
impression of having seen the four-wheeler run over the
woman's body, and should have been obliged to swear
accordingly, there could be no doubt that it was really
the hansom that had done so.   This was not only the
evidence of the neighbours, which I suspected at the time
of being a trick, but of the cabdriver, who had stopped
at the moment to abide the results of the accident.   I
afterwards had the curiosity to ask an eminent police
magistrate, Sir John Bridge, whether this illusion of
memory on my part —which I can only account for by
supposing that my eyes had been fixed on the sufferer
and that I had unconsciously referred her injuries to
the heavier vehicle — would have entirely discredited
my testimony in his Court.   His answer was that it
would not ; that he was constantly meeting with such
errors, and that if he found a number of witnesses of
the same occurrence exactly agreed in every particular,
he would suspect that they had talked the matter over

and agreed upon what they were to say. This was the opinion of an experienced judge, a skilled critic of the defects of personal observation. An Old Bailey counsel for the defence, who is equally acquainted with the weakness of human memory, takes advantage of the fact that it is not generally understood by a Jury, and makes the fallacious assumption that glaring discrepancies are irreconcilable with the good faith of the witnesses who differ.[1]

II.—TRADITION.—HEARSAY EVIDENCE.

Next in value to personal observation, we must place the report, oral or written, of an eye-witness. This is the best evidence we can get if we have not witnessed an occurrence ourselves. Yet Courts of Law, which in consideration of the defects of personal observation require more than one witness to establish the truth, exclude hearsay evidence altogether in certain cases, and not without reason.

---

[1] The truth is, that we see much less than is commonly supposed. Not every impression is attended to that is made on the retina, and unless we do attend we cannot, properly speaking, be said to see. Walking across to college one day, I was startled by seeing on the face of a clock in my way that it was ten minutes to twelve, whereas I generally passed that spot about twenty minutes to twelve. I hurried on, fearing to be late, and on my arrival found myself in very good time. On my way back, passing the clock again, I looked up to see how much it was fast. It marked ten minutes to eight. It had stopped at that time. When I passed before I had really seen only the minute hand. The whole dial must have been on my retina, but I had looked at or attended to only what I was in doubt about, taking the hour for granted. I am bound to add that my business friends hint that it is only absorbed students that are capable of such mistakes, and that alert men of business are more circumspect. That can only be because they are more alive to the danger of error.

In hearing a report we are in the position of observers of a series of significant sounds, and we are subject to all the fallacies of observation already mentioned.   In an aggravated degree, for words are harder to observe than visible things.   Our attention is apt to be more listless than in presence of the actual events.   Our minds dwell upon parts of the narrative to the neglect of other parts, and in the coherent story or description that we retain in our memories, sequences are apt to be altered and missing links supplied in accordance with what we were predisposed to hear.   Thus hearsay evidence is subject to all the imperfections of the original observer, in addition to the still more insidious imperfections of the second observer.

How quickly in the course of a few such transmissions hearsay loses all evidentiary value is simply illustrated by the game known as Russian Scandal.   One of a company, A, writes down a short tale or sketch, and reads it to B.   B repeats it to C, C to D, and so on. When it has thus gone the round of the company, the last hearer writes down his version, and it is compared with the original.   With every willingness to play fair, the changes are generally considerable and significant.

Sometimes it is possible to compare an oral tradition with a contemporary written record.   In one of Mr. Hayward's Essays—"The Pearls and Mock Pearls of History"—there are some examples of this disenchanting process.   There is, for instance, a pretty story of an exchange of courtesies between the leaders of the French and English Guards at the battle of Fontenoy. The tradition runs that Lord Charles Hay stepped in front of his men and invited the French Guards to fire, to which M. d'Auteroche with no less chivalry responded : " Monsieur, we never fire first ;

you fire ". What really passed we learn from a letter from Lord Charles Hay to his mother, which happens to have been preserved. " I advanced before our regiment, and drank to the Frenchmen, and told them we were the English Guards, and hoped they would stand till we came, and not swim the Scheldt as they did the Maine at Dettingen." Tradition has changed this lively piece of buffoonery into an act of stately and romantic courtesy. The change was probably made quite unconsciously by some tenth or hundredth transmitter, who remembered only part of the story, and dressed the remainder to suit his own fancy.

The question has been raised, For how long can oral tradition be trusted? Newton was of opinion that it might be trusted for eighty years after the event. Others have named forty years. But if this means that we may believe a story that we find in circulation forty years after the alleged events, it is wildly extravagant. It does injustice to the Mythopœic Faculty of man. The period of time that suffices for the creation of a full-blown myth, must be measured by hours rather than by years. I will give an instance from my own observation, if that has not been entirely discredited by my previous confessions. The bazaars of the East are generally supposed to be the peculiar home of myth, hotbeds in which myths grow with the most amazing speed, but the locality of my myth is Aberdeen. In the summer of 1887 our town set up in one of its steeples a very fine carillon of Belgian bells. There was much public excitement over the event: the descriptions of enthusiastic promoters had prepared us to hear silvery music floating all over the town and filling the whole air. On the day fixed for the inauguration, four hours after the time announced for the first ceremonial peal, not having heard the bells, I was in a shop and asked if anything had happened to put off the ceremony. "Yes," I was told; "there had been an accident; they had not been properly hung, and when the wife of the Lord Provost had taken hold of a string to give the first pull, the whole machinery had come down." As a matter of fact all that had happened was that the sound of the bells was faint, barely audible a hundred yards from the belfry, and not at all like what had been expected. There were hundreds of people in the streets, and the myth had originated somehow among those who had not heard what they went out to hear. The shop where it was repeated circumstantially to me was in the main street, not more than a quarter of a mile from where the carillon had been played in the hearing of a large but disappointed crowd. I could not help reflecting that if I had been a mediæval chronicler, I should have gone home and recorded the story, which continued to circulate for some days in spite of the newspapers: and two hundred years hence no historian would have ventured to challenge the truth of the contemporary evidence.

III.—Method of Testing Traditional Evidence.

It is obvious that the tests applied to descriptive testimony in Courts of Law cannot be applied to the assertions of History. It is a supreme canon of historical evidence that only the statements of contemporaries can be admitted: but most even of their statements must rest on hearsay, and even when the historian professes to have been an eye-witness, the range of his observation is necessarily limited, and he cannot be put into the witness-box and cross-examined. Is there then no way of ascertaining historical fact? Must we reject history as altogether unworthy of credit?

The rational conclusion only is that very few facts can be established by descriptive testimony such as would satisfy a Court of Law. Those who look for such ascertainment are on a wrong track, and are doomed to disappointment. It is told of Sir Walter Raleigh that when he was writing his History of the World, he heard from his prison in the Tower a quarrel outside, tried to find out the rights and the wrongs and the course of it, and failing to satisfy himself after careful inquiry, asked in despair how he could pretend to write the history of the world when he could not find out the truth about what occurred under his own windows. But this was really to set up an impossible standard of historical evidence.

The method of testing historical evidence follows rather the lines of the Newtonian method of Explanation, which we shall afterwards describe. We must treat any historical record as being itself in the first place a fact to be explained. The statement at least is extant: our first question is, What is the most rational way of accounting for it? Can it be accounted for most probably by supposing the event stated to have really occurred with all the circumstances alleged? Or is it a more probable hypothesis that it was the result of an illusion of memory on the part of the original observer, if it professes to be the record of an eye-witness, or on the part of some intermediate trans-mitter, if it is the record of a tradition? To qualify ourselves to answer the latter kind of question with reasonable probability we must acquaint ourselves with the various tendencies to error in personal observation and in tradition, and examine how far any of them are likely to have operated in the given case. We must study the operation of these tendencies within our experience, and apply the knowledge thus gained. We must learn from actual observation of facts what the Mythopœic Faculty is capable of in the way of creation and transmutation, and what feats are beyond its powers, and then determine with as near a probability as we can how far it has been active in the particular case before us.

Chapter III.

ASCERTAINMENT OF FACTS OF CAUSATION.

I.—*Post Hoc ergo Propter Hoc.*

ONE of the chief contributions of the Old Logic to Inductive Method was a name for a whole important class of misobservations. The fallacy entitled *Post Hoc ergo Propter Hoc*—"After, therefore, Because of"—consisted in alleging mere sequence as a proof of consequence or causal sequence. The sophist appeals to experience, to observed facts : the sequence which he alleges has been observed. But the appeal is fallacious : the observation on which he relies amounts only to this, that the one event has followed upon the other. This much must be observable in all cases of causal sequence, but it is not enough for proof. *Post hoc ergo propter hoc* may be taken as a generic name for imperfect proof of causation from observed facts of succession.

The standard example of the fallacy is the old Kentish peasant's argument that Tenterden Steeple was the cause of Goodwin Sands. Sir Thomas More (as Latimer tells the story in one of his Sermons to ridicule incautious inference) had been sent down into Kent as a commissioner to inquire into the cause of the silting up of Sandwich Haven. Among those who came to his court was the oldest inhabitant, and thinking that he from his great age must at least have seen more than anybody else, More asked him what he had to say as to the cause of the sands. " Forsooth, sir," was the greybeard's answer, " I am an old man : I think that Tenterden Steeple is the cause of Goodwin Sands. For I am an old man, and I may remember the building of Tenterden Steeple, and I may remember when there was no steeple at all there. And before that Tenterden Steeple was in building, there was no manner of speaking of any flats or sands that stopped the haven ; and, therefore, I think that Tenterden Steeple is the cause of the destroying and decaying of Sandwich Haven."

This must be taken as Latimer meant it to be, a ridiculous example of a purely imbecile argument from observation, but the appeal to experience may have more show of reason and yet be equally fallacious. The believers in Kenelm Digby's " Ointment of Honour" appealed to experience in support of its efficacy. The treatment was to apply the ointment, not to the wound, but to the sword that had inflicted it, to dress this carefully at regular intervals, and, meantime, having bound up the wound, to leave it alone for seven days. It was observed that many cures followed upon this treatment. But those who inferred that the cure was due to the bandaging of the sword, failed to observe that there was another circumstance that might have been instrumental, namely, the exclusion of the air and the leaving of the wound undisturbed while the natural healing processes went on. And it was found upon further observation that binding up the wound alone answered the purpose equally well whether the sword was dressed or not.

In cases where *post hoc* is mistaken for *propter hoc,*

simple sequence for causal sequence, there is commonly some bias of prejudice or custom which fixes
observation on some one antecedent and diverts
attention from other circumstances and from what
may be observed to follow in other cases. In the
minds of Digby and his followers there was probably
a veneration for the sword as the weapon of honour,
and a superstitious belief in some secret sympathy
between the sword and its owner. So when the
practice of poisoning was common, and suspicion was
flurried by panic fear, observation was often at fault.
Pope Clement VIII. was said to have been killed by
the fumes of a poisoned candle which was placed in
his bedroom. Undoubtedly candles were there, but
those who attributed the Pope's death to them took no
notice of the fact that a brazier of burning charcoal was
at the same time in the apartment with no sufficient
outlet for its fumes. Prince Eugene is said to have
received a poisoned letter, which he suspected and immediately threw from him. To ascertain whether his
suspicions were well founded the letter was administered
to a dog, which, to make assurance doubly sure, was
fortified by an antidote. The dog died, but no inquiry
seems to have been made into the character of the
antidote.

Hotspur's retort to Glendower showed a sound sense
of the true value to be attached to mere priority.

Glendower. At my nativity
The front of heaven was full of fiery shapes,
Of burning cressets: and at my birth
The frame and huge foundation of the earth
Shaked like a coward.
Hotspur. Why so it would have done at the same season, if
your mother's cat had but kittened, though yourself had never
been born. 1 Hen. IV., 3, 1, 13.

We all admit at once that the retort was just. What principle of sound conclusion was involved in it ?   It is the business of Inductive Logic to make such principles explicit.

Taking *Post Hoc ergo Propter Hoc* as a generic name for fallacious arguments of causation based on observed facts, for the fallacious proof of causation from experience, the question for Logic is, What more than mere *sequence* is required to prove *consequence ?* When do observations of *Post Hoc* warrant the conclusion *Propter Hoc ?*

II.—Meaning of "Cause".—Methods of Observation.—Mill's Experimental Methods.

The methods formulated by Mill under the name of Experimental Methods are methods actually practised by men of science with satisfactory results, and are perfectly sound in principle.   They were, indeed, in substance, taken by him from the practice of the scientific laboratory and study as generalised by Herschel.   In effect what Mill did was to restate them and fit them into a system.   But the controversies into which he was tempted in so doing have somewhat obscured their exact function in scientific inquiry. Hostile critics, finding that they did not serve the ends that he seemed to claim for them, have jumped to the conclusion that they are altogether illusory and serve no purpose at all.

First, we must dismiss the notion, encouraged by Mill's general theory of Inference, that the Experimental Methods have anything special to do with the observation and inferential extension of uniformities such as that death is common to all organised beings.

One of the Methods, as we shall see, that named by Mill the Method of Agreement, does incidentally and collaterally establish empirical laws in the course of its observations, and this probably accounts for the prominence given to it in Mill's system.   But this is not its end and aim, and the leading Method, that named by him the Method of Difference, establishes as fact only a particular case of causal coincidence. It is with the proof of theories of causation that the Experimental Methods are concerned :   they are methods of observing with a view to such proof.[1]

The next point to be made clear is that the facts of causation with which the Methods are concerned are observable facts, relations among phenomena, but that the causal relations or conditions of which they are the proof are not phenomena, in the meaning of being manifest to the senses, but rather noumena, inasmuch as they are reached by reasoning from what is manifest.

Take, for example, what is known as the *quaquaversus* principle in Hydrostatics, that pressure upon a liquid is propagated equally in all directions.   We cannot observe this extension of pressure among the liquid particles directly.   It cannot be traced among the particles by any of our senses.   But we can assume that it is so, consider what ought to be visible if it is so, and then observe whether the visible facts are in accordance with the hypothesis.   A box can be made, filled with water, and so fitted with pistons on top and bottom and on each of its four sides that they will

---

[1] This is implied, as I have already remarked, in the word Experimental.   An experiment is a proof or trial : of what ?   Of a theory, a conjecture.

indicate the amount of pressure on them from within. Let pressure then be applied through a hole in the top, and the pistons show that it has been communicated to them equally. The application of the pressure and the yielding of the pistons are observable facts, facts in causal sequence : what happens among the particles of the liquid is not observed but reasonably conjectured, is not *phenomenal* but *noumenal*.

This distinction, necessary to an understanding of the scope of the Methods, was somewhat obscured by Mill in his preliminary discussion of the meaning of "cause". Very rightly, though somewhat inconsistently with his first theory of Induction, he insists that " the notion of Cause being the root of the whole theory of Induction, it is indispensable that this idea should at the very outset of our inquiry be, with the utmost practicable degree of precision, fixed and determined ". But in this determination, not content with simply recognising that it is with phenomena that the Experimental Methods primarily deal, it being indeed only phenomena that can be the subjects of experi ital management and observation, he starts by declaring that science has not to do with any causes except such as are phenomenal--" when I speak of the cause of any phenomenon, I do not mean a cause which is not itself a phenomenon "—and goes on to define as the only correct meaning of cause "the sum total of conditions," including among them conditions which are not phenomenal, in the sense of being directly open to observation.

When Mill protested that he had regard only to phenomenal causes, he spoke as the partisan of a philosophical tradition. It would have been well if he had acted upon his own remark that the proper understanding of the scientific method of investigating cause is independent of metaphysical analysis of what cause means. Curiously enough, this remark is the preface to an analysis of cause which has but slight relevance to science, and is really the continuation of a dispute begun by Hume. This is the key to his use of the word phenomenon : it must be interpreted with reference to this : when he spoke of causes as phenomenal, he opposed the word to " occult " in some supposed metaphysical sense.[1] And this irrelevant discussion, into the vortex of which he allowed himself to be carried, obscured the fact, elsewhere fully recognised by Mill himself, that science does attempt to get beyond phenomena at ultimate laws which are not themselves phenomena though they bind phenomena together. The " colligation " of the facts, to use Whewell's phrase, is not a phenomenon, but a noumenon.

The truth is that a very simple analysis of " cause " is sufficient for the purposes of scientific inquiry. It is enough to make sure that causal sequence or conse-quence shall not be confounded with simple sequence. Causal sequence is simple sequence and something more, that something more being expressed by calling it causal. What we call a cause is not merely antecedent or prior in time to what we call its effect : it is so related to the effect that if it or an equivalent event had not happened the effect would not have happened. Anything in the absence of which a

---

[1] If we remember, as becomes apparent on exact psychological analysis, that things and their qualities are as much *noumena* and not, strictly speaking, *phenomena* as the attraction of gravity or the quaquaversus principle in liquid pressure, the prejudice against occultism is mitigated.

phenomenon would not have come to pass as it did come to pass is a cause in the ordinary sense. We may describe it as an indispensable antecedent, with this reservation (which will be more fully understood afterwards), that if we speak of a general effect, such as death, the antecedents must be taken with corresponding generality.

It is misleading to suggest, as Mill does, by defining cause as " the sum total of conditions "—a definition given to back up his conception of cause as phenomenal —that science uses the word cause in a different meaning from that of ordinary speech. It is quite true that " the cause, philosophically speaking, is the sum total of the conditions, positive and negative, taken together: the whole of the contingencies of every description, which being realised, the consequent invariably follows ". But this does not imply any discrepancy between the scientific or philosophical meaning and the ordinary meaning. It is only another way of saying that the business of science or philosophy is to furnish a complete explanation of an event, an account of all its indispensable antecedents. The plain man would not refuse the name of cause to anything that science or philosophy could prove to be an indispensable antecedent, but his interest in explanation is more limited. It is confined to what he wants to know for the purpose he has in hand. Nor could the man of science consistently refuse the name of cause to what the plain man applies it to, if it really was something in consequence of which the event took place. Only his interest in explanation is different. The indispensable antecedents that he wants to know may not be the same. Science or philosophy applies itself to the satisfaction of a wider curiosity : it wants to know all the causes, the whole why, the sum total of conditions. To that end the various departments of science interest themselves in various species of conditions. But all understand the word cause in the ordinary sense.

We must not conclude from accidental differences in explanation or statement of cause, dependent on the purpose in view, that the word Cause is used in different senses. In answering a question as to the cause of anything, we limit ourselves to what we suppose our interrogator to be ignorant of and desirous of knowing. If asked why the bells are ringing, we mention a royal marriage, or a victory, or a church meeting, or a factory dinner hour, or whatever the occasion may be. We do not consider it necessary to mention that the bells are struck by a clapper. Our hearer understands this without our mentioning it. Nor do we consider it necessary to mention the acoustic condition, that the vibration of the bells is communicated to our ears through the air, or the physiological condition, that the vibrations in the drums of our ears are conveyed by a certain mechanism of bone and tissue to the nerves. Our hearer may not care to know this, though quite prepared to admit that these conditions are indispensable antecedents. Similarly, a physiographer, in stating the cause of the periodical inundation of the Nile, would consider it enough to mention the melting of snow on the mountains in the interior of Africa, without saying anything of such conditions as the laws of gravity or the laws of liquefaction by heat, though he knows that these conditions are also indispensable. Death is explained by the doctor when referred to a gunshot wound, or a poison, or a virulent disease. The Pathologist may inquire further, and the Moral Philosopher further still. But all inquiries into indispensable conditions are inquiries into cause. And all alike have to be on their guard against mistaking simple sequence for consequence.

To speak of the sum total of conditions, as the Cause in a distinctively scientific sense, is misleading in another direction. It rather encourages the idea that science investigates conditions in the lump, merely observing the visible relations between sets of antecedents and their consequents. Now this is the very thing that science must avoid in order to make progress. It analyses the antecedent situation, tries to separate the various coefficients, and finds out what they are capable of singly. It must recognise that some of the antecedents of which it is in search are not open to observation. It is these, indeed, for the most part that constitute the special subject-matter of the sciences in Molar as well as in Molecular Physics. For practical every-day purposes, it is chiefly the visible succession of phenomena that concerns us, and we are interested in the latent conditions only in as far as they provide safer ground for inference regarding such visible succession. But to reach the latent conditions is the main work of science.

It is, however, only through observation of what is open to the senses that science can reach the underlying conditions, and, therefore, to understand its methods we must consider generally what is open to observation in causal succession. What can be observed when phenomena follow one another as cause and effect, that is, when the one happens in consequence of the happening of the other? In Hume's theory, which Mill formally adopted with a modification,[1] there is nothing observable but the constancy or invariability of the connexion. When we say that Fire burns, there is nothing to be observed except that a certain sensation invariably follows upon close proximity to fire. But this holds good only if our observation is arbitrarily limited to the facts enounced in the expression. If this theory were sound, science would be confined to the observation of empirical laws. But that there is something wrong with it becomes apparent when we reflect that it has been ascertained beyond doubt that in many observed changes, and presumably in all, there is a transference of energy from one form to another. The paralogism really lies in the assumption from which Hume deduced his theory, namely, that every idea is a copy of some impression. As a matter of fact, we have ideas that are not copies of any one impression, but a binding together, colligation, or intellection of several impressions. Psychological analysis shows us that even when we say that things exist with certain qualities, we are expressing not single impressions or mental phenomena, but supposed causes and conditions of such, *noumena* in short, which connect our recollections of many separate impressions and expectations of more.

The Experimental Methods proceed on the assumption that there is other outward and visible evidence

[1] The modification was that causation is not only "invariable" but also "unconditional" sequence. This addition of unconditionality as part of the meaning of cause, after defining cause as the sum total of the conditions, is very much like arguing in a circle. After all, the only point recognised in the theory as observable is the invariability of the sequence. But this is less important than the fact that in his canons of the Experimental Methods Mill recognised that more is observable.

of causal connexion than invariability of sequence.   In the leading Method it is assumed that when events may be observed to follow one another in a certain way, they are in causal sequence.   If we can make sure that an antecedent change is the only change that has occurred in an antecedent situation, we have proof positive that any immediately subsequent change in the situation is a consequent, that the successive changes are in causal sequence.   Thus when Pascal's barometer was carried to the top of Puy le Dome, and the mercury in it fell, the experimenters argued that the fall of the mercury was causally connected with the change of elevation, all the other circumstances remaining the same.   This is the foundation of the so-called Method of Difference.   To determine that the latent condition was a difference in the weight of the atmosphere, needed other observations, calculations and inferences ; but if it could be shown that the elevation was the only antecedent changed in a single instance, causal connexion was established between this and the phenomenon of the fall of the barometer.

It is obvious that in coming to this conclusion we assume what cannot be demonstrated but must simply be taken as a working principle to be confirmed by its accordance with experience, that nothing comes into being without some change in the antecedent circumstances.   This is the assumption known as the Law of Causation—*ex nihilo nihil fit.*

Again, certain observable facts are taken as evidence that there is no causal connexion.   On the assumption that any antecedent in whose absence a phenomenon takes place is not causally connected with it, we set aside or eliminate various antecedents as fortuitous or non-causal.   This negative principle, as we shall see,

is the foundation of what Mill called the Method of
Agreement.

Be it remarked, once for all, that before coming to
a conclusion on the Positive Method or Method of
Difference, we may often have to make many observations on the Negative Method. Thus Pascal's experimenters, before concluding that the change of altitude
was the only influential change, tried the barometer in
exposed positions and in sheltered, when the wind
blew and when it was calm, in rain and in fog, in
order to prove that these circumstances were indifferent.
We must expound and illustrate the methods separately, but every method known to science may have
in practice to be employed in arriving at a single
conclusion.

Chapter IV.

METHODS OF OBSERVATION.—SINGLE DIFFERENCE.

I.—The Principle of Single Difference.— Mill's " Canon ".

On what principle do we decide, in watching a succession of phenomena, that they are connected as cause and effect, that one happened in consequence of the happening of another?   It may be worded as follows :—

> *When the addition of an agent is followed by the appearance or its subtraction by the disappearance of a certain effect, no other influential circumstance having been added or subtracted at the same time or in the meantime, and no change having occurred among the original circumstances, that agent is a cause of the effect.*

On this principle we would justify our belief in the causal properties of common things—that fire burns, that food appeases hunger, that water quenches thirst, that a spark ignites gunpowder, that taking off a tight shoe relieves a pinched foot. We have observed the effect following when there was no other change in the antecedent circumstances, when the circumstance to which we refer it was simply added to or subtracted from the prior situation.

Suppose we doubt whether a given agent is or is not capable of producing a certain effect in certain circumstances, how do we put it to the proof? We add it singly or subtract it singly, taking care that everything else remains as before, and watch the result. If we wish to know whether a spoonful of sugar can sweeten a cup of tea, we taste the tea without the sugar, then add the sugar, and taste again. The isolated introduction of the agent is the proof, the experiment. If we wish to know whether a pain in the foot is due to a tight lacing, we relax the lacing and make no other change : if the pain then disappears, we refer it to the lacing as the cause. The proof is the disappearance of the pain on the subtraction of the single antecedent.

The principle on which we decide that there is causal connexion is the same whether we make the experimental changes ourselves or merely watch them as they occur—the only course open to us with the great forces of nature which are beyond the power of human manipulation. In any case we have proof of causation when we can make sure that there was only one difference in the antecedent circumstances corresponding to the difference of result.

Mill's statement of this principle, which he calls the Canon of the Method of Difference, is somewhat more abstract, but the proof relied upon is substantially the same.

If an instance in which the phenomenon under investigation occurs, and an instance in which it does not occur, have every circumstance in common save one, that one occurring only in the former, the circumstance in which alone the two instances differ is [the effect, or] [1] *the cause, or an indispensable part of the cause, of the phenomenon.*

Mill's statement has the merit of exactness, but besides being too abstract to be easy of application, the canon is apt to mislead in one respect. The wording of it suggests that the two instances required must be two separate sets of circumstances, such as may be put side by side and compared, one exhibiting the phenomenon and the other not. Now in practice it is commonly one set of circumstances that we observe with a special circumstance introduced or withdrawn : the two instances, the data of observation, are furnished by the scene before and the scene after the experimental interference. In the case, for example, of a man shot in the head and falling dead, death being the phenomenon in question, the instance where it does not occur is the man's condition before he received the wound, and the instance where it does occur is his condition after, the single circumstance of difference being the wound, a difference produced by the addition or introduction of a new circumstance. Again, take the common coin and feather experiment, contrived to show that the resistance of the air is the cause of the

---

[1] Prof. Bain, who adopts Mill's Canon, silently drops the words within brackets. They seem to be an inadvertence. The "circumstance," in all the examples that Mill gives, is an antecedent circumstance. Herschel's statement, of which Mill's is an adaptation, runs as follows: "If we can either find produced by nature, or produce designedly for ourselves, two instances which agree exactly in all but one particular and differ in that one, its influence in producing the phenomenon, if it have any, must thereby be rendered apparent ".

feather's falling to the ground more slowly than the coin. The phenomenon under investigation is the retardation of the feather. When the two are dropped simultaneously in the receiver of an air-pump, the air being left in, the feather flutters to the ground after the coin. This is the instance where the phenomenon occurs. Then the air is pumped out of the receiver, and the coin and the feather being dropped at the same instant reach the ground together. This is the instance where the phenomenon does not occur. The single circumstance of difference is the presence of air in the former instance, a difference produced by the subtraction of a circumstance.

Mill's Canon is framed so as to suit equally whether the significant difference is produced by addition to or subtraction from an existing sum of circumstances. But that it is misleading in so far as it suggests that the two instances must be separate sets of circumstances, is shown by the fact that it misled himself when he spoke of the application of the method in social investigations, such as the effect of Protection on national wealth. " In order," he says, "to apply to the case the most perfect of the methods of experimental inquiry, the Method of Difference, we require to find two instances which tally in every particular except the one which is the subject of inquiry. We must have two nations alike in all natural advantages and disadvantages; resembling each other in every quality physical and moral; habits, usages, laws, and institutions, and differing only in the circumstance that the one has a prohibitory tariff and the other has not." It being impossible ever to find two such instances, he concluded that the Method of Difference could not be applied in social inquiries. But really it is not necessary in order to have two instances that we should have two different nations: the same nation before and after a new law or institution fulfils that requirement. The real difficulty, as we shall see, is to satisfy the paramount condition that the two instances shall differ in a single circumstance. Every new enactment would be an experiment after the Method of Difference, if all circumstances but it remained the same till its results appeared. It is because this seldom or never occurs that decisive observation is difficult or impossible, and the simple method of difference has to be supplemented by other means.

To introduce or remove a circumstance singly is the typical application of the principle; but it may be employed also to compare the effects of different agents, each added alone to exactly similar circumstances. A simple example is seen in Mr. Jamieson's agricultural experiments to determine the effects of different manures, such as coprolite and superphosphate, on the growth of crops. Care is taken to have all the antecedent circumstances as exactly alike as possible, except as regards the agency whose effects are to be observed. A field is chosen of uniform soil and even exposure and divided into plots: it is equally drained so as to have the same degree of moisture throughout; the seed is carefully selected for the whole sowing. Between the sowing and the maturing of the crop all parts of the field are open to the same weather. Each plot may thus be regarded as practically composing the same set of conditions, and any difference in the product may with reasonable probability be ascribed to the single difference in the antecedents, the manures which it is desired to compare.

II.—APPLICATION OF THE PRINCIPLE.

The principle of referring a phenomenon to the only immediately preceding change in antecedent circumstances that could possibly have affected it, is so simple and so often employed by everybody every day, that at first we do not see how there can be any difficulty about it or any possibility of error. And once we understand how many difficulties there are in reaching exact knowledge even on this simple principle, and what care has to be taken, we are apt to overrate its value, and to imagine that it carries us further than it really does. The scientific expert must know how to apply this principle, and a single application of it with the proper precautions may take him days or weeks, and yet all that can be made good by it may carry but a little way towards the knowledge of which he is in search.

When the circumstances are simple and the effect follows at once, as when hot water scalds, or a blow with a stick breaks a pane of glass, there can be no doubt of the causal connexion so far, though plenty of room for further inquiry into the why. But the mere succession of phenomena may be obscure. We may introduce more than one agent without knowing it, and if some time elapses between the experimental interference and the appearance of the effect, other agents may come in without our knowledge.

We must know exactly what it is that we introduce and all the circumstances into which we introduce it. We are apt to ignore the presence of antecedents that are really influential in the result. A man heated by work in the harvest field hastily swallows a glass of water, and drops down dead. There is no doubt that the drinking of the water was a causal antecedent, but the influential circumstance may not have been the quantity or the quality of the liquid but its temperature, and this was introduced into the situation as well as a certain amount of the liquid components. In making tea we put in so much tea and so much boiling water. But the temperature of the pot is also an influential circumstance in the resulting infusion. So in chemical experiments, where one might expect the result to depend only upon the proportions of the ingredients, it is found that the quantity is also influential, the degree of heat evolved entering as a factor into the result. Before we can apply the principle of single difference, we must make sure that there is really only a single difference between the instances that we bring into comparison.

The air-pump was invented shortly before the foundation of the Royal Society, and its members made many experiments with this new means of isolating an agent and thus discovering its potentialities. For example, live animals were put into the receiver, and the air exhausted, with the result that they quickly died. The absence of the air being the sole difference, it was thus proved to be indispensable to life. But air is a composite agent, and when means were contrived of separating its components, the effects of oxygen alone and of carbonic acid alone were experimentally determined.

A good example of the difficulty of excluding agencies other than those we are observing, of making sure that none such intrude, is found in the experiments that have been made in connexion with spontaneous generation. The question to be decided is whether life ever comes into existence without the antecedent presence of living germs. And the method of determining this is to exclude all germs rigorously from a compound of inorganic matter, and observe whether life ever appears. If we could make sure in any one case that no germs were antecedently present, we should have proved that in that case at least life was spontaneously generated. ·

The difficulty here arises from the subtlety of the agent under observation. The notion that maggots are spontaneously generated in putrid meat, was comparatively easy to explode. It was found that when flies were excluded by fine wire-gauze, the maggots did not appear. But in the case of microscopic organisms proof is not so easy. The germs are invisible, and it is difficult to make certain of their exclusion. A French experimenter, Pouchet, thought he had obtained indubitable cases of spontaneous generation. He took infusions of vegetable matter, boiled them to a pitch sufficient to destroy all germs of life, and hermetically sealed up the liquid in glass flasks. After an interval, micro-organisms appeared. Doubts as to the conclusion that they had been spontaneously generated turned upon two questions : whether all germs in the liquid had been destroyed by the preliminary boiling, and whether germs could have found access in the course of the interval before life appeared. At a certain stage in Pouchet's process he had occasion to dip the mouths of the flasks in mercury. It occurred to Pasteur in repeating the experiments that germs might have found their way in from the atmospheric dust on the surface of this mercury. That this was so was rendered probable by his finding that when he carefully cleansed the surface of the mercury no life appeared afterwards in his flasks.

The application of the principle in human affairs is rendered uncertain by the immense complication of the phenomena, the difficulty of experiment, and the special liability of our judgments to prejudice. That men and communities of men are influenced by circumstances is not to be denied, and the influence of circumstances, if it is to be traced at all, must be traced through observed facts. Observation of the succession of phenomena must be part at least of any method of tracing cause and effect. We must watch what follows upon the addition of new agencies to a previously existing sum. But we can seldom or never get a decisive observation from one pair of instances, a clear case of difference of result preceded by a single difference in the antecedents. The simple Method of Experimental Addition or Subtraction is practically inapplicable. We can do nothing with a man analogous to putting him into a hermetically sealed retort. Any man or any community that is the subject of our observations must be under manifold influences. Each of them probably works some fraction of the total change observable, but how are they to be disentangled? Consider, for example, how impossible it would be to prove in an individual case, on the strict principle of Single Difference, that Evil communications corrupt good manners. Moral deterioration may be observed following upon the introduction of an evil companion, but how can we make sure that no other degrading influence has operated, and that no original depravity has developed itself in the interval? Yet such propositions of moral causation can be proved from experience with reasonable probability. Only it must be by more extended observations than the strict Method of Difference takes into account. The method is to observe repeated coincidences between evil companionship and moral deterioration, and to account for this in accordance with still wider observations of the interaction of human personalities.

For equally obvious reasons the simple Method of Difference is inapplicable to tracing cause and effect in communities. Every new law or repeal of an old law is the introduction of a new agency, but the effects of it are intermixed with the effects of other agencies that operate at the same time. Thus Professor Cairnes remarks, concerning the introduction of a high Protective Tariff into the United States in 1861, that before its results could appear in the trade and manufacture of the States, there occurred (1) The great Civil War, attended with enormous destruction of capital; (2) Consequent upon this the creation of a huge national debt, and a great increase of taxation; (3) The issue of an inconvertible paper currency, deranging prices and wages; (4) The discovery of great mineral resources and oil-springs; (5) A great extension of railway enterprise. Obviously in such circumstances other methods than the Method of Difference must be brought into play before there can be any satisfactory reasoning on the facts observed. Still what investigators aim at is the isolation of the results of single agencies.

CHAPTER V.

METHODS OF OBSERVATION.—ELIMINATION.—
SINGLE AGREEMENT.

I.—The Principle of Elimination.

The essence of what Mill calls the Method of Agreement is really the elimination[1] of accidental, casual, or fortuitous antecedents. It is a method employed when we are given an effect and set to work to discover the cause. It is from the effect that we start and work back. We make a preliminary analysis of the antecedents; call the roll, as it were, of all circumstances present before the effect appeared. Then we proceed to examine other instances of the same effect, and other instances of the occurrence of the various antecedents, and bring to bear the principle that any antecedent in the absence of which the effect has appeared or on the presence of which it has not appeared may be set aside as fortuitous, as being not

---

[1] Elimination, or setting aside as being of no concern, must not be confounded with the exclusion of agents practised in applying the Method of Difference. We use the word in its ordinary sense of putting outside the sphere of an argument. By a curious slip, Professor Bain follows Mill in applying the word sometimes to the process of singling out or disentangling a causal circumstance. This is an inadvertent departure from the ordinary usage, according to which elimination means discarding from consideration as being non-essential.

an indispensable antecedent. This is really the guiding principle of the method as a method of observation.

Let the inquiry, for example, be into the cause of Endemic Goitre. Instances of the disease have been collected from the medical observations of all countries over many years. Why is it endemic in some localities and not in others? We proceed on the assumption that the cause, whatever it is, must be some circumstance common to all localities where it is endemic. If any such circumstance is obvious at once, we may conclude on the mere principle of repeated coincidence that there is causal connexion between it and the disease, and continue our inquiry into the nature of the connexion. But if no such circumstance is obvious, then in the course of our search for it we eliminate, as fortuitous, conditions that are present in some cases but absent in others. One of the earliest theories was that endemic goitre was connected with the altitude and configuration of the ground, some notorious centres of it being deeply cleft mountain valleys, with little air and wind and damp marshy soil. But wider observation found it in many valleys neither narrower nor deeper than others that were exempt, and also in wide exposed valleys such as the Aar. Was it due to the geological formation? This also had to be abandoned, for the disease is often incident within very narrow limits, occurring in some villages and sparing others though the geological formation is absolutely the same. Was it due to the character of the drinking-water? Especially to the presence of lime or magnesia? This theory was held strongly, and certain springs characterised as goitre-springs. But the springs in some goitre centres show not a trace of magnesia. The comparative immunity of coast regions suggested that it might be owing to a deficiency of iodine in the drinking-water and the air, and many instances were adduced in favour of this. But further inquiries made out the presence of iodine in considerable quantities, in the air, the water, and the vegetation of districts where goitre was widely prevalent ; while in Cuba it is said that not a trace of iodine is discoverable either in the air or the water, and yet it is quite free from goitre. After a huge multiplication of instances, resulting in the elimination of every local condition that had been suggested as a possible cause, Hirsch came to the conclusion that the true cause must be a morbid poison, and that endemic goitre has to be reckoned among the infectious diseases.[1]

On this negative principle, that if a circumstance comes and goes without bringing the phenomenon in its train, the phenomenon is causally independent of it, common-sense is always at work disconnecting events that are occasionally coincident in time. A bird sings at our window, for example, and the clock ticks on the mantelpiece. But the clock does not begin to tick when the bird begins to sing, nor cease to tick when the bird flies away. Accordingly, if the clock should stop at any time, and we wished to inquire into the cause, and anybody were to suggest that the stoppage of the clock was caused by the stoppage of a bird's song outside, we should dismiss the suggestion at once. We should eliminate this circumstance from our inquiry, on the ground that from other observations we knew it to be a casual or fortuitous concomitant.

[1] Hirsch's *Geographical and Historical Pathology*, Creighton's translation, vol. ii. pp. 121-202.

Hotspur's retort to Glendover (p. 297) was based on this principle. When poetic sentiment or superstition rejects a verdict of common-sense or science, it is because it imagines a causal connexion to exist that is not open to observation, as in the case of the grandfather's clock which stopped short never to go again when the old man died.

II.—THE PRINCIPLE OF SINGLE AGREEMENT.

The procedure in Mill's "Method of Agreement" consists in thus eliminating fortuitous antecedents or concomitants till only one remains. We see the nature of the proof relied upon when we ask, How far must elimination be carried in order to attain proof of causal connexion? The answer is that we must go on till we have eliminated all but one. We must multiply instances of the phenomenon, till we have settled of each of the antecedents except one that it is not the cause. We must have taken account of all the antecedents, and we must have found in our observations that all but one have been only occasionally present.

> *When all the antecedents of an effect except one can be absent without the disappearance of the effect, that one is causally connected with the effect, due precautions being taken that no other circumstances have been present besides those taken account of.*

Mill's Canon of the Method of Agreement is substantially identical with this :—

> When two or more instances of the phenomenon under investigation have only one circumstance in common, the circumstance in which alone all the instances agree is the cause (or effect) of the given phenomenon.

Herschel's statement, on which this canon is founded, runs as follows: " Any circumstance in which all the facts without exception agree, may be the cause in question, or if not, at least a collateral effect of the same cause: if there be but one such point of agreement, the possibility becomes a certainty ".

All the instances examined must agree in one circumstance—hence the title Method of Agreement. But it is not in the agreement merely that the proof consists, but the agreement in one circumstance combined with difference in all the other circumstances, when we are certain that every circumstance has come within our observation. It is the singleness of the agreement that constitutes the proof just as it is the singleness of the difference in the Method of Difference.[1]

It has been said that Mill's Method of Agreement amounts after all only to an uncontradicted *Inductio per enumerationem simplicem*, which he himself stigmatised as Induction improperly so called. But this is not strictly correct. It is a misunderstanding probably caused by calling the method that of agreement simply, instead of calling it the Method of Single Agreement, so as to lay stress upon the process of elimination by which the singleness is established. It is true that in the course of our observations we do perform an induction by simple enumeration. In eliminating, we

---

[1] The bare titles Difference and Agreement, though they have the advantage of simplicity, are apt to puzzle beginners inasmuch as in the Method of Difference the agreement among the instances is at a maximum, and the difference at a minimum, and *vice versâ* in the Method of Agreement. In both Methods it is really the isolation of the connexion between antecedent and sequent that constitutes the proof.

at the same time generalise. That is to say, in multiplying instances for the elimination of non-causes, we necessarily at the same time multiply instances where the true causal antecedent, if there is only one possible, is present. An antecedent containing the true cause must always be there when the phenomenon appears, and thus we may establish by our eliminating observations a uniformity of connexion between two facts.

Take, for example, Roger Bacon's inquiry into the cause of the colours of the rainbow. His first notion seems to have been to connect the phenomenon with the substance crystal, probably from his thinking of the crystal firmament then supposed to encircle the universe. He found the rainbow colours produced by the passage of light through hexagonal crystals. But on extending his observations, he found that the passage of light through other transparent mediums was also attended by the phenomenon. He found it in dewdrops, in the spray of waterfalls, in drops shaken from the oar in rowing. He thus eliminated the substance crystal, and at the same time established the empirical law that the passage of light through transparent mediums of a globular or prismatic shape was a causal antecedent of the rainbow colours.[1]

Ascertainment of invariable antecedents may thus proceed side by side with that of variable antecedents, the use of the elimination being simply to narrow the scope of the inquiry. But the proof set forth in Mill's Canon does not depend merely on one antecedent or

---

[1] That rainbows in the sky are produced by the passage of light through minute drops in the clouds was an inference from this observed uniformity.

concomitant being invariably present, but also on the assumption that all the influential circumstances have been within our observation. Then only can we be sure that the instances have *only one* circumstance in common.

The truth is that owing to the difficulty of fulfilling this condition, proof of causation in accordance with Mill's Canon is practically all but impossible. It is not attained in any of the examples commonly given. The want of conclusiveness is disguised by the fact that both elimination and positive observation of mere agreement or uniform concomitance are useful and suggestive in the search for causes, though they do not amount to complete proof such as the Canon describes. Thus in the inquiry into the cause of goitre, the elimination serves some purpose though the result is purely negative. When the inquirer is satisfied that goitre is not originated by any directly observable local conditions, altitude, temperature, climate, soil, water, social circumstances, habits of exertion, his search is profitably limited. And mere frequency, much more constancy of concomitance, raises a presumption of causal connexion, and looking out for it is valuable as a-mode of reconnoitring. The first thing that an inquirer naturally asks when confronted by numerous instances of a phenomenon is, What have they in common ? And if he finds that they have some one circumstance invariably or even frequently present, although he cannot prove that they have no other circumstance in common as the Canon of Single Agreement requires, the presumption of causal connexion is strong enough to furnish good ground for further inquiry. If an inquirer finds an illness with marked symptoms in a number of different households, and finds also that all the households get their milk supply from the same source, this is not conclusive proof of causation, but it is a sufficient presumption to warrant him in examining whether there is any virulent ingredient in the milk.

Thus varying the circumstances so as to bring out a common antecedent, though it does not end in exact proof, may indicate causal connexion though it does not prove what the nature of the connexion is. Roger Bacon's observations indicated that the production of rainbow colours was connected with the passage of light through a transparent globe or prism. It was reserved for Newton to prove by other methods that white light was composed of rays, and that those rays were differently refracted in passing through the transparent medium. We have another example of how far mere agreement, revealed by varying the circumstances, carries us towards discovery of the cause, in Wells's investigation of the cause of dew. Comparing the numerous instances of dew appearing without visible fall of moisture, Wells found that they all agreed in the comparative coldness of the surface dewed. This was all the agreement that he established by observation; he did not carry observation to the point of determining that there was absolutely no other common circumstance : when he had simply discovered or detected that this circumstance was common to dewed surfaces, he tried next to show by reasoning from other known facts how the coldness of the surface affected the aqueous vapour of the neighbouring air. He did not establish his Theory of Dew by the Method of Agreement: but the observation of an agreement or common feature in a number of instances was a stage in the process by which he reached his theory.

III.—Mill's "Joint Method of Agreement and Difference".

After examining a variety of instances in which an effect appears, and finding that they all agree in the antecedent presence of some one circumstance, we may proceed to examine instances otherwise similar (*in pari materia*, as Prof. Fowler puts it) where the effect does not appear. If these all agree in the absence of the circumstance that is uniformly present with the effect, we have corroborative evidence that there is causal connexion between this circumstance and the effect.

The principle of this method seems to have been suggested to Mill by Wells's investigations into Dew. Wells exposed a number of polished surfaces of various substances, and compared those in which there was a copious deposit of dew with those in which there was little or none. If he could have got two surfaces, one dewed and the other not, identical in every concomitant but one, he would have attained complete proof on the principle of Single Difference. But this being impracticable, he followed a course which approximated to the method of eliminating every circumstance but one from instances of dew, and every circumstance but one in instances of no-dew. Mill sums up as follows the results of his experiments: "It appears that the instances in which much dew is deposited, which are very various, agree in this, and, *so far as we are able to observe, in this only*, that they either radiate heat rapidly or conduct it slowly : qualities between which there is no other circumstance of agreement than that by virtue of either, the body tends to lose heat from the surface more rapidly than it can be restored from within. The instances, on the contrary, in which no dew, or but a small quantity of it, is formed, and which are also extremely various, agree *(as far as we can observe) in nothing except* in *not* having this same property. We seem therefore to have detected the characteristic difference between the substances on which the dew is produced, and those on which it is not produced. And thus have been realised the requisitions of what we have termed the Indirect Method of Difference, or the Joint Method of Agreement and Difference." The Canon of this Method is accordingly stated by Mill as follows :—

> If two or more instances in which the phenomenon occurs have only one circumstance in common, while two or more instances in which it does not occur have nothing in common save the absence of that circumstance ; the circumstance in which alone the two sets of instances differ, is the effect, or the cause, or an indispensable part of the cause, of the phenomenon.

In practice, however, this theoretical standard of proof is never attained. What investigators really proceed upon is the presumption afforded, to use Prof. Bain's terms, by Agreement in Presence combined with Agreement in Absence. When it is found that all substances which have a strong smell agree in being readily oxidisable, and that the marsh gas or carbonetted hydrogen which has no smell is not oxidisable at common temperatures, the presumption that oxidation is one of the causal circumstances in smell is strengthened, even though we have not succeeded in eliminating every circumstance but this one from either the positive or the negative instances. So in the following examples given by Prof. Fowler there is not really a compliance with the theoretical requirements of Mill's Method : there is only an increased presumption from the double agreement. " The Joint Method of Agreement and Difference (or the Indirect Method of Difference, or, as I should prefer to call it, the Double Method of Agreement) is being continually employed by us in the ordinary affairs of life. If when I take a particular kind of food, I find that I invariably suffer from some particular form of illness, whereas, when I leave it off, I cease to suffer, I entertain a double assurance that the food is the cause of my illness. I have observed that a certain plant is invariably plentiful on a particular soil; if, with a wide experience, I fail to find it growing on any other soil, I feel confirmed in my belief that there is in this particular soil some chemical constituent, or some peculiar combination of chemical constituents, which is highly favourable, if not essential, to the growth of the plant."

CHAPTER VI.

METHODS OF OBSERVATION.—MINOR METHODS.

I.—CONCOMITANT VARIATIONS.

Whatever phenomenon varies in any manner whenever another phenomenon varies in some particular manner, is either a cause or an effect of that phenomenon, or is connected with it through some fact of causation.

THIS simple principle is constantly applied by us in connecting and disconnecting phenomena. If we hear a sound which waxes and wanes with the rise and fall of the wind, we at once connect the two phenomena. We may not know what the causal connexion is, but if they uniformly vary together, there is at once a presumption that the one is causally dependent on the other, or that both are effects of the same cause.

This principle was employed by Wells in his researches into Dew. Some bodies are worse conductors of heat than others, and rough surfaces radiate heat more rapidly than smooth. Wells made observations on conductors and radiators of various degrees, and found that the amount of dew deposited was greater or less according as the objects conducted heat slowly or radiated heat rapidly. He thus established what Herschel called a " scale of intensity " between the conducting and radiating properties of the bodies bedewed, and the amount of the dew deposit. The explanation was that in bad conductors the surface cools more quickly than in good conductors because heat is more slowly supplied from within. Similarly in rough surfaces there is a more rapid cooling because heat is given off more quickly. But whatever the explanation might be, the mere concomitant variation of the dew deposit with these properties showed that there was some causal connexion between them.

It must be remembered that the mere fact of concomitant variation is only an index that some causal connexion exists. The nature of the connexion must be ascertained by other means, and may remain a problem, one of the uses of such observed facts being indeed to suggest problems, for inquiry. Thus a remarkable concomitance has been observed between spots on the sun, displays of Aurora Borealis, and magnetic storms. The probability is that they are causally connected, but science has not yet discovered how. Similarly in the various sciences properties are arranged in scales of intensity, and any correspondence between two scales becomes a subject for investigation on the assumption that it points to a causal connexion. We shall see afterwards how in social investigations concomitant variations in averages furnish material for reasoning.

When two variants can be precisely measured, the ratio of their variation may be ascertained by the Method of Single Difference. We may change an antecedent in degree, and watch the corresponding change in the effect, taking care that no other agent influences the effect in the meantime. Often when we cannot remove an agent altogether, we may remove it in a measurable amount, and observe the result. We cannot remove friction altogether, but the more it is diminished, the further will a body travel under the impulse of the same force.

Until a concomitant variation has been fully explained, it is merely an empirical law, and any inference that it extends at the same rate beyond the limits of observation must be made with due caution. " Parallel variation," says Professor Bain, " is sometimes interrupted by critical points, as in the expansion of bodies by heat, which suffers a reverse near the point of cooling. Again, the energy of a solution does not always follow the strength; very dilute solutions occasionally exercise a specific power not possessed in any degree by stronger. So, in the animal body, food and stimulants operate proportionally up to a certain point, at which their further operation is checked by the peculiarities in the structure of the living organs. . . . We cannot always reason from a few steps in 'a' series to the whole series, partly because of the occurrence of critical points, and partly from the development at the extremes of new and unsuspected powers. Sir John Herschel remarks that until very recently ' the formulæ empirically deduced for the elasticity of steam, those for the resistance of fluids, and on other similar subjects, have almost invariably failed to support the theoretical structures that have been erected upon them '." [1]

II.—SINGLE RESIDUE.

Subduct from any phenomenon such part as previous induction has shown to be the effect of certain antecedents, and the residue of the phenomenon is the effect of the remaining antecedents.

" Complicated phenomena, in which several causes

[1] Bain's *Logic*, vol. ii. p. 64.

concurring, opposing, or quite independent of each other, operate at once, so as to produce a compound effect, may be simplified by subducting the effect of all the known causes, as well as the nature of the case permits, either by deductive reasoning or by appeal to experience, and thus leaving as it were a *residual phenomenon* to be explained.   It is by this process, in fact, that science, in its present advanced state, is chiefly promoted.   Most of the phenomena which nature presents are very complicated ; and when the effects of all known causes are estimated with exactness, and subducted, the residual facts are constantly appearing in the form of phenomena altogether new, and leading to the most important conclusions." [1]

It is obvious that this is not a primary method of observation, but a method that may be employed with great effect to guide observation when a considerable advance has been made in accurate knowledge of agents and their mode of operation.   The greatest triumph of the method, the discovery of the planet Neptune, was won some years after the above passage from Herschel's Discourse was written.   Certain perturbations were observed in the movements of the planet Uranus : that is to say, its orbit was found not to correspond exactly with what it should be when calculated according to the known influences of the bodies then known to astronomers.   These perturbations were a residual phenomenon.   It was supposed that they might be due to the action of an unknown planet, and two astronomers, Adams and Le Verrier, simultaneously calculated the position of a body such as would account for the observed deviations.   When

---

[1] Herschel's *Discourse*, § 158.

telescopes were directed to the spot thus indicated, the planet Neptune was discovered. This was in September, 1846: before its actual discovery, Sir John Herschel exulted in the prospect of it in language that strikingly expresses the power of the method. "We see it," he said, "as Columbus saw America from the shores of Spain. Its movements have been felt, trembling along the far-reaching line of our analysis, with a certainty hardly inferior to that of ocular demonstration."[1]

Many of the new elements in Chemistry have been discovered in this way. For example, when distinctive spectrums had been observed for all known substances, then on the assumption that every substance has a distinctive spectrum, the appearance of lines not referable to any known substance indicated the existence of hitherto undiscovered substances and directed search for them. Thus Bunsen in 1860 discovered two new alkaline metals, Cæsium and Rubidium. He was examining alkalies left from the evaporation of a large quantity of mineral water from Durkheim. On applying the spectroscope to the flame which this particular salt or mixture of salts gave off, he found that some bright lines were visible which he had never observed before, and which he knew were not produced either by potash or soda. He then set to work to analyse the mixture, and ultimately succeeded in separating two new alkaline substances. When he had succeeded in getting them separate, it was of course by the Method of Difference that he ascertained them to be capable of producing the lines that had excited his curiosity.

---

[1] De Morgan's *Budget of Paradoxes*, p. 237.

CHAPTER VII.

THE METHOD OF EXPLANATION.

GIVEN perplexity as to the cause of any phenomenon, what is our natural first step? We may describe it as searching for a clue : we look carefully at the circumstances with a view to finding some means of assimilating what perplexes us to what is already within our knowledge. Our next step is to make a guess, or conjecture, or, in scientific language, a hypothesis. We exercise our Reason or *Nous*, or Imagination, or whatever we choose to call the faculty, and try to conceive some cause that strikes us as sufficient to account for the phenomenon. If it is not at once manifest that this cause has really operated, our third step is to consider what appearances ought to present themselves if it did operate. We then return to the facts in question, and observe whether those appearances do present themselves. If they do, and if there is no other way of accounting for the effect in all its circumstances, we conclude that our guess is correct, that our hypothesis is proved, that we have reached a satisfactory explanation.

These four steps or stages may be distinguished in most protracted inquiries into cause. They correspond to the four stages of what Mr. Jevons calls the Inductive Method *par excellence*, Preliminary Observation,

Hypothesis, Deduction and Verification. Seeing that the word Induction is already an overloaded drudge, perhaps it would be better to call these four stages the Method of Explanation. The word Induction, if we keep near its original and most established meaning, would apply strictly only to the fourth stage, the Verification, the bringing in of the facts to confirm our hypothesis. We might call the method the Newtonian method, for all four stages are marked in the prolonged process by which he made good his theory of Gravitation.

To give the name of Inductive Method simply to all the four stages of an orderly procedure from doubt to a sufficient explanation is to encourage a widespread misapprehension. There could be no greater error than to suppose that only the senses are used in scientific investigation. There is no error that men of science are so apt to resent in the mouths of the non-scientific. Yet they have partly brought it on themselves by their loose use of the word Induction, which they follow Bacon in wresting from the traditional meaning of Induction, using it to cover both Induction or the bringing in of facts—an affair mainly of Observation—and Reasoning, the exercise of Nous, the process of constructing satisfactory hypotheses. In reaction against the popular misconception which Bacon encouraged, it is fashionable now to speak of the use of Imagination in Science. This is well enough polemically. Imagination as commonly understood is akin to the constructive faculty in Science, and it is legitimate warfare to employ the familiar word of high repute to force general recognition of the truth. But in common usage Imagination is appropriated to creative genius in the Fine Arts, and to speak of Imagination in Science is to suggest that Science deals in fictions, and has discarded Newton's declaration *Hypotheses non fingo.* In a fight for popular respect, men of science may be right to claim for themselves Imagination ; but in the interests of clear understanding, the logician must deplore that they should defend themselves from a charge due to their abuse of one word by making an equally unwarrantable and confusing extension of another.

Call it what we will, the faculty of likely guessing, of making probable hypotheses, of conceiving in all its circumstances the past situation or the latent and supramicroscopical situation out of which a phenomenon has emerged, is one of the most important of the scientific man's special gifts. It is by virtue of it that the greatest advancements of knowledge have been achieved, the cardinal discoveries in Molar and Molecular Physics, Biology, Geology, and all departments of Science. We must not push the idea of stages in explanatory method too far : the right explanation may be reached in a flash. The idea of stages is really useful mainly in trying to make clear the various difficulties in investigation, and the fact that different men of genius may show different powers in overcoming them. The right hypothesis may occur in a moment, as if by simple intuition, but it may be tedious to prove, and the gifts that tell in proof, such as Newton's immense mathematical power in calculating what a hypothesis implies, Darwin's patience in verifying, Faraday's ingenuity in devising experiments, are all great gifts, and may be serviceable at different stages. But without originality and fertility in probable hypothesis, nothing can be done.

The dispute between Mill and Whewell as to the place and value of hypotheses in science was in the main a dispute about words. Mill did not really undervalue hypothesis, and he gave a most luminous and accurate account of the conditions of proof. But here and there he incautiously spoke of the "hypothetical method" (by which he meant what we have called the method of Explanation) as if it were a defective kind of proof, a method resorted to by science when the "experimental methods" could not be applied. Whether his language fairly bore this construction is not worth arguing, but this was manifestly the construction that Whewell had in his mind when he retorted, as if in defence of hypotheses, that " the inductive process consists in framing successive hypotheses, the comparison of these with the ascertained facts of nature, and the introduction into them of such modifications as the comparison may render necessary". This is a very fair description of the whole method of explanation. There is nothing really inconsistent with it in Mill's account of his " hypothetical method " ; only he erred himself or was the cause of error in others in suggesting, intentionally or unintentionally, that the Experimental Methods were different methods of proof. The "hypothetical method," as he described it, consisting of Induction, Ratiocination, and Verification, really comprehends the principles of all modes of observation, whether naturally or artificially experimental. We see this at once when we ask how the previous knowledge is got in accordance with which hypotheses are framed. The answer must be, by Observation. However profound the calculations, it must be from observed laws, or supposed analogues of them, that we start. And it is always by Observation that the results of these calculations are verified.

Both Mill and Whewell, however, confined themselves too exclusively to the great hypotheses of the Sciences, such as Gravitation and the Undulatory Theory of Light. In the consideration of scientific method, it is a mistake to confine our attention to these great questions, which from the multitude of facts embraced can only be verified by prolonged and intricate inquiry. Attempts at the explanation of the smallest phenomena proceed on the same plan, and the verification of conjectures about them is subject to the same conditions, and the methods of investigation and the conditions of verification can be studied most simply in the smaller cases. Further, I venture to think it a mistake to confine ourselves to scientific inquiry in the narrow sense, meaning thereby inquiry conducted within the pale of the exact sciences. For not merely the exact sciences but all men in the ordinary affairs of life must follow the same methods or at least observe the same principles and conditions, in any satisfactory attempt to explain.

Tares appear among the wheat. Good seed was sown : whence, then, come the tares ? " An enemy has done this." If an enemy has actually been observed sowing the tares, his agency can be proved by descriptive testimony. But if he has not been seen in the act, we must resort to what is known in Courts of Law as circumstantial evidence. This is the " hypothetical method" of science. That the tares are the work of an enemy is a hypothesis : we examine all the circumstances of the case in order to prove, by inference from our knowledge of similar cases, that thus, and thus only, can those circumstances be accounted for. Similarly, when a question is raised as to the authorship of an anonymous book. We first search for a clue by carefully noting the diction, the structure of the sentences, the character and sources of the illustration, the special tracks of thought. We proceed upon the knowledge that every author has characteristic turns of phrase and imagery and favourite veins of thought, and we look out for such internal evidence of authorship in the work before us. Special knowledge and acumen may enable us to detect the authorship at once from the general resemblance to known work. But if we would have clear proof, we must show that the resemblance extends to all the details of phrase, structure and imagery: we must show that our hypothesis of the authorship of XYZ explains all the circumstances. And even this is not sufficient, as many erroneous guesses from internal evidence may convince us. We must establish further that there is no other reasonable way of accounting for the matter and manner of the book; for example, that it is not the work of an imitator. An imitator may reproduce all the superficial peculiarities of an author with such fidelity that the imitation can hardly be distinguished from the original: thus few can distinguish between Fenton's work and Pope's in the translation of the Odyssey. We must take such known facts into account in deciding a hypothesis of authorship. Such hypotheses can seldom be decided on internal evidence alone: other circumstantial evidence—other circumstances that ought to be discoverable if the hypothesis is correct—must be searched for.

The operation of causes that are manifest only in their effects must be proved by the same method as the operation of past causes that have left only their effects behind them. Whether light is caused by a projection of particles from a luminous body or by an agitation communicated through an intervening medium cannot be directly observed.   The only proof open is to calculate what should occur on either hypothesis, and observe whether this does occur.   In such a case there is room for the utmost calculating power and experimental ingenuity.   The mere making of the general hypothesis or guess is simple enough, both modes of transmitting influence, the projection of moving matter and the travelling of an undulation or wave movement, being familiar facts.   But it is not so easy to calculate exactly how a given impulse would travel, and what phenomena of ray and shadow, of reflection, refraction and diffraction ought to be visible in its progress.   Still, no matter how intricate the calculation, its correspondence with what can be observed is the only legitimate proof of the hypothesis.

II.—Obstacles to Explanation.—Plurality of Causes and Intermixture of Effects.

There are two main ways in which explanation may be baffled.   There may exist more than one cause singly capable of producing the effect in question, and we may have no means of determining which of the equally sufficient causes has actually been at work. For all that appears the tares in our wheat may be the effect of accident or of malicious design : an anonymous book may be the work of an original author or of an imitator.   Again, an effect may be the joint result of several co-operating causes, and it may be impossible to determine their several potencies.   The bitter article in the *Quarterly* may have helped to kill John Keats, but it co-operated with an enfeebled constitution and a naturally over-sensitive temperament, and we cannot assign its exact weight to each of these coefficients. Death may be the result of a combination of causes ; organic disease co-operating with exposure, over-fatigue co-operating with the enfeeblement of the system by disease.

The technical names for these difficulties, Plurality of Causes and Intermixture of Effects, are apt to confuse without some clearing up. In both kinds of difficulty more causes than one are involved : but in the one kind of case there is a plurality of possible or equally probable causes, and we are at a loss to decide which : in the other kind of case there is a plurality of co-operating causes ; the effect is the result or product of several causes working conjointly, and we are unable to assign to each its due share.

It is with a view to overcoming these difficulties that Science endeavours to isolate agencies and ascertain what each is capable of singly. Mill and Bain treat Plurality of Causes and Intermixture of Effects in connexion with the Experimental Methods. It is better, perhaps, to regard them simply as obstacles to explanation, and the Experimental Methods as methods of overcoming those obstacles. The whole purpose of the Experimental Methods is to isolate agencies and effects : unless they can be isolated, the Methods are inapplicable. In situations where the effects observable may be referred with equal probability to more than one cause, you cannot eliminate so as to obtain a single agreement. The Method of Agreement is frustrated. And an investigator can get no light from mixed effects, unless he knows enough of the causes at work to be able to apply the Method of Residues. If he does not, he must simply look out for or devise instances where the agencies are at work separately, and apply the principle of Single Difference.

Great, however, as the difficulties are, the theory of Plurality and Intermixture baldly stated makes them appear greater than they are in practice. There is a consideration that mitigates the complication, and renders the task of unravelling it not altogether hopeless. This is that different causes have distinctive ways of operating, and leave behind them marks of their presence by which their agency in a given case may be recognised.

An explosion, for example, occurs. There are several explosive agencies, capable of causing as much destruction as meets the eye at the first glance. The agent in the case before us may be gunpowder or it may be dynamite. But the two agents are not so alike in their mode of operation as to produce results identical in every circumstance. The expert inquirer knows by previous observation that when gunpowder acts the objects in the neighbourhood are blackened; and that an explosion of dynamite tears and shatters in a way peculiar to itself. He is thus able to interpret the traces, to make and prove a hypothesis.

A man's body is found dead in water. It may be a question whether death came by drowning or by previous violence. He may have been suffocated and afterwards thrown into the water. But the circumstances will tell the true story. Death by drowning has distinctive symptoms. If drowning was the cause, water will be found in the stomach and froth in the trachea.

Thus, though there may be a plurality of possible causes, the causation in the given case may be brought home to one by distinctive accompaniments, and it is the business of the scientific inquirer to study these. What is known as the " ripple-mark " in sandstone surfaces may be produced in various ways. The most familiar way is by the action of the tides on the sand of the sea-shore, and the interpreter who knows this way only would ascribe the marks at once to this agency. But ripple-marks are produced also by the winds on drifting sands, by currents of water where no tidal influence is felt, and in fact by any body of water in a state of oscillation. Is it, then, impossible to decide between these alternative possibilities of causation ? No : wind-ripples and current-ripples and tidal-ripples have each their own special character and accompanying conditions, and the hypothesis of one rather than another may be made good by means of these. " In rock-formations," Mr. Page says,[1] " there are many things which at first sight seem similar, and yet on more minute examination, differences are detected and conditions discovered which render it impossible that these appearances can have arisen from the same causation."

The truth is that generally when we speak of plurality of causes, of alternative possibilities of causation, we are not thinking of the effect in its individual entirety, but only of some general or abstract aspect of it. When we say, *e.g.*, that death may be produced by a great many different causes, poison, gunshot wounds, disease of this or that organ, we are thinking of death in the abstract, not of the particular case under consideration, which as an individual case, has characters so distinctive that only one combination of causes is possible.

[1] Page's *Philosophy of Geology*, p. 38.

The effort of science is to become less and less abstract in this sense, by observing agencies or combinations of agencies apart and studying the special characters of their effects. That knowledge is then applied, on the assumption that where those characters are present, the agent or combination of agencies has been at work. Given an effect to be explained, it is brought home to one out of several possible alternatives by *circumstantial evidence*.

Bacon's phrase, *Instantia Crucis*,[1] or Finger-post Instance, might be conveniently appropriated as a technical name for a circumstance that is decisive between rival hypotheses. This was, in effect, proposed by Sir John Herschel,[2] who drew attention to the importance of these crucial instances, and gave the following example : " A curious example is given by M. Fresnel, as decisive, in his mind, of the question between the two great opinions on the nature of light, which, since the time of Newton and Huyghens, have divided philosophers. When two very clean glasses are laid one on the other, if they be not perfectly flat, but one or both in an almost imperceptible degree convex or prominent, beautiful and vivid colours will be seen between them ; and if these be viewed through a red glass, their appearance will be that of alternate dark and bright stripes. . . . Now, the coloured stripes thus produced are explicable on both theories, and are appealed to by both as strong confirmatory facts ; but there is a difference in one circumstance according as one or the other theory is employed to explain them. In the case of the Huyghenian doctrine, the intervals

---

[1] Crux in this phrase means a cross erected at the parting of ways, with arms to tell whither each way leads.

[2] *Discourse*, § 218.

between the bright stripes ought to appear *absolutely black;* in the other, *half bright*, when viewed [in a particular manner] through a prism. This curious case of difference was tried as soon as the opposing consequences of the two theories were noted by M. Fresnel, and the result is stated by him to be decisive in favour of that theory which makes light to consist in the vibrations of an elastic medium."

III.—THE PROOF OF A HYPOTHESIS.

The completest proof of a hypothesis is when that which has been hypothetically assumed to exist as a means of accounting for certain phenomena is afterwards actually observed to exist or is proved by descriptive testimony to have existed. Our argument, for example, from internal evidence that Mill in writing his Logic aimed at furnishing a method for social investigations is confirmed by a letter to Miss Caroline Fox, in which he distinctly avowed that object.

The most striking example of this crowning verification in Science is the discovery of the planet Neptune, in which case an agent hypothetically assumed was actually brought under the telescope as calculated. Examples almost equally striking have occurred in the history of the Evolution doctrine. Hypothetical ancestors with certain peculiarities of structure have been assumed as links between living species, and in some cases their fossils have actually been found in the geological register.

Such triumphs of verification are necessarily rare. For the most part the hypothetical method is applied to cases where proof by actual observation is impossible, such as prehistoric conditions of the earth or of life upon the earth, or conditions in the ultimate constitution of matter that are beyond the reach of the strongest microscope. Indeed, some would confine the word hypothesis to cases of this kind. This, in fact, was done by Mill: hypothesis, as he defined it, was a conjecture not completely proved, but with a large amount of evidence in its favour. But seeing that the procedure of investigation is the same, namely, conjecture, calculation and comparison of facts with the calculated results, whether the agency assumed can be brought to the test of direct observation or not, it seems better not to restrict the word hypothesis to incompletely proved conjectures, but to apply it simply to a conjecture made at a certain stage in whatever way it may afterwards be verified.

In the absence of direct verification, the proof of a hypothesis is exclusive sufficiency to explain the circumstances. The hypothesis must account for all the circumstances, and there must be no other way of accounting for them. Another requirement was mentioned by Newton in a phrase about the exact meaning of which there has been some contention. The first of his Regulæ Philosophandi laid down that the cause assumed must be a *vera causa*. "We are not," the Rule runs, "to admit other causes of natural things than such as both are true, and suffice for explaining their phenomena."[1]

It has been argued that the requirement of "verity" is superfluous; that it is really included in the requirement of sufficiency; that if a cause is sufficient to explain the phenomena it must *ipso facto* be the true

[1] Causas rerum naturalium non plures admitti debere quam quæ et veræ sint et earum phenomenis explicandis sufficiant.

cause. This may be technically arguable, given a sufficient latitude to the word sufficiency : nevertheless, it is convenient to distinguish between mere sufficiency to explain the phenomena in question, and the proof otherwise that the cause assigned really exists *in rerum natura*, or that it operated in the given case. The frequency with which the expression *vera causa* has been used since Newton's time shows that a need is felt for it, though it may be hard to define " verity " precisely as something apart from "sufficiency". If we examine the common usage of the expression we shall probably find that what is meant by insisting on a *vera causa* is that we must have some evidence for the cause assigned outside the phenomena in question. In seeking for verification of a hypothesis we must extend our range beyond the limited facts that have engaged our curiosity and that demand explanation.

There can be little doubt that Newton himself aimed his rule at the Cartesian hypothesis of Vortices. This was an attempt to explain the solar system on the hypothesis that cosmic space is filled with a fluid in which the planets are carried round as chips of wood in a whirlpool, or leaves or dust in a whirlwind. Now this is so far a *vera causa* that the action of fluid vortices is a familiar one : we have only to stir a cup of tea with a bit of stalk in it to get an instance. The agency supposed is sufficient also to account for the revolution of a planet round the sun, given sufficient strength in the fluid to buoy up the planet. But if there were such a fluid in space there would be other phenomena : and in the absence of these other phenomena the hypothesis must be dismissed as imaginary. The fact that comets pass into and out of spaces where the vortices must be assumed to be in action without exhibiting any perturbation is an *instantia crucis* against the hypothesis.

If by the requirement of a *vera causa* were meant that the cause assigned must be one directly open to observation, this would undoubtedly be too narrow a limit. It would exclude such causes as the ether which is assumed to fill interstellar space as a medium for the propagation of light. The only evidence for such a medium and its various properties is sufficiency to explain the phenomena. Like suppositions as to the ultimate constitution of bodies, it is of the nature of what Professor Bain calls a " Representative Fiction ": the only condition is that it must explain all the phenomena, and that there must be no other way of explaining all. When it is proved that light travels with a finite velocity, we are confined to two alternative ways of conceiving its transmission, a projection of matter from the luminous body and the transference of vibrations through an intervening medium. Either hypothesis would explain many of the facts : our choice must rest with that which best explains all. But supposing that all the phenomena of light were explained by attributing certain properties to this intervening medium, it would probably be held that the hypothesis of an ether had not been fully verified till other phenomena than those of light had been shown to be incapable of explanation on any other hypothesis. If the properties ascribed to it to explain the phenomena of light sufficed at the same time to explain otherwise inexplicable phenomena connected with Heat, Electricity, or Gravity, the evidence of its reality would be greatly strengthened.

Not only must the circumstances in hand be explained, but other circumstances must be found to be such as we should expect if the cause assigned really operated. Take, for example, the case of Erratic blocks or boulders, huge fragments of rock found at a distance from their parent strata. The lowlands of England, Scotland, and Ireland, and the great central plain of Northern Europe contain many such fragments. Their composition shows indubitably that they once formed part of hills to the northward of their present site. They must somehow have been detached and transported to where we now find them. How? One old explanation is that they were carried by witches, or that they were themselves witches accidentally dropped and turned into stone. Any such explanation by supernatural means can neither be proved nor disproved. Some logicians would exclude such hypotheses altogether on the ground that they cannot be rendered either more or less probable by subsequent examination.[1] The proper scientific limit, however, is not to the making of hypotheses, but to the proof of them. The more hypotheses the merrier: only if such an agency as witchcraft is suggested, we should expect to find other evidence of its existence in other phenomena that could not otherwise be explained. Again, it has been suggested that the erratic boulders may have been transported by water. Water is so far a *vera causa* that currents are known to be capable of washing huge blocks to a great distance. But blocks transported in this way have the edges worn off by the friction of their passage : and, besides, currents strong enough to dislodge and force along for miles blocks as big as cottages must have left other marks of their

[1] See Prof. Fowler on the Conditions of Hypotheses, *Inductive Logic*, pp. 100-115.

presence.   The explanation now received is that glaciers and icebergs were the means of transport. But this explanation was not accepted till multitudes of circumstances were examined all tending to show that glaciers had once been present in the regions where the erratic blocks are found.   The minute habits of glaciers have been studied where they still exist: how they slowly move down carrying fragments of rock ; how icebergs break off when they reach water, float off with their load, and drop it when they melt ; how they grind and smooth the surfaces of rocks over which they pass or that are frozen into them : how they undercut and mark the faces of precipices past which they move ; how moraines are formed at the melting ends of them, and so forth.   When a district exhibits all the circumstances that are now observed to attend the action of glaciers the proof of the hypothesis that glaciers were once there is complete.

Chapter VIII.

Supplementary Methods of Investigation.

I.—The Maintenance of Averages.—Supplement to the Method of Difference.

A CERTAIN amount of law obtains among events that are usually spoken of as matters of chance or accident in the individual case. Every kind of accident recurs with a certain uniformity. If we take a succession of periods, and divide the total number of any kind of event by the number of periods, we get what is called the average for that period : and it is observed that such averages are maintained from period to period. Over a series of years there is a fixed proportion between good harvests and bad, between wet days and dry : every year nearly the same number of suicides takes place, the same number of crimes, of accidents to life and limb, even of suicides, crimes, or injuries by particular means : every year in a town nearly the same number of children stray from their parents and are restored by the police : every year nearly the same number of persons post letters without putting an address on them.

This maintenance of averages is simple matter of observation, a datum of experience, an empirical law. Once an average for any kind of event has been noted, we may count upon its continuance as we count upon the continuance of any other kind of observed

352 *Inductive Logic, or the Logic of Science.*

uniformity. Insurance companies proceed upon such empirical laws of average in length of life and immunity from injurious accidents by sea or land: their prosperity is a practical proof of the correctness and completeness of the observed facts and the soundness of their inference to the continuance of the average.

The constancy of averages is thus a guide in practice. But in reasoning upon them in investigations of cause, we make a further assumption than continued uniformity. We assume that the maintenance of the average is due to the permanence of the producing causes. We regard the average as the result of the operation of a limited sum of forces and conditions, incalculable as regards their particular incidence, but always pressing into action, and thus likely to operate a certain number of times within a limited period.

Assuming the correctness of this explanation, it would follow that *any change in the average is due to some change in the producing conditions;* and this derivative law is applied as a help in the observation and explanation of social facts. Statistics are collected and classified: averages are struck: and changes in the average are referred to changes in the concomitant conditions.

With the help of this law, we may make a near approach to the precision of the Method of Difference. A multitude of unknown or unmeasured agents may be at work on a situation, but we may accept the average as the result of their joint operation. If then a new agency is introduced or one of the known agents is changed in degree, and this is at once followed by a change in the average, we may with fair probability refer the change in the result to the change in the antecedents.

The difficulty is to find a situation where only one antecedent has been changed before the appearance of the effect. This difficulty may be diminished in practice by eliminating changes that we have reason to know could not have affected the circumstances in question. Suppose, for example, our question is whether the Education Act of 1872 had an influence in the decrease of juvenile crime. Such a decrease took place *post hoc;* was it *propter hoc?* We may at once eliminate or put out of account the abolition of Purchase in the Army or the extension of the Franchise as not having possibly exercised any influence on juvenile crime. But with all such eliminations, there may still remain other possible influences, such as an improvement in the organisation of the Police, or an expansion or contraction of employment. " Can you tell me in the face of chronology," a leading statesman once asked, " that the Crimes Act of 1887 did not diminish disorder in Ireland ? " But chronological sequence alone is not a proof of causation as long as there are other contemporaneous changes of condition that may also have been influential.

The great source of fallacy is our proneness to eliminate or isolate in accordance with our prejudices. This has led to the gibe that anything can be proved by statistics. Undoubtedly statistics may be made to prove anything if you have a sufficiently low standard of proof and ignore the facts that make against your conclusion. But averages and variations in them are instructive enough if handled with due caution. The remedy for rash conclusions from statistics is not no statistics, but more of them and a sound knowledge of the conditions of reasonable proof.

II.—THE PRESUMPTION FROM EXTRA-CASUAL COINCIDENCE.

We have seen that repeated coincidence raises a presumption of causal connexion between the coinciding events. If we find two events going repeatedly together, either abreast or in sequence, we infer that the two are somehow connected in the way of causation, that there is a reason for the coincidence in the manner of their production. It may not be that the one produces the other, or even that their causes are in any way connected : but at least, if they are independent one of the other, both are tied down to happen at the same place and time,—the coincidence of both with time and place is somehow fixed.

But though this is true in the main, it is not true without qualification. We expect a certain amount of repeated coincidence without supposing causal connexion. If certain events are repeated very often within our experience, if they have great positive frequency, we may observe them happening together more than once without concluding that the coincidence is more than fortuitous.

For example, if we live in a neighbourhood possessed of many black cats, and sally forth to our daily business in the morning, a misfortune in the course of the day might more than once follow upon our meeting a black cat as we went out without raising in our minds any presumption that the one event was the result of the other.

Certain planets are above the horizon at certain periods of the year and below the horizon at certain other periods. All through the year men and women are born who afterwards achieve distinction in various walks of life, in love, in war, in business, at the bar, in the pulpit. We perceive a certain number of coincidences between the ascendancy of certain planets and the birth of distinguished individuals without suspecting that planetary inference was concerned in their superiority.

Marriages take place on all days of the year: the sun shines on a good many days at the ordinary time for such ceremonies; some marriages are happy, some unhappy; but though in the case of many happy marriages the sun has shone upon the bride, we regard the coincidence as merely accidental.

Men often dream of calamities and often suffer calamities in real life: we should expect the coincidence of a dream of calamity followed by a reality to occur more than once as a result of chance. There are thousands of men of different nationalities in business in London, and many fortunes are made: we should expect more than one man of any nationality represented there to make a fortune without arguing any connexion between his nationality and his success.

We allow, then, for a certain amount of repeated coincidence without presuming causal connexion: can any rule be laid down for determining the exact amount?

Prof. Bain has formulated the following rule: " Consider the positive frequency of the phenomena themselves, and how great frequency of coincidence must follow from that, supposing there is neither connexion nor repugnance. If there be greater frequency, there is connexion; if less, repugnance."

I do not know that we can go further in definite precept. The number of casual coincidences bears a certain proportion to the positive frequency of the

coinciding phenomena : that proportion is to be determined by common-sense in each case.   It may be
possible, however, to bring out more clearly the principle on which common-sense proceeds in deciding
what chance will and will not account for, although
our exposition amounts only to making more clear
what it is that we mean by chance as distinguished
from assignable reason.   I would suggest that in
deciding what chance will not account for, we make
regressive application of a principle which may be
called the principle of Equal and Unequal Alternatives,
and which may be worded as follows :—

> Of a given number of possible alternatives, all equally
> possible, one of which is bound to occur at a given
> time, we expect each to have its turn an equal
> number of times in the long run.   If several of the
> alternatives are of the same kind, we expect an
> alternative of that kind to recur with a frequency
> proportioned to their greater number.   If any of
> the alternatives has an advantage, it will recur with
> a frequency proportioned to the strength of that
> advantage.

Situations in which alternatives are absolutely equal
are rare in nature, but they are artificially created for
games " of chance," as in tossing a coin, throwing
dice, drawing lots, shuffling and dealing a pack of
cards.   The essence of all games of chance is to construct a number of equal alternatives, making them as
nearly equal as possible, and to make no prearrange-
ment which of the number shall come off.   We then
say that this is determined by chance.   If we ask why
we believe that when we go on bringing off one alternative at a time, each will have its turn, part of

the answer undoubtedly is that given by De Morgan, namely, that we know no reason why one should be chosen rather than another. This, however, is probably not the whole reason for our belief. The rational belief in the matter is that it is only in the long run or on the average that each of the equal alternatives will have its turn, and this is probably founded on the experience of actual trial. The mere equality of the alternatives, supposing them to be perfectly equal, would justify us as much in expecting that each would have its turn in a single revolution of the series, in one complete cycle of the alternatives. This, indeed, may be described as the natural and primitive expectation which is corrected by experience. Put six balls in a wicker bottle, shake them up, and roll one out : return this one, and repeat the operation : at the end of six draws we might expect each ball to have had its turn of being drawn if we went merely on the abstract equality of the alternatives. But experience shows us that in six successive draws the same ball may come out twice or even three or four times, although when thousands of drawings are made each comes out nearly an equal number of times. So in tossing a coin, heads may turn up ten or twelve times in succession, though in thousands of tosses heads and tails are nearly equal. Runs of luck are thus within the rational doctrine of chances : it is only in the long run that luck is equalised supposing that the events are pure matter of chance, that is, supposing the fundamental alternatives to be equal.

If three out of six balls are of the same colour, we expect a ball of that colour to come out three times as often as any other colour on the average of a long succession of tries. This illustrates the second clause of our principle.   The third is illustrated by a loaded coin or die.

By making regressive application of the principle thus ascertained by experience, we often obtain a clue to special causal connexion.   We are at least enabled to isolate a problem for investigation.   If we find one of a number of alternatives recurring more frequently than the others, we are entitled to presume that they are not equally possible, that there is some inequality in their conditions.

The inequality may simply lie in the greater possible frequency of one of the coinciding events, as when there are three black balls in a bottle of six.   We must therefore discount the positive frequency before looking for any other cause.   Suppose, for example, we find that the ascendancy of Jupiter coincides more frequently with the birth of men afterwards distinguished in business than with the birth of men otherwise distinguished, say in war, or at the bar, or in scholarship.   We are not at liberty to conclude planetary influence till we have compared the positive frequency of the different modes of distinction. The explanation of the more frequently repeated coincidence may simply be that more men altogether are successful in business than in war or law or scholarship.   If so, we say that chance accounts for the coincidence, that is to say, that the coincidence is casual as far as planetary influence is concerned.

So in epidemics of fever, if we find on taking a long average that more cases occur in some streets of a town than in others, we are not warranted in concluding that the cause lies in the sanitary conditions of those streets or in any special liability to infection without first taking into account the number of families in the different streets. If one street showed on the average ten times as many cases as another, the coincidence might still be judged casual if there were ten times as many families in it.

Apart from the fallacy of overlooking the positive frequency, certain other fallacies or liabilities to error in applying this doctrine of chances may be specified.

1. We are apt, under the influence of prepossession or prejudice, to remember certain coincidences better than others, and so to imagine extra-casual coincidence where none exists. This bias works in confirming all kinds of established beliefs, superstitious and other, beliefs in dreams, omens, retributions, telepathic communications, and so forth. Many people believe that nobody who thwarts them ever comes to good, and can produce numerous instances from experience in support of this belief.

2. We are apt, after proving that there is a residuum beyond what chance will account for on due allowance made for positive frequency, to take for granted that we have proved some particular cause for this residuum. Now we have not really explained the residuum by the application of the principle of chances : we have only isolated a problem for explanation. There may be more than chance will account for : yet the cause may not be the cause that we assign off-hand. Take, for example, the coincidence that has been remarked between race and different forms of Christianity in Europe. If the distribution of religious systems were entirely independent of race, it might be said that you would expect one system to coincide equally often with different races in proportion to the positive number of their communities. But the Greek system is found almost solely among Slavonic peoples, the Roman

among Celtic, and the Protestant among Teutonic. The coincidence is greater than chance will account for. Is the explanation then to be found in some special adaptability of the religious system to the character of the people? This may be the right explanation, but we have not proved it by merely discounting chance. To prove this we must show that there was no other cause at work, that character was the only operative condition in the choice of system, that political combinations, for example, had nothing to do with it. The presumption from extra-casual coincidence is only that there is a special cause: in determining what that is we must conform to the ordinary conditions of explanation.

So coincidence between membership of the Government and a classical education may be greater than chance would account for, and yet the circumstance of having been taught Latin and Greek at school may have had no special influence in qualifying the members for their duties. The proportion of classically educated in the Government may be greater than the proportion of them in the House of Commons, and yet their eminence may be in no way due to their education. Men of a certain social position have an advantage in the competition for office, and all those men have been taught Latin and Greek as a matter of course. Technically speaking, the coinciding phenomena may be independent effects of the same cause.

3. Where the alternative possibilities are very numerous, we are apt not to make due allowance for the number, sometimes overrating it, sometimes under-rating it.

The fallacy of underrating the number is often seen in games of chance, where the object is to create a vast number of alternatives, all equally possible, equally open to the player, without his being able to affect the advent of one more than another. In whist, for example, there are some six billions of possible hands. Yet it is a common impression that, one night with another, in the course of a year, a player will have dealt to him about an equal number of good and bad hands. This is a fallacy. A very much longer time is required to exhaust the possible combinations. Suppose a player to have 2000 hands in the course of a year: this is only one "set," one combination, out of thousands of millions of such sets possible. Among those millions of sets, if there is nothing but chance in the matter, there ought to be all proportions of good and bad, some sets all good, some all bad, as well as some equally divided between good and bad.[1]

Sometimes, however, the number of possible alternatives is overrated. Thus, visitors to London often remark that they never go there without meeting somebody from their own locality, and they are surprised at this as if they had the same chance of meeting their fellow-visitors and any other of the four millions of the metropolis. But really the possible alternatives of rencounter are far less numerous. The places frequented by visitors to London are filled by much more limited numbers: the possible rencounters are to be counted by thousands rather than by millions.

---

[1] See De Morgan's *Essay on Probabilities*, c. vi., "On Common Notions of Probability".

CHAPTER IX

PROBABLE INFERENCE TO PARTICULARS.—THE MEASUREMENT OF PROBABILITY.

UNDOUBTEDLY there are degrees of probability. Not only do we expect some events with more confidence than others : we may do so, and our confidence may be misplaced : but we have reason to expect some with more confidence than others. There are different degrees of rational expectation. Can those degrees be measured numerically?

The question has come into Logic from the mathematicians. The calculation of Probabilities is a branch of Mathematics. We have seen how it may be applied to guide investigation by eliminating what is due to chance, and it has been vaguely conceived by logicians that what is called the calculus of probabilities might be found useful also in determining by exact numerical measurement the probability of single events. Dr. Venn, who has written a separate treatise on the Logic of Chance, mentions "accurate quantitative apportionment of our belief" as one of the goals which Logic should strive to attain. The following passage will show his drift.[1]

A man in good health would doubtless like to know whether he will be alive this time next year. The fact

---

[1] *Empirical Logic*, p. 556.

will be settled one way or the other in due time, if he can afford to wait, but if he wants a present decision, Statistics and the Theory of Probability can alone give him any information. He learns that the odds are, say five to one that he will survive, and this is an answer to his question as far as any answer can be given. Statisticians are gradually accumulating a vast mass of data of this general character. What they may be said to aim at is to place us in the position of being able to say, in any given time or place, what are the odds for or against any at present indeterminable fact which belongs to a class admitting of statistical treatment.

Again, outside the regions of statistics proper—which deal, broadly speaking, with events which can be numbered or measured, and which occur with some frequency—there is still a large field as to which some better approach to a reasoned intensity of belief can be acquired. What will be the issue of a coming war? Which party will win in the next election? Will a patient in the crisis of a given disease recover or not? That statistics are lying here in the background, and are thus indirectly efficient in producing and graduating our belief, I fully hold; but there is such a large intermediate process of estimating, and such scope for the exercise of a practised judgment, that no direct appeal to statistics in the common sense can directly help us. In sketching out therefore the claims of an Ideal condition of knowledge, we ought clearly to include a due apportionment of belief to every event of such a class as this. It is an obvious defect that one man should regard as almost certain what another man regards as almost impossible. Short, therefore, of certain prevision of the future, we want complete agreement as to the degree of probability of every future event: and for that matter of every past event as well.

Technically speaking, if we extend the name Modality (see p. 78) to any qualification of the certainty of a statement of belief, what Dr. Venn here desiderates, as he has himself suggested, is a more exact measurement of the Modality of propositions. We speak of things as being certain, possible, impossible, probable, extremely probable, faintly probable, and so forth: taking certainty as the highest degree of probability [1] shading gradually down to the zero of the impossible, can we obtain an exact numerical measure for the gradations of assurance?

To examine the principles of all the cases in which chances for and against an occurrence have been calculated from real or hypothetical data, would be to trespass into the province of Mathematics, but a few simple cases will serve to show what it is that the calculus attempts to measure, and what is the practical value of the measurement as applied to the probability of a single event.

Suppose there are 100 balls in a box, 30 white and 70 black, all being alike except in respect of colour, we say that the chances of drawing a black ball as against a white are as 7 to 3, and the probability of drawing black is measured by the fraction $\frac{7}{10}$. In believing this we proceed on the principle already explained (p. 356) of Proportional Chances. We do not know for certain whether black or white will emerge, but knowing the antecedent situation we expect black

---

[1] Mr. Jevons held that all inference is merely probable and that no inference is certain. But this is a purposeless repudiation of common meaning, which he cannot himself consistently adhere to. We find him saying that if a penny is tossed into the air it will *certainly* come down on one side or the other, on which side being a matter of probability. In common speech probability is applied to a degree of belief short of certainty, but to say that certainty is the highest degree of probability does no violence to the common meaning.

rather than white with a degree of assurance corresponding to the proportions of the two in the box. It is our degree of rational assurance that we measure by this fraction, and the rationality of it depends on the objective condition of the facts, and is the same for all men, however much their actual degree of confidence may vary with individual temperament. That black will be drawn seven times out of every ten on an average if we go on drawing to infinity, is as certain as any empirical law : it is the probability of a single draw that we measure by the fraction $\frac{7}{10}$.

When we build expectations of single events on statistics of observed proportions of events of that kind, it is ultimately on the same principle that rational expectation rests. That the proportion will obtain on the average we regard as certain : the ratio of favourable cases to the whole number of possible alternatives is the measure of rational expectation or probability in regard to a particular occurrence. If every year five per cent. of the children of a town stray from their guardians, the probability of this or that child's going astray is $\frac{1}{20}$. The ratio is a correct measure only on the assumption that the average is maintained from year to year.

Without going into the combination of probabilities, we are now in a position to see the practical value of such a calculus as applied to particular cases. There has been some misunderstanding among logicians on the point. Mr. Jevons rebuked Mill for speaking disrespectfully of the calculus, eulogised it as one of the noblest creations of the human intellect, and quoted Butler's saying that " Probability is the guide of life ". But when Butler uttered this famous saying he was probably not thinking of the mathematical calculus of probabilities as applied to particular cases, and it was this special application to which Mill attached comparatively little value.

The truth is that we seldom calculate or have any occasion to calculate individual chances except as a matter of curiosity. It is true that insurance offices calculate probabilities, but it is not the probability of this or that man dying at a particular age. The precise shade of probability for the individual, in so far as this depends on vital statistics, is a matter of indifference to the company as long as the average is maintained. Our expectations about any individual life cannot be measured by a calculation of the chances because a variety of other elements affect those expectations. We form beliefs about individual cases, but we try to get surer grounds for them than the chances as calculable from statistical data. Suppose a person were to institute a home for lost dogs, he would doubtless try to ascertain how many dogs were likely to go astray, and in so doing would be guided by statistics. But in judging of the probability of the straying of a particular dog, he would pay little heed to statistics as determining the chances, but would proceed upon empirical knowledge of the character of the dog and his master. Even in betting on the field against a particular horse, the bookmaker does not calculate from numerical data such as the number of horses entered or the number of times the favourite has been beaten : he tries to get at the pedigree and previous performances of the various horses in the running. We proceed by calculation of chances only when we cannot do better.

CHAPTER X.

INFERENCE FROM ANALOGY.

THE word Analogy was appropriated by Mill, in accordance with the usage of the eighteenth century, to designate a ground of inference distinct from that on which we proceed in extending a law, empirical or scientific, to a new case. But it is used in various other senses, more or less similar, and in order to make clear the exact logical sense, it is well to specify some of these. The original word ἀναλογία, as employed by Aristotle, corresponds to the word Proportion in Arithmetic : it signified an equality of ratios, ἰσότης λόγων : two compared with four is analogous to four compared with eight. There is something of the same meaning in the technical use of the word in Physiology, where it is used to signify similarity of function as distinguished from similarity of structure, which is called homology : thus the tail of a whale is analogous to the tail of a fish, inasmuch as it is similarly used for motion, but it is homologous with the hind legs of a quadruped ; a man's arms are homologous with a horse's fore legs, but they are not analogous inasmuch as they are not used for progression. Apart from these technical employments, the word is loosely used in common speech for any kind of resemblance. Thus De Quincey speaks of the " analogical " power in memory, meaning thereby the power of recalling things by their inherent likeness as distinguished from their casual connexions or their order in a series. But even in common speech, there is a trace of the original meaning: generally when we speak of analogy we have in our minds more than one pair of things, and what we call the analogy is some resemblance between the different pairs. This is probably what Whately had in view when he defined analogy as " resemblance of relations ".

In a strict logical sense, however, as defined by Mill, sanctioned by the previous usage of Butler and Kant, analogy means more than a resemblance of relations. It means a preponderating resemblance between two things such as to warrant us in inferring that the resemblance extends further. This is a species of argument distinct from the extension of an empirical law. In the extension of an empirical law, the ground of inference is a coincidence frequently repeated within our experience, and the inference is that it has occurred or will occur beyond that experience: in the argument from analogy, the ground of inference is the resemblance between two individual objects or kinds of objects in a certain number of points, and the inference is that they resemble one another in some other point, known to belong to the one, but not known to belong to the other. " Two things go together in many cases, therefore in all, including this one," is the argument in extending a generalisation : " Two things agree in many respects, therefore in this other," is the argument from analogy.

The example given by Reid in his *Intellectual Powers* has become the standard illustration of the peculiar argument from analogy.

We may observe a very great similitude between this

earth which we inhabit, and the other planets, Saturn, Jupiter, Mars, Venus and Mercury. They all revolve round the sun, as the earth does, although at different distances and in different periods. They borrow all their light from the sun, as the earth does. Several of them are known to revolve round their axis like the earth, and by that means have like succession of day and night. Some of them have moons, that serve to give them light in the absence of the sun, as our moon does to us. They are all, in their motions, subject to the same law of gravitation as the earth is. From all this similitude it is not unreasonable to think that these planets may, like our earth, be the habitation of various orders of living creatures. There is some probability in this conclusion from analogy.[1]

The argument from analogy is sometimes said to range through all degrees of probability from certainty to zero. But this is true only if we take the word analogy in its loosest sense for any kind of resemblance. If we do this, we may call any kind of argument an argument from analogy, for all inferences turn upon resemblance. I believe that if I throw my pen in the air it will come down again, because it is like other ponderable bodies. But if we use the word in its limited logical sense, the degree of probability is much nearer zero than certainty. This is apparent from the conditions that logicians have formulated of a strict argument from analogy.

1. The resemblance must be preponderating. In estimating the value of an argument from analogy, we must reckon the points of difference as counting against the conclusion, and also the points in regard to which we do not know whether the two objects agree or differ. The numerical measure of value is the ratio of

---

[1] Hamilton's *Reid*, p. 236.

the points of resemblance to the points of difference *plus* the unknown points. Thus, in the argument that the planets are inhabited because they resemble the earth in some respects and the earth is inhabited, the force of the analogy is weakened by the fact that we know very little about the surface of the planets.

2. In a numerical estimate all circumstances that hang together as effects of one cause must be reckoned as one. Otherwise, we might make a fallaciously imposing array of points of resemblance. Thus in Reid's enumeration of the agreements between the earth and the planets, their revolution round the sun and their obedience to the law of gravitation should count as one point of resemblance. If two objects agree in a, b, c, d, e, but b follows from a, and d and e from c, the five points count only as two.

3. If the object to which we infer is known to possess some property incompatible with the property inferred, the general resemblance counts for nothing. The moon has no atmosphere, and we know that air is an indispensable condition of life. Hence, however much the moon may resemble the earth, we are debarred from concluding that there are living creatures on the moon such as we know to exist on the earth. We know also that life such as it is on the earth is possible only within certain limits of temperature, and that Mercury is too hot for life, and Saturn too cold, no matter how great the resemblance to the earth in other respects.

4. If the property inferred is known or presumed to be a concomitant of one or more of the points of resemblance, any argument from analogy is superfluous. This is, in effect, to say that we have no occasion to argue from general resemblance when we have

reason to believe that a property follows from something that an object is known to possess. If we knew that any one of the planets possessed all the conditions, positive and negative, of life, we should not require to reckon up all the respects in which it resembles the earth in order to create a presumption that it is inhabited. We should be able to draw the conclusion on other grounds than those of analogy. Newton's famous inference that the diamond is combustible is sometimes quoted as an argument from analogy. But, technically speaking, it was rather, as Professor Bain has pointed out, of the nature of an extended generalisation. Comparing bodies in respect of their densities and refracting powers, he observed that combustible bodies refract more than others of the same density ; and observing the exceptionally high refracting power of the diamond, he inferred from this that it was combustible, an inference afterwards confirmed by experiment. "The concurrence of high refracting power with inflammability was an empirical law ; and Newton, perceiving the law, extended it to the adjacent case of the diamond. The remark is made by Brewster that had Newton known the refractive powers of the minerals *greenockite* and *octohedrite*, he would have extended the inference to them, and would have been mistaken." [1]

From these conditions it will be seen that we cannot conclude with any high degree of probability from analogy alone. This is not to deny, as Mr. Jevons seems to suppose, that analogies, in the sense of general resemblances, are often useful in directing investigation. When we find two things very much alike, and ascertain that one of them possesses a

[1] Bain's *Logic*, ii. 145.

certain property, the presumption that the other has the same is strong enough to make it worth while trying whether as a matter of fact it has. It is said that a general resemblance of the hills near Ballarat in Australia to the Californian hills where gold had been found suggested the idea of digging for gold at Ballarat. This was a lucky issue to an argument from analogy, but doubtless many have dug for gold on similar general resemblances without finding that the resemblance extended to that particular. Similarly, many of the extensions of the Pharmacopeia have proceeded upon general resemblances, the fact that one drug resembles another in certain properties being a sufficient reason for trying whether the resemblance goes further. The lucky guesses of what is known as natural sagacity are often analogical. A man of wide experience in any subject-matter such as the weather, or the conduct of men in war, in business, or in politics, may conclude to the case in hand from some previous case that bears a general resemblance to it, and very often his conclusions may be perfectly sound though he has not made a numerical estimate of the data.

The chief source of fallacy in analogical argument is ignoring the number of points of difference. It often happens that an amount of resemblance only sufficient for a rhetorical simile is made to do duty as a solid argument. Thus the resemblance between a living body and the body politic is sometimes used to support inferences from successful therapeutic treatment to State policy. The advocates of annual Parliaments in the time of the Commonwealth based their case on the serpent's habit of annually casting its skin.

Wisest of beasts the serpent see,
Just emblem of eternity,
   And of a State's duration ;
Each year an annual skin he takes,
And with fresh life and vigour wakes
   At every renovation.

Britain ! that serpent imitate.
Thy Commons House, that skin of State,
   By annual choice restore ;
So choosing thou shalt live secure,
And freedom to thy sons inure,
   Till Time shall be no more.

Carlyle's saying that a ship could never be taken round Cape Horn if the crew were consulted every time the captain proposed to alter the course, if taken seriously as an analogical argument against Representative Government, is open to the objection that the differences between a ship and a State are too great for any argument from the one to the other to be of value. It was such fallacious analogies as these that Heine had in view in his humorous prayer, " Heaven defend us from the Evil One and from metaphors "

Aberdeen University Press.

29176979R00218

Made in the USA
Lexington, KY
15 January 2014